# PAUL KRETZMANN

# 1 and 2 Samuel

Just and Sinner

Ithaca, NY 14850

www.JustandSinner.org

First edition

ISBN: 978-1-952295-38-6

This book was professionally typeset on Reedsy. Find out more at reedsy.com

# Contents

# 1 Samuel Introduction

The First Book of Samuel is really only the first part of a larger history, which was later divided into two parts. When the Greek translation of the Hebrew Bible was made, the translators divided both the Book of Samuel and the Book of Kings into two, and each of the four parts was called a book of the Kings, for which reason the subtitle in the Authorized Version is retained, "The First Book of the Kings." Books of Samuel the historical account is called, not because Samuel was the author, although he may have left some written notes, but because he is the prominent figure in the earlier history and because he exerted a very pronounced influence in Israel even when the form of government had been changed to a monarchy. "The influence of Samuel, who had called and anointed both Saul and David, was felt in Israel throughout the reign of Saul, and must have been a decisive factor in the training of David for his future task. Beginning with a biographical sketch of Samuel's life before he became the last Judge of Israel, the author takes up the thread of history at the point where the Book of Judges drops it after relating the end of Samson, and carries it forward to the close of David's reign." Samuel, the last Judge of Israel, Saul, the first king of Israel, and David, the greatest king of Israel, are the three leading characters. But the book was not merely written "to be a record of the lives of three great men whom God gave to

His people, although their story is full of human interest. The Christian reader will retain the proper point of view, that this story sets forth the providential control which God exercised over the affairs of His people, achieving His purposes without fail."

The author of the book does not mention his name, and it is impossible from the contents to make a definite statement regarding the authorship except this, that it was not composite. Samuel himself could not have written the entire history, since his death is related, 1 Sam. 25, 1; 28, 3; also the division of the people into two separate kingdoms is referred to, which took place long after Samuel's death, 1 Sam. 11, 8; 15, 4; cp. 27, 6. It is probable that some prophet living not long after the time of Solomon is the author. The First Book of Samuel is easily divisible into two parts, the restoration of the theocratic government in Israel under Samuel, the last Judge, who also was a prophet of the Lord; the history of Saul's reign, namely, his first campaigns," disobedience, and rejection, his persecution of David, his war against the Philistines, and his death. 1) The lessons of this history are readily applied.

I

1 Samuel

# 1

# 1 Samuel 1

**S**amuel's Birth and Presentation to the Lord.
THE UNHAPPINESS AND THE PRAYER OF HANNAH.
— V. 1. **Now there was a certain man of Ramathaim-zophim, of Mount Ephraim,** usually called Ramah, some six miles northwest of Jerusalem, in the territory of Benjamin, **and his name was Elkanah, the son of Jeroham, the son of Elihu, the son of Tohu, the son of Zuph,** after whom this special region was named, **an Ephrathite,** cp. 1 Chron. 6, 22-27, belonging to the tribe of Levi; **v. 2. and he had two wives: the name of the one was Hannah** (charm, grace), **and the name of the other Peninnah** (coral, pearl); **and Peninnah had children, but Hannah had no children.** The bigamy of Elkanah, though tolerated by God among the Jews, was opposed to the original divine institution of monogamy, and the misfortune which attached to this relation appeared in Elkanah's married and family life. **V. 3. And this man went up out of his city yearly,** year after year, **to worship and to sacrifice unto the Lord of hosts in Shiloh,** evidently at the Feast of Passover and of Unleavened Bread, since he

3

took his whole household along. **And the two sons of Eli, Hophni and Phinehas, the priests of the Lord, were there.** This notice is here inserted by the author to prepare for the subsequent history. Elkanah, as a true Israelite, worshiped the great Lord of hosts, the one true God, and be brought his sacrifices of peace offerings in order to strengthen his fellowship with this God. **V. 4. And when the time was that Elkanah offered,** it happened on the day that he brought his sacrifice, **he gave to Peninnah, his wife, and to all her sons and her daughters, portions,** as their part of the sacrificial feast, Deut. 12, 11–13; **v. 5. but unto Hannah he gave a worthy portion,** a double portion; **for he loved Hannah,** she was his favorite wife, as Rachel had been Jacob's; **but the Lord had shut up her womb,** He had given her no children, and childlessness was rightly held to be a great misfortune, a reproach, even a divine punishment, Gen. 19, 31; 30,1. 23. **V. 6. And her adversary,** Peninnah, who was jealous of Elkanah's special love for Hannah, **also provoked her sore for to make her fret,** to make her worried and excited, **because the Lord had shut up her womb,** while Peninnah, more fortunate in child-bearing and therefore boastful, made it a point to vex her with her childlessness. **V. 7. And as he,** Elkanah, **did so year by year,** followed the same custom, **when she went up to the house of the Lord, so she,** Peninnah, **provoked her,** for she had her flock of children about her and made use of the occasion to sneer at lonely Hannah; **therefore she wept and did not eat,** she was too deeply hurt to have any appetite. **V. 8. Then said Elkanah, her husband, to her, Hannah, why weepest thou, and why eatest thou not, and why is thy heart grieved?** This is a climax showing his deep anxiety and solicitude for her. **Am I not better to thee than ten sons?**

The deep and tender love of the husband tried to console her in her great disappointment. **V. 9. So Hannah rose up after they had eaten in Shiloh, and after they had drunk,** at the conclusion of the sacrificial meal. **Now Eli, the priest,** the high priest at that time, **sat upon a seat by a post of the Temple of the Lord,** at the entrance to the Tabernacle of Jehovah, the palace of the Lord. **V. 10. And she was in bitterness of soul,** on account of the continuance of her hopelessness and of the vexations which she suffered from her adversary, **and prayed unto the Lord, and wept sore,** her many tears being an expression of her grief because all her petitions up to that time had been unheard. **V. 11. And she vowed a vow and said, O Lord of hosts,** Jehovah of Sabbath, **if Thou wilt indeed look on the affiliation of Thine handmaid,** the misery of her childlessness, **and remember me, and not forget Thine handmaid, but wilt give unto Thine handmaid a man child, then I will give him unto the Lord all the days of his life,** consecrate him for lifelong service in the Tabernacle, to which the Levites were not pledged otherwise; **and there shall no razor come upon his head,** he was to be a perpetual Nazarite, Num. 6, 2 ff. **V. 12. And it came to pass, as she continued praying before the Lord,** in a long and urgent prayer, **that Ell marked her mouth,** for she was evidently out in the court of the Tabernacle, not far from the altar of burnt offerings. **V. 13. Now Hannah, she spake in her heart,** literally, "to her heart"; she was so deeply engrossed with her trouble that she forgot her surroundings. Her face was full of expressive eagerness and emotion, but her communing with the Lord was all in her heart. **Only her lips moved,** in the intensity of her fervor, **but her voice was not heard. Therefore Ell,** drawing a. rash and profane conclusion, **thought she had**

5

**been drunken,** having partaken of too much wine at the sacrificial meal. **V. 14. And Eli said unto her, How long wilt thou be drunken?** **Put away thy wine from thee,** namely, by sleeping off its effects in secret, where her supposed condition would offend no one. **V. 15. And Hannah answered and said, No, my lord; I am a Woman.** **of a sorrowful spirit,** in deep trouble, this being an emphatic and indignant denial of Eli's suspicions; **I have drunk neither wine nor strong drink,** a very intoxicating beverage made of barley, dates, and honey, **but have poured out my soul before the Lord.** Cp. Ps. 42,5. **V. 16. Count not thine handmaid for a daughter of Belial,** be was not to place her on a level with worthless bad women; **for out of the abundance of my complaint and grief have I spoken hitherto,** while Eli had observed her. **V. 17. Then Eli answered and said,** not only retracting his accusation, but remembering the dignity of his office, **Go in peace; and the God of Israel grant thee thy petition that thou hast asked of Him.** not a prophecy, but a sincere wish and prayer. **V. 18. And she said, Let thine handmaid find grace in thy sight,** she showed her modesty, reverence, and humility in accepting the kind wishes of the high priest. **so the woman went her way and did eat,** her heart was eased, so she could partake of food, **and her countenance was no more sad.** The right conclusion of a prayer is a confident Amen, which testifies that we are sure of the hearing of our prayer by God in advance.

SAMUEL BORN AND BROUGHT TO SHILOH. — **V. 19. And they rose up in the morning early, and worshiped before the Lord,** took part in the morning service, **and returned, and came to their house to Ramah. And Elkanah knew Hannah, his wife; and the Lord remembered her,** for it is He alone whole gift children are in marriage. **V. 20. Wherefore it came** to pass, when the time was come about after Hannah had conceived, at the end of the period of pregnancy, that she bare a son, and called his name Samuel (asked of God), saying, Because I have asked him of the Lord, he was a perpetual reminder of the fact that God hears prayers, even for temporal blessings. V. 21. And the man Elkanah and all his house went up to offer unto the Lord the yearly sacrifice and his vow, for apparently he also had made a promise to the Lord and now offered this in the form of a sacrifice in addition to those portions of his property which belonged to the Lord by law. Samuel may, at that time, have been two or three months old. V. 22. But Hannah went not up; for she said unto her husband, I will not go up until the child be weaned, which occurred at the age of three years, and then I will bring him that he may appear before the Lord and there abide forever, consecrated to the Lord's service all his life. V. 23. And Elkanah, her husband, said unto her, Do what seemeth thee good, he was in entire sympathy with his wife in this matter; tarry until thou have weaned him; only the Lord establish His word, fulfill it, bring it to completion, namely, so far as his destination for the Lord's service was concerned. So the woman abode, and gave her son suck until she weaned him. V. 24. And when she had weaned him, she took him up with her, with three bullocks, one for each year of the boy's life, and one ephah of flour (about 26 quarts), three-tenth deals being required for each bullock, and a bottle of wine, for a drink-offering, and brought him unto the house of the Lord in Shiloh; and the child was young, having probably just turned three years. V. 25. And they slew a bullock, as a burnt offering to accompany the consecration of Samuel, and brought the child to Eli, for both parents presented him to the

Lord. **V. 26. And she said, O my lord, as thy soul liveth, my lord, I am the woman that stood by thee here, praying unto the Lord,** the circumstance by which Eli was to remember her. **V. 27. For this child I prayed, and the Lord hath given me my petition which I asked of him; v. 28. therefore also I have lent him to the Lord,** given him to the Lord in turn; **as long as he liveth, he shall be lent to the Lord,** given to the Lord as one that had been granted by the Lord. **And he,** Elkanah, as the father of the house, **worshiped the Lord there.** It. is pleasing to God if parents consecrate their sons for the service of the Church. But the main thing is for all men who have experienced God's love and faithfulness in their lives to place themselves in the Lord's service, both body and soul.

# 2

# 1 Samuel 2

Hannah's Song.
The Wickedness of Eli's Sons.

HANNAH'S SONG OF THANKFULNESS. — **V. 1. And Hannah prayed and said,** in an exaltation of spirit brought about by the Holy Ghost, **My heart rejoiceth in the Lord, mine horn is exalted in the Lord,** said of vigorous courage and consciousness of power; **my mouth is enlarged over mine enemies,** being opened widely to praise the salvation of the Lord; **because I rejoice in Thy salvation,** in the merciful kindness which Jehovah had shown her. **V. 2. There is none holy as the Lord; for there is none beside Thee,** His holiness being the reflection of His majesty; **neither is there any rock like our God,** in whom the believers may always place their trust with firm confidence, Deut. 32, 4. 15. **V. 3. Talk no more so exceeding proudly,** these words being addressed to the godless, to the enemies of Jehovah; **let not arrogancy come out of your mouth,** anything which savors of impertinence against Jehovah; **for the Lord is a God of knowledge,** an omniscient God, **and by Him actions are**

9

**weighed,** or, all His doing is weighed by Him, is right and true. **V. 4. The bows of the mighty men are broken,** all human power being helpless before Him, **and they that stumbled are girded with strength,** prepared for battle by virtue of their trust in Jehovah. **V. 5. They that were full have hired out themselves for bread,** having been reduced to the most pitiful straits; **and they that were hungry ceased,** receiving the food which they need by the mercy of God, **so that the barren hath born seven,** Ps. 113, 9; **and she that hath many children is waxed feeble,** having been bereaved of her children in her old age, Jer. 15, 9. **V. 6. The Lord killeth and maketh alive,** sending danger and distress, but also delivering those that trust in Him, Ps. 30, 3. 4; **He bringeth down to the grave and bringeth up,** extricating His children from deadly sorrow, from extreme misfortune, and placing them in safety and joy. **V. 7. The Lord maketh poor and maketh rich,** for in His hands are all the treasures of the world; **He bringeth low and lifteth up. V. 8. He raiseth up the poor out of the dust and lifteth up the beggar from the dunghill,** from the deepest dishonor and disgrace, in which one is, as it were, trodden under foot, **to set them among princes,** on seats of honor, such as are occupied by the nobility, **and to make them inherit the throne of glory,** to hold the very opposite position of that which formerly was theirs; **for the pillars of the earth are the Lord's,** having been erected by Him and being held in place by His almighty power, **and He bath set the world upon them,** as the Creator and Sustainer of the world. **V. 9. He will keep the feet of His saints,** to guard them from tottering and falling, **and the wicked shall be silent in darkness,** deprived of the light of God's mercy; **for by strength shall no man prevail;** it is impossible for man, in his own might, to defy the storms of life. **V. 10. The adversaries of the Lord shall be broken to pieces** for Jehovah will destroy and annihilate those who lift up their voices to challenge Him; **out of heaven shall He thunder upon them,** as a warning of the nearness of His judgment; **the Lord shall judge the ends of the earth; and He shall give strength unto His King,** to His Anointed, the future Messiah of Israel. **and exalt the horn of His Anointed.** The kingdom of Christ extends to the ends of the earth, which He will judge on the Last Day. Then the unbelievers, the godless, will be condemned to everlasting damnation, but the power of the Christ of God will be established throughout eternity. Thus the inspired song reached its wonderful climax. **V. 11. And Elkanah, with his household, went to Ramah to his house. And the child,** Samuel, **did minister unto the Lord before Eli, the priest.**

THE WICKED PRACTICES OF ELI'S SONS. — **V. 12. Now the sons of Eli were sons of Belial,** worthless, profitless rascals; **they knew not the Lord,** they did not fear Him, they had no faith in Him. **V. 13. And the priest's custom with the people was that, when any man offered sacrifice, the priest's servant came, while the flesh was in seething, with a flesh-hook of three teeth,** a trident, or three-pronged fork, **in his hand; v. 14. and he struck it into the pan, or kettle, or caldron, or pot; all that the flesh-hook brought up the priest took for himself.** That was the greedy conduct of the priests in the preparation of the sacrificial meal after the sacrifice proper had been brought. This manner of acting had already become the rule. **So they did in Shiloh unto all the Israelites that came thither,** thus robbing the people and the Lord, instead of confining themselves to the wave-breast, the heave-shoulder, and certain other perquisites, Lev. 7, 28-36; Num. 18. **V. 15.**

**Also before they burned the fat,** before the sacrifice proper, which included the fat, Lev. 3, 3-5, **the priest's servant came, and said to the man that sacrificed, Give flesh to roast for the priest,** for they did not want boiled meat all the time; **for he will not have sodden flesh of' thee, but raw,** such as was still full of strength and juice. **V. 16. And if any man said unto him, Let them not fail to burn the fat presently,** that is, he was about to have the fat of his offering burned, according to law, **and then take as much as thy soul desireth; then he,** the priests' servant, **would answer him, Nay; but thou shalt give it me now; and if not, I will take it by force.** These abuses had been introduced by Eli's sons in connection with the peace-offerings, with which a sacrificial meal was connected. **V. 17. Wherefore the sin of the young men was very great before the Lord,** it was an outrage equivalent to sacrilege; **for men abhorred the offering of the Lord,** they despised and blasphemed it as a form of graft in holy places. That is the height of corruption in the Church, when the servants of the sanctuary themselves are godless rascals, having only their temporal advancement in view, and thus give the enemies of the Lord occasion to blaspheme.

HANNAH BLESSED BY THE LORD. — **V. 18. But Samuel ministered before the Lord, being a child, girded with a linen ephod,** a garment for the shoulders patterned after the ephod of the high priest, worn by all priests as a sign of their calling. **V. 19. Moreover, his mother made him a little coat,** an every-day garment, **and brought it to him from year to year, when she came up with her husband to offer the yearly sacrifice,** a close connection thus being maintained between the home of the parents and the lad in the Tabernacle. **V. 20. And Eli blessed Elkanah and his wife and said, The Lord**

**give thee seed of this woman for the loan which is lent to the Lord,** or, instead of the begged one, Samuel, whom she begged from the Lord, in place of the gift which was asked for Jehovah. **And they went unto their own home. V. 21. And the Lord visited Hannah** once more in merciful goodness, **so that she conceived and bare three sons and two daughters.** That was the Lord's reward for her pious confidence in Him. **And the child Samuel grew before the Lord,** in wisdom and knowledge, which flowed from the fear of the Lord. That is a blessing of the Lord, when a boy, a young man, grows up in the fear of the Lord, increases in knowledge and in favor with God and men.

THE PROPHECY AGAINST ELI. — **V. 22. Now Eli was very old and heard all that his sons did unto all Israel,** as described above, **and how they lay with the women that assembled at the door of the Tabernacle of the Congregation,** women who performed certain services in the court of the Tabernacle, Ex. 38, 8, so that the Sanctuary was desecrated by the sensual lusts of these men, by their seduction of the serving women. **V. 23. And he said unto them, Why do ye such things? For I hear of your evil dealings by all this people,** the report of the wickedness having been brought to him. **V. 24. Nay, my sons; for it is no good report that I hear; ye make the Lord's people to transgress,** for many took offense and followed the evil example set before them. **V. 25. If one man sin against another, the judge shall judge him,** in case of transgressions between men, God, as the chief Judge, adjudicates the matter through the government instituted by Him; **but if a man sin against the Lord, who shall intreat for him,** in that case no man can act as intercessor. **Notwithstanding, they hearkened not unto the voice of their father,** to his mild reproaches, **because the Lord would slay them,** they had gone so far in willful sinning that they had become obdurate, they were on their way to perdition. **V. 26. And the child Samuel grew on, and was in favor both with the Lord and also with men,** this being noted here once more by way of effective contrast. **V. 27. And there came a man of God,** a prophet, **unto Eli and said unto him, Thus saith the Lord, Did I plainly appear,** reveal Myself, **unto the house of thy father,** Aaron, through his direct ancestor Ithamar, the son of Aaron, **when they were in Egypt in Pharaoh's house? V. 28. And did I choose him,** rather, affirmatively, "I did choose him," Aaron, **out of all the tribes of Israel to be My priest, to offer upon Mine altar, to burn incense, to wear an ephod before Me,** Ex. 28, 1. 4; Num. 16, 5; 18, 1. 7. **And did I give unto the house of thy father all the offerings made by fire of the children of Israel?** Lev. 2, 3. 10; 6, 16. **V. 29. Wherefore kick ye at My sacrifice and at Mine offering,** treading them under foot, **which I have commanded in My habitation,** in the Tabernacle (this was done by the contemptuous, blasphemous behavior of the priests**), and honorest thy sons above Me,** by not taking an energetic stand against them, **to make yourselves fat with the chiefest of all the offerings of Israel, My people,** by taking all the choicest parts of the sacrificial animals? **V. 30. Wherefore the Lord God of Israel saith, I said indeed that thy house and the house of thy father should walk before Me forever,** in performing the service of priests; for the; fact that Eli, of the family of Ithamar, was high priest at this time, was only a temporary arrangement, the descendants of Phinehas probably lacking the energy needed for the office at that time. **But now the Lord saith, Be it far from Me; for them that honor Me I will honor, and they that despise Me shall be**

**lightly esteemed,** covered with contempt and shame. **V. 31. Behold, the days come, that I will cut off thine arm,** the word here standing for might, power, influence, authority, **and the arm of thy father's house, that there shall not be an old man in thine house,** as long as the family existed, none of its members would reach a ripe old age. **V. 32. And thou shalt see an enemy in My habitation, in all the wealth which God shall give Israel,** he would, so far as his own family was concerned, see distress and affliction for the inhabitants of the Tabernacle in all the blessings which the Lord would show His people, since they would not share in the national prosperity and the consequent rejoicing; **and there shall not be an old man in thine house forever. V. 33. And the man,** the descendant, **of thine whom I shall not cut off from Mine altar shall be to consume thine eyes and to grieve thine heart; and all the increase of thine house shall die in the flower of their age.** So there would always be a descendant of the house of Eli serving at the Tabernacle, to be a witness of the decay of the true worship, thus being consumed with anxiety and worry over the fate of the Tabernacle. **V. 34. And this shall be a sign unto thee,** an earnest of the fulfilment of His threat, **that shall come upon thy two sons, on Hophni and Phinehas: in one day they shall die both of them.** That is the invariable consequence, when parents hold their peace at the sins of their children or venture only a faint objection, omit reproof and correction, love or fear their children more than God. **V. 35. And I will raise Me up a faithful priest that shall do according to that which is in Mine heart and in My mind,** one upon whom He could rely absolutely, and who would perform all his work exactly in the manner most pleasing to the Lord. **And I will build him a sure house; and he shall walk before Mine**

**Anointed forever.** This is a prophecy of Christ, who is Priest and King in one person. **V. 36. And it shall come to pass that every one that is left in thine house shall come and crouch to him,** in the position of a suppliant, with bended knee, **for a piece of silver and a morsel of bread, and shall say, Put me, I pray thee, into one of the priests' offices that I may eat a piece of bread.** He who takes his refuge to Messiah, the great Priest-king, confessing the need brought upon him by reason of his sinfulness, will find in Him grace and mercy and peace without end.

# 1 Samuel 3

**S**amuel's Call.

THE LORD REVEALS HIMSELF TO SAMUEL. — **V. 1. And the child Samuel ministered unto the Lord before Eli,** as a special servant of the Sanctuary, under the immediate direction of the high priest. **And the Word of the Lord was precious in those days,** it rarely happened that the Lord sent a message by direct prophetic announcement; **there was no open vision,** literally, "there was no vision spread abroad," made public frequently. There was lacking, on the one hand, a pious, God-fearing priesthood and, on the other hand, an appreciation of the divine Spirit's work through the Word. "Jehovah had indeed promised His people to send prophets, who should reveal to them His will and counsel, Deut. 18, 15 ff.; cp. Num. 23, 23; but since divine revelation presupposes willingness to accept the truth on the part of man, the unbelief and the disobedience of the people was able to hinder the fulfillment of this and similar prophecies, and God could in punishment deprive the idolatrous people of His Word." (Keil.) **V. 2. And it came to pass at that time, when**

**Eli was laid down in his place,** namely, to sleep at night in the room reserved for him, **and his eyes began to wax dim that he could not see,** this being added by way of parenthesis, in order to explain the action of Samuel, who supposed that Eli was calling him to assist him in some manner, **v. 3. and ere the lamp of God,** the large candlestick with its seven lamps, whose oil was replenished every morning, since they went out toward morning, **went out in the Temple of the Lord, where the ark of God was, and Samuel was laid down to sleep, v. 4. that the Lord called Samuel; and he answered, Here am I.** So Samuel was sleeping in one of the rooms which were built in the court of the Tabernacle for the use of the priests and Levites who happened to be on duty, and it was toward morning. **V. 5. And he ran unto Eli and said, Here am I; for thou calledst me.** That was the conclusion which he naturally drew, and his faithful willingness took him to the room of Eli as quickly as he could get there – a fine example to many a young man of our days. **And he,** Eli, **said, I called not; lie down again,** evidently supposing that Samuel had merely dreamed he was being called. **And he went and lay down. V. 6. And the Lord called yet again, Samuel! And Samuel arose, and went to Eli, and said, Here am I; for thou didst call me.** He was again, as a faithful servant, ready to do his master's bidding; there was no peevish discontent in his voice for having been called out of his rest. **And he,** Eli, **answered, I called not, my son; lie down again,** still believing that the young man was being misled by some illusion of the senses. **V. 7. Now, Samuel did not yet know the Lord, neither was the Word of the Lord yet revealed unto him.** This is added by way of explanation. Samuel did not yet possess the special, direct knowledge of God, for this was given only by an extraordinary revelation of Jehovah, in dreams and in visions, and this form of manifestation was at that time practically unknown in Israel; hence his ignorance. **V. 8. And the Lord called Samuel again the third time. And he arose and went to Eli,** still with the same cheerful willingness which disregarded its own comfort, **and said, Here am I; for thou didst call me.** He was ready for service day or night, and without the slightest irritation. **And Eli perceived that the Lord had called the child.** This was the conclusion which Eli reached from his knowledge of God's manner of dealing with His prophets. **V. 9. Therefore Eli said unto Samuel, Go, lie down; and it shall be, if He call thee, that thou shalt say, Speak, Lord, for Thy servant heareth. So Samuel,** ever obedient, even while he may have wondered about the strangeness of the command, **went and lay down in his place. V. 10. And the Lord,** who had at first manifested Himself merely by His voice, **came, and stood,** in a vision which must have been plainly visible to Samuel upon awakening, **and called as at other times, Samuel! Samuel! Then Samuel answered, Speak, for Thy servant heareth.** Samuel is not only an example of obedience, but also of willingness to hear the voice of the Lord. Like him all believers should open their ears and hearts to God and give heed to the voice which comes to us in the Word.

THE PROPHECY AGAINST ELI. — **V. 11. And the Lord said to Samuel,** in a revelation which was his call to the office of prophet in Israel, **Behold, I will do a thing in Israel at which both the ears of every one that heareth it shall tingle,** with sudden dread and horror, which almost cause a person to lose his senses over the fearfulness of the impending doom. **V. 12. In that day I will perform against Eli all things which I have spoken concerning his house,** the destruction foretold by the prophet, chap. 2, 27-36; **when I begin, I will also make an end,** He would both begin and also conclude what He had decided upon as punishment. **V. 13. For I have told him that I will judge his house forever for the iniquity which he knoweth,** punish him and his entire family on account of the transgression of his sons, of whose guilt he had become a partaker; **because his sons made themselves vile,** deliberately placed themselves under the curse of the Law, **and he restrained them not,** made no serious, emphatic move to interfere with them. **V. 14. And therefore I have sworn unto the house of Eli,** by an oath which made the sentence of punishment irrevocable, **that the iniquity of Eli's house shall not be purged with sacrifice nor offering forever.** It was no longer a warning, but a definite statement of a curse which was about to descend upon Eli and his house for his neglect of the duty which he should have performed to his sons as father, high priest, and judge, by employing severe chastisement und punishment upon them. The harm done by the crimes of the priests affected the whole family, even their descendants. This story should be heeded more in our days, when mawkish sentimentality is making a farce of bringing up children. **V. 15. And Samuel lay until the morning,** sleeping in his bed, untroubled by an evil conscience, **and opened the doors of the house of the Lord,** those of the entrance to the court, so the people might come in for the morning worship. **And Samuel feared to tell Eli the vision,** the revelation which he had received, since it. threatened evil to the house of his master. **V. 16. Then Eli called Samuel and said. Samuel, my son! And he answered, Here am I.** Even the divine revelation which had been vouchsafed him did not change the simple obedience of Samuel. **V. 17. And he,** Eli, said. **What is the**

20

**thing that the Lord hath said unto thee?** He felt that the revelation concerned him, and he was eager to know it. **I pray thee hide it not from me; God do so to thee, and more also,** in a severe punishment, **if thou hide anything from me of all the things that He said unto thee.** Eli's excitement is seen in the climax formed by his words. "He asks for the word of the Lord; he demands an exact and complete statement; he adjures Samuel not to conceal anything from him." (Lange.) **V. 18. And Samuel told him every whit,** placing the pathetic demand of Eli above his own fear and sorrow, **and hid nothing from him.** Thus Samuel entered upon his prophetic office. **And he,** Eli, **said, It is the Lord; let Him do what seemeth Him good.** He expressed his humble submission to the will of the Lord, for with all his weakness and in spite of his transgression he was a believer in Jehovah of Israel, and he realized the justice of the punishment. **V. 19. And Samuel grew,** he reached full manhood, **and the Lord was with him,** not only by general manifestations of His goodness and mercy, but also by special revelations and gifts of the Spirit which the Lord imparted to him as His prophet, **and did let none of his words fall to the ground,** what he prophetically announced as the Word of Jehovah was fulfilled. **V. 20. And all Israel from Dan,** on the extreme northern boundary, **even to Beersheba,** the city in the extreme south, **knew that Samuel was established to be a prophet of the Lord,** throughout all Israel, in the entire land of Canaan, Samuel was known as a faithful, trustworthy prophet, upon whose words one could depend. **V. 21. And the Lord appeared again in Shiloh,** He continued to manifest Himself there; **for the Lord revealed Himself to Samuel in Shiloh by the Word of the Lord.** God made known His will to the people by the revelation of His Word to Samuel, who was thus the first exponent of the permanent prophetic order. It has happened repeatedly in history that the Lord graciously visited His people after a season of spiritual drought and gave them His Gospel in rich measure.

# 4

# 1 Samuel 4

War with the Philistines.

THE ARK OF THE COVENANT IN CAMP. — **V. 1. And the word of Samuel came to all Israel,** it was heard throughout the nation and served for the guidance of Israel, the people accepted it without question as the Word of Jehovah. **Now, Israel went out against the Philistines,** who at that time were their oppressors, **to battle, and pitched beside Ebenezer,** a place between Mizpeh and Shen which was afterwards given this name, chap. 7, 12; **and the Philistines pitched in Aphek,** also some distance west or northwest of Jerusalem. **V. 2. And the Philistines put themselves in array against Israel; and when they joined battle,** the charge being made from both sides at the same time, **Israel was smitten before the Philistines,** they were worsted in the encounter; **and they slew of the army,** while the Israelites were trying to hold their line of battle, **in the field,** out on the plain where the battle was fought, **about four thousand men.** They did not, however, put the Israelites to rout that day. **V. 3. And when the people were come into the camp,** in an orderly retreat, withdrawing their forces before the superior strength of the enemy, **the elders of Israel said, Wherefore hath the Lord smitten us today before the Philistines?** They felt that this was the only explanation of. their failure, for they had apparently undertaken the campaign at the suggestion of Samuel. **Let us fetch the Ark of the Covenant of the Lord out of Shiloh into us, that, when it cometh among us, it may save us out of the hand of our enemies.** Instead of turning to the Lord in true sorrow and repentance over their sins, the people placed their trust, in a superstitious manner, in the material vessel, as in a fetish. Their faith was obscured by this heathenish feature. It was in vain for them to trust in God, when they were not purged from their sins. **V. 4. So the people sent to Shiloh that they might bring from thence the Ark of the Covenant of the Lord of hosts, which dwelleth between the cherubims,** the very name intimating their hope that God would join their forces by this mere outward act on their part; for God had revealed Himself to Moses from the cover of the ark, from between the cherubim, Ex. 25, 22. **And the two sons of Eli, Hophin and Phinehas, were there with the Ark of the Covenant of God,** men whose acts in desecrating the Sanctuary of the Lord were notorious. **V. 5. And when the Ark of the Covenant of the Lord came into the camp,** borne an the shoulders of the reprobate priests, **all Israel shouted with a great shout, so that the earth rang again,** resounding and reverberating from the shouting of the army. **V. 6. And when the Philistines heard the noise of the shout,** the confident cry of victory, **they said, What meaneth the noise of this great shout in the camp of the Hebrews? And they understood,** found out, **that the ark of the Lord was come into the camp. V. 7. And the Philistines were afraid,**

**for they said, God is come into the camp.** Like all heathen, they had a superstitious fear of the supernatural, also of the deities of their enemies. Moreover, the Philistines feared the power of the God of the Israelites all the more, since the fame of His powerful deeds in former times had come to their ears. **And they said,** in consternation and fear, **Woe unto us! For there hath not been such a thing heretofore.** This expedient had never been adopted by Israel before this. **V. 8. Woe unto us! Who shall deliver us out of the hands of these mighty Gods? These are the Gods that smote the Egyptians with all the plagues in the wilderness.** As heathen they speak of the true God in the plural, and in their excitement they express a confused view. by combining the recollection of the plagues in Egypt and the destruction of the Egyptian army in the Red Sea into one statement. But the very fear, consternation, and despair of the Philistines encouraged them to make a last supreme effort to break the power of Israel. **V. 9. Be strong, and quit yourselves like men, O ye Philistines, that ye be not servants unto the Hebrews, as they have been to you; quit yourselves like men and fight!** A decisive victory on the part of Israel would have turned the tables and made the Philistines tributary, and the fear of such a contingency was another factor in strengthening their arms. **V. 10. And the Philistines fought,** in a bitter attack; **and Israel was smitten, and they fled every man into his tent,** back to his home. **And there was a very great slaughter; for there fell of Israel thirty thousand footmen,** a total of thirty thousand (for Israel had no cavalry). **V. 11. And the ark of God was taken,** as a welcome prize; **and the two sons of Eli, Hophni and Phinehas,** the guardians of the ark, **were slain**. Thus the Lord gave His people evidence that He had indeed withdrawn His merciful presence from them, in spite of the fact that they had the ark in their camp. This is a serious warning to all who boast of their orthodoxy in a mere fleshly manner. relying upon this fact to give them a standing before God, just as many have the name of Christ in their mouths, but are far from accepting Him as their personal Savior. God wants true repentance, faith, fear of His Word. A dead orthodoxy without true piety of the heart avails nothing.

DEATH OF ELI AND OF HIS DAUGHTER-IN-LAW. — **V. 12. And there ran a man of Benjamin out of the army,** which was now in utter rout, **and came to Shiloh the same day with his clothes rent and with earth upon his head,** as signs of a sudden deep grief, in which the heart is rent with sorrow. **V. 13. And when he came, lo, Eli sat upon a seat by the wayside watching,** straining his feeble eyes as much as their remaining strength permitted; **for his heart trembled for the ark of God,** especially since it had been taken without divine permission, and he was its real guardian, responsible for it. **And when the man came into the city and told it,** brought the news of the defeat of Israel's army, **all the city cried out,** in sorrow, fear, and dread. **V. 14. And when Eli heard the noise of the crying, he said, What meaneth the noise of this tumult?** The very sound of the cries filled him with grave forebodings. **And the man came in hastily and told Eli. v. 15. Now, Eli was ninety and eight years old; and his eyes were dim that he could not see;** they were set in the lifeless, motionless appearance found in the extremely old, just before total blindness ensues. **V. 16. And the man said unto Eli, I am he that came out of the army, and I fled today out of the army.** He was in a position to give authentic news. **And he said, What is there done, my son?** What news is there? What happened? **V. 17. And the messenger answered**

26

**and said, Israel is fled before the Philistines, and there hath been also a great slaughter among the people, and thy two sons also, Hophni and Phinehas, are dead, and the ark of God is taken.** The fugitive poured forth his news in four sharp sentences, every succeeding blow being harder, until the force of the message reached its climax in the crushing report that the ark was lost to the enemies. **V. 18. And it came to pass, when he made mention of the ark of God,** all the other blows having been expected by Eli, **that he fell from off the seat backward by the side of the gate,** evidently at the entrance to the court of the Tabernacle, **and his neck brake, and he died; for he was an old man and heavy.** It was the beginning of the divine judgment upon Eli and his family, although he himself seems to have died in the fear of God. **And he had judged Israel forty years. V. 19. And his daughter-in-law, Phinehas' wife, was with child, near to be delivered; and when she heard the tidings that the ark of God was taken and that her father-in-law and her husband were dead, she bowed herself and travailed; for her pains came upon her,** literally, "turned upon her in a sudden attack," came upon her prematurely. **V. 20. And about the time of her death,** for her strength was not able to bear the blow, **the women that stood by her said unto her, Fear not; for thou hast born a son,** the message being intended to comfort and strengthen her. **But she answered not, neither did she regard it;** she entirely ignored this information, since her mind was occupied with the more serious matter of the ark. **V. 21. And she named the child Ichabod** (not-glory), **saying, The glory is departed from Israel,** is carried into captivity, **because the ark of God was taken, and because of her father-in-law and her husband. V. 22. And she said,** repeating her

27

complaint in a dull repetition, as though unable to grasp the magnitude of the horror which had come upon Israel, **The glory is departed from Israel; for the ark of God is taken.** "With the abandonment of the earthly throne of His glory the Lord seemed to have annulled His covenant of grace with Israel; for the ark, with the tables of the Law and the mercy-seat, was the visible pledge of the covenant of grace which Jehovah had made with Israel." (Keil.) The account of this death contains a great deal of comfort for poor sinners. He who in the hour of death clings to the Word of God and the covenant of His mercy dies a blessed death. God's Word is the power of God unto salvation to everyone that believeth.

# 1 Samuel 5

**T**he Philistines Smitten because of the Ark.
THE ARK IN ASHDOD. — **V. l. And the philistines took the ark of God,** which they had captured in the great battle, **and brought it from Ebenezer,** as the place was afterward called, **unto Ashdod,** a city of Philistia almost due west of the battlefield, on the Mediterranean, apparently the leading city in the federation of city-states among the Philistines. **V. 2. When the Philistines took the ark of God, they brought it into the house of Dagon,** their chief idol, to whose honor they had erected sanctuaries in all their principal cities, Judg. 16, 23, **and set it by Dagon,** near the picture or statue of this deity, which had a human head and hands, but a fish-body, to symbolize the fruitfulness of the sea, as represented by the fish. **V. 3. And when they of Ashdod arose early on the morrow, behold, Dagon,** to whom they ascribed their victory over the Israelites, **was fallen upon his face to the earth before the ark of the Lord,** in an attitude of worship, this being intended as a sign to the Philistines that the God of Israel was not to be conquered, but that every idol and

so-called deity would have to sink to the ground before His majesty and power. **And they,** the priests of the Philistines, **took Dagon and set him in his place again,** apparently under the impression that the figure had toppled over by chance, not having been set up securely. **V. 4. And when they arose early on the morrow morning,** the second morning after the arrival of the ark, **behold, Dagon was fallen upon his face to the ground before the ark of the Lord,** in the same posture of abject adoration; **and the head of Dagon and both the palms of his hands,** the hollow forms of his hands, **were cut off,** severed as by a clean stroke, **upon the threshold,** namely, that of the inner sanctuary, in which the idol was placed, where the parts might be trodden on by everyone who entered; **only the stump of Dagon,** his fish-body, that which was properly the Fish-god, **was left to him. V. 5. Therefore neither the priests of Dagon,** of whom there seems to have been a special order, **nor any that come into Dagon's house, tread on the threshold of Dagon in Ashdod unto this day,** all visitors to his shrine carefully stepped over the door-sill, lest they should desecrate the place where the head of the god had lain. **V. 6. But the hand of the Lord was heavy upon them of Ashdod,** in an oppressive visitation, probably in the form of a plague of field-mice, to which the context seems to point, **and he destroyed them,** caused the death of many of them, **and smote them with emerods,** with an infectious skin-disease in the form of boils and ulcers, **even Ashdod and the coast thereof,** the entire vicinity. **V. 7. And when the men of Ashdod saw that it was so, they said,** rightly concluding that it was the God of Israel who was striking them, **The ark of the God of Israel shall not abide with us,** they regarded it as the medium, as the bearer of all the evils; **for His hand is**

**sore upon us and upon Dagon, our god.** Thus God proved to the heathen, as He does to the unbelievers at times to this day, that all idols are nothing before Him, that those things in which the world places its trust crumble to pieces before the manifestation of His majesty and righteousness.

THE ARK IN GATH AND EKRON. — V. 8. **They sent, therefore, and gathered all the lords of the Philistines,** the heads of their five city-states, **unto them and said, What shall we do with the ark of the God of Israel?** As eager as they were to have the ark in their city as a trophy of their great victory, so eager were they now to get rid of the unlucky piece of furniture. **And they answered, Let the ark of the God of Israel be carried about unto Gath.** The princes of the Philistines intended to make an experiment, in order to determine whether the misfortunes which struck Ashdod were really to be attributed to the ark or were the result of chance. **And they carried the ark of the God of Israel about thither,** farther to the east. **V. 9. And it was so that, after they had carried it about,** caused it to be taken in the indicated direction, to this second city, **the hand of the Lord was against the city with a very great destruction,** disquietude, consternation taking hold upon all the inhabitants, a feeling of impending disaster; **and He smote the men of the city, both small and great, and they had emerods in their secret parts,** they were plagued with the same eruption of boils as the people of Ashdod had been, and the boils apparently broke open, causing painful ulcers. **V. 10. Therefore they sent the ark of God to Ekron,** the chief city in the northwestern part of the Philistine country. **And it came to pass, as the ark of God came to Ekron,** by the command of the Philistine chiefs, **that the Ekronites cried out,** for they had been informed of the plague which had struck Ashdod and

Gath, **saying, They have brought about the ark of the God of Israel to us to slay us and our people.** But their protest was ignored, and the ark was brought into their city. **V. 11. So they sent and gathered together all the lords of the Philistines,** for a second conference, **and said, Send away the ark of the God of Israel, and let it go again to his own place, that it slay us not and our people.** The plague was not only generally prevalent, but also especially malignant, the effects being exceptionally deadly; **for there was a deadly destruction,** a consternation of terror on account of the sudden death of so many people, **throughout all the city; the hand of God was very heavy there,** the severity of the plague here reached its greatest height. **V. 12. And the men that died not were smitten with the emerods,** being extremely ill with the boil-sickness; **and the cry of the city went up to heaven,** for the Philistines were forced to acknowledge that in this place the almighty hand of the God of Israel was revealed. Thus the Lord revenged the sacrilege of the heathen in laying their hands upon the ark consecrated to Him. When unbelievers presume to attack the Word of God, to blaspheme and persecute the Word of Salvation, and, in addition, refuse to bow under the chastening hand of God, He often visits them with very severe plagues and terrors.

# 6

# 1 Samuel 6

**eturn of the Ark to Israel.**
THE ARK SENT BACK TO BETH-SHEMESH. — **V. 1. And the ark of the Lord was in the country of the Philistines seven months,** in the three cities of the Philistine territory which were named in the preceding chapter. **V. 2. And the Philistines,** as represented by their five lords, **called for the priests and the diviners,** all of whom were supposed to possess soothsaying power to reveal the counsel of the deity, **saying, What shall we do to the ark of the Lord?** What form of procedure was advisable in the circumstances? **Tell us wherewith we shall send it to his place.** They were especially anxious to find out what gifts of atonement must accompany the ark on its return in order that the plague might be stopped. **V. 3. And they,** the soothsayers, **said, If ye send away the ark of the God of Israel, send it not empty,** without some expiatory gift; **but in any wise return Him a trespass-offering,** a sacrifice or gift to atone for their offense, to wipe out their debt; **then ye shall be healed, and it shall be known to you why His hand is not removed from**

**you;** by the cure which the soothsayers expected to follow this course the people would learn that it was actually God's hand which was smiting them, a matter which the priests themselves were not yet quite ready to concede. **V. 4. Then said they, What shall be the trespass-offering which we shalt return to Him? They answered, Five golden emerods and five golden mice, according to the number of the lords of the Philistines,** which, in turn, agreed with that of the city-states in the federation; **for one plague was on you all and on your lords.** In suggesting five golden boils and five golden mice the soothsayers followed the ancient custom by which likenesses of the diseased parts were dedicated to the deity to whom the sickness was ascribed. **V. 5. Wherefore ye shall make images,** carved or engraved likenesses, **of your emerods and images of your mice that mar the land; and ye shall give glory unto the God of Israel,** confessing that the plagues with which they had been smitten had been laid upon them in justice; **peradventure He will lighten His hand from off you,** by causing the punishment to stop, **and from off your gods, and from off your land,** the burden of the chastisement thus being taken from their entire nation. Still they are careful to speak conditionally, in order to have an excuse if their plan should fail. **V. 6. Wherefore, then, do ye harden your hearts, as the Egyptians and Pharaoh hardened their hearts,** Ex. 7, 13? **When He had wrought wonderfully among them,** carried out His avenging purpose upon them, **did they not let the people go and they departed?** Cp. Ex. 12, 31 ff. The Philistines were urged to profit by the example of the Egyptians, not as a matter of conviction or of confession of the true God, but of expediency, the God of Israel apparently being the stronger God, who therefore had to be humored.

34

**V. 7. Now, therefore, make a new cart,** take and prepare in the proper manner, **and take two milch kine on which there hath come no yoke,** cp. Deut. 21, 3, **and tie the kine to the cart,** hitching them before the cart to draw it, **and bring their calves home from them,** holding them back in the barn; **v. 8. and take the ark of the Lord, and lay it upon the cart; and put the jewels of gold which ye return Him for a trespass-offering,** the five golden boils and the five golden mice, **in a coffer,** a small chest, **by the side thereof; and send it away that it may go,** giving the strange draft-animals their head. Only such things were to be used as had not been desecrated by profane use, in order to show proper honor to the dreaded God of Israel. **V. 9. And see, if it,** the cart as thus prepared, **goeth up by the way of his own coast to Beth-shemesh,** within the territory of Israel, **then He,** the God of Israel, **hath done us this great evil; but if not, then we shall know that it is not His hand that smote us; it was a chance that happened to us.** The crafty priests of Dagon, who feared for their prestige, had purposely specified cows with calves, since it was probable that their instinct, their natural impulse, would tend to make them turn back to their stalls, unless a higher power restrained them, compelling them to take the road to Beth-shemesh and hold it. **V. 10. And the men did so; and took two milch kine, and tied them to the cart, and shut up their calves at home; v. 11. and they laid the ark of the Lord upon the cart and the coffer with the mice of gold and the images of their emerods. V. 12. And the kine took the straight way to the way of Beth-shemesh,** headed directly for the highway leading to the nearest city of Israel, just beyond the boundary, **and went along the highway,** keeping to the road, **lowing as they went,** because they wanted their calves, **and turned not**

**aside to the right hand or to the left,** made no attempt to go back to their stalls; **and the lords of the Philistines went after them unto the border of Beth-shemesh,** to find out where the animals would take the ark. It was evident that the living God directed the course of the cart, and that it was He who had sent the punishment upon the Philistines. It may well be that this realization caused at least some of the Philistines to turn to the true God. Thus many a national calamity has, in the hands of God, been a means of making people realize their sinfulness and turn to the living God for their salvation.

THE ARK ACCEPTED, BUT THE PEOPLE SLAIN. — **V. 13. And they of Beth-shemesh,** which was a city set aside for priests on the boundary between Judah and Dan, Josh. 15, 10; 21, 16, **were reaping their wheat-harvest in the valley,** about the beginning of June; **and they lifted up their eyes, and saw the ark, and rejoiced to see it,** very much pleased to know that it had been returned to Israel. **V. 14. And the cart came into the field of Joshua, a Beth-shemite, and stood there, where there was a great stone,** the cows came to a halt there of their own free will; **and they,** the inhabitants of the city, **clave the wood of the cart and offered the kine a burnt offering unto the Lord. V. 15. And the Levites,** who also were living in the city, **took down the ark of the Lord,** had taken it down as soon as they received news of the joyful happening, **and the coffer that was with it, wherein the jewels of gold were, and put them on the great stone; and the men of Beth-shemesh,** in a second sacrificial act, **offered burnt offerings,** thus consecrating themselves anew to the service of the Lord, **and sacrificed sacrifices the same day unto the Lord,** the sacrificial meals being intended to renew their fellowship with Jehovah, who had proved Himself such a mighty God, the only true Lord. **V. 16. And when the five lords of the Philistines had seen it,** being witnesses of this revelation of the God of Israel, **they returned to Ekron the same day,** having followed the instructions of their priests. **V. 17. And these are the golden emerods which the Philistines returned for a trespass-offering unto the Lord,** as expiatory gifts: **for Ashdod one, for Gaza one, for Askelon one, for Gath one, for Ekron one,** these being the five city-states of the Philistines; **v. 18. and the golden mice, according to the number of all the cities of the Philistines belonging to the five lords, both of fenced cities and of country villages,** every city and town in the five states thus being represented by a figure, evidently because the plague of the mice had extended over the entire country, **even unto the great stone of Abel,** that mighty attar like ledge in the field of Joshua, **whereon they set the ark of the Lord; which stone remaineth unto this day in the field of Joshua, the Beth-shemite,** a mute witness and monument of the event as here recorded. **V. 19. And he,** God, **smote the men of Beth-shemesh, because they,** overcome by a blasphemous curiosity, **had looked into the ark of the Lord,** in a manner which did not agree with the holiness of Jehovah, to whom the ark was dedicated, **even He smote of the people fifty thousand and threescore and ten men. And the people lamented because the Lord had smitten many of the people with a great slaughter** 2) Apparently the presence of the ark attracted a great many sightseers from the entire surrounding country, who came with anything but a reverent mind and were therefore punished by Jehovah. **V. 20. And the men of Beth-shemesh said, Who is able to stand before this holy Lord God? And to whom shall He go up from us?** They were afraid to keep the ark in their own midst after the great tragedy had occurred. **V. 21. And they sent messengers to the inhabitants of Kirjath-jearim,** a city of Judah somewhat farther to the east, **saying, The Philistines have brought again the ark of the Lord; come ye down and fetch it up to you.** The Beth-shemites felt that they were no better than the men who had been killed, and they dreaded a recurrence of the tragedy. All those who dare to draw near to the means of grace, the Word and the Sacrament, with fleshly minds, with sacrilegious hearts, will receive no blessing, but only God's judgment and condemnation.

# 7

# 1 Samuel 7

Israel's Repentance and Victory over the Philistines. REFORMATION IN ISRAEL. — **V. 1. And the men of Kirjath-jearim,** to whom the Bethshemites had sent word of the return of the ark, chap. 6, 21, **came, and fetched up the ark of the Lord, and brought it into the house of Abinadab in the hill,** on an elevation near the city, **and sanctified Eleazar, his son, to keep the ark of the Lord,** for he was probably of Levitical descent, otherwise he would hardly have been entrusted with this office. **v. 2. And it came to pass, while the ark abode in Kirjath-jearim, that the time was long,** its length, on account of conditions in Israel and on account of the oppression of the Philistines, seemed unusually great; **for it was twenty years,** twenty years of servitude and disgrace; **and all the house of Israel lamented after the Lord,** turning to Him again and entreating Him to deliver them **V. 3. And Samuel spake unto all the house of Israel, saying,** with reference to the apparent sincere sorrow of the people, **If ye do return unto the Lord with all your hearts,** if their lamenting was no mere sham and hypocrisy,

**then put away the strange gods and Ashtaroth,** the male and female idols of the heathen nations of Canaan, **from among you, and prepare your hearts unto the Lord,** firmly established in faith and trust in Him, **and serve Him only,** for the service of the true God and of false deities of any kind does not agree together; **and He will deliver you out of the hand of the Philistines,** announcing His relation as covenant God to them by saving them from their enemies and once more establishing them as an independent people. **V. 4. Then the children of Israel,** heeding the earnest words of their great prophet and leader, **did put away Baalim and Ashtaroth,** they completely did away with the worship of strange gods, **and served the Lord only,** they restored His exclusive worship. Here again the fact is brought out that idolatry had been practiced, but in such a manner that the Jehovah worship had outwardly been kept up. It was the same mixture of true and false religion which is now found in so many parts of Christendom, where antichristian religious societies are existing in the very midst of so-called Christian congregations. **V. 5. And Samuel said, Gather all Israel to Mizpeh,** which was used as a place of assembly at other times also, Judg. 20, 1, **and I will pray for you unto the Lord,** principally with the object of restoring them to the covenant relation with Jehovah, now that their conversion had been shown to be sincere. **V. 6. And they gathered together to Mizpeh, and drew water, and poured it out before the Lord,** a symbolic act of penitence as expressing their deep misery, care, and anxiety, Ps. 22, 15, **and fasted on that day,** to express the deep humiliation of their souls, **and said there, We have sinned against the Lord.** It was a frank, unequivocal confession of their guilt, accompanied by such outward acts of mourning and sorrow as showed the sincerity of their conversion to Jehovah. **And Samuel judged the children of Israel in Mizpeh,** exercising the functions of his judicial position in Israel, he administered right and justice, and proposed measures that looked to the good of the people. **V. 7. And when the Philistines heard that the children of Israel were gathered together to Mizpeh, the lords of the Philistines went up against Israel,** they mobilized an army to attack the children of Israel, for they considered the great assembly a hostile demonstration, if not an actual mustering for war. **And when the children of Israel heard it,** not being in readiness, evidently, for such an attack, **they were afraid of the Philistines. V. 8. And the children of Israel said to Samuel,** the sincerity of their recent conversion showing also in the fact that they now relied entirely upon Jehovah, **Cease not to cry unto the Lord, our God, for us,** by keeping silence for so much as one moment, **that He will save us out of the hand of the Philistines.** That is genuine repentance, if a sinner is truly sorrowful over his sins, makes a frank confession of his transgressions, puts away from him everything that displeases God, and places his trust in the Lord alone.

THE PHILISTINES OVERTHROWN. — **V. 9. And Samuel took a sucking lamb,** one having been about seven days with its mother, Lev. 22, 27, **and offered it for a burnt offering wholly unto the Lord,** without having divided it according to the usual form of burnt offerings. **And Samuel cried unto the Lord for Israel; and the Lord heard him,** gave him an answer in the defeat of their enemies, as now related. **V. 10. And as Samuel was offering up the burnt offering,** while this act of worship was still going on, **the Philistines drew near to battle against Israel; but the Lord thundered with a**

**great thunder,** with terrific peals, which followed one after another, **on that day upon the Philistines and discomfited them,** so that they were terrified, confused, and confounded; **and they were smitten before Israel,** literally, "before the face of Israel," while the Israelites were looking on in wonder. **V. 11. And the men of Israel,** while the enemies turned away in confusion, **went out of Mizpeh, and pursued the Philistines, and smote them until they came under Bethcar,** below a city at some distance from the field of battle. **V. 12. Then Samuel took a stone, and set it between Mizpeh and Shen,** at the place where the two former battles with the Philistines had also been fought, **and called the name of it Ebenezer** (stone of help), **saying, Hitherto hath the Lord helped us.** Although the victory did not complete the deliverance from the oppression of the Philistines, yet it pointed to the fact that Jehovah was once more with the army of Israel, and therefore this token of thanksgiving in the name of the whole people properly expressed the sentiments which were stirring their hearts. **V. 13. So the Philistines were subdued,** in consequence of this victory, **and they came no more into the coast of Israel,** all attempts made by them with this object in view were promptly frustrated; **and the hand of the Lord was against the Philistines all the days of Samuel;** while he lived, they did not regain the supremacy over Israel which they once held. **V. 14. And the cities which the Philistines had taken from Israel were restored to Israel, from Ekron even unto Gath,** these cities being on the Philistine frontier. These cities themselves were clearly not included in the territory which they yielded, the text merely stating that Israel recovered the land on the Philistine borders between Ekron and Gath, which had originally been subdued by the armies of Judah and Simeon, Judg. 1, 18. **And the coasts thereof did Israel deliver out of the hands of the Philistines. And there was peace between Israel and the Amorites;** the other Canaanitish nations, among whom the Amorites were the strongest, thought it the best policy not to undertake any campaigns against the children of Israel. **V. 15. And Samuel judged Israel all the days of his life,** rendering decisions in difficult matters and proposing measures for the benefit of the people even when Saul had been made king. **V. 16. And he went from year to year in circuit to Bethel,** toward the north, **and Gilgal,** in the valley of Jordan near Jericho, **and Mizpeh,** toward the southwest, **and judged Israel in all those places. V. 17. And his return was to Ramah,** to this city he always came back; **for there was his house; and there he judged Israel,** when not absent on one of his circuit-court trips; **and there he built an altar unto the Lord.** Although the Tabernacle remained at Shiloh for the time being, public worship was, for a number of years, carried on in other places as well. Thus Samuel, as judge, prophet, and priest, performed the work of his office and taught Israel the ways of the Lord. Herein he is a type of the Messiah, Jesus Christ, who is Priest, Prophet, and King in one person, who sacrificed Himself for the sins of all men, gives knowledge of the salvation gained by Him through the Gospel, and lives and reigns throughout eternity.

# 8

# 1 Samuel 8

**I**srael Demands a King.

SAMUEL DISPLEASED AT THE INSISTENT DESIRE. — **V. 1. And it came to pass, when Samuel was old, that he made his sons judges over Israel,** the increasing infirmities of old age prompting him to take this step, whereby his sons became his assistants. **V. 2. Now, the name of his first-born was Joel** (Jehovah is God), **and the name of his second, Abiah** (Jehovah is Father); **they were judges in Beersheba,** in the extreme southern part of Canaan, important in those days as a station on the trade-route between Asia and Egypt. The very names which Samuel gave his sons are an evidence of his piety even in the days of Israel's misery and disgrace. **V. 3. And his sons walked not in his ways,** they did not follow the pious example of their father, **but turned aside after lucre,** they were covetous, avaricious, they desired money, **and took bribes, and perverted judgment,** thereby transgressing the Law of the Lord, Ex. 23, 6. 8; Deut. 16, 19, and bringing the judicial office into disrepute in the eyes of the people, thus causing the latter to desire a higher authority to guide the affairs of the nation. **V. 4. Then all the elders of Israel gathered themselves together and came to Samuel unto Ramah,** as a delegation representing the whole people, **v. 5. and said unto him, Behold, thou art old, and thy sons walk not in thy ways,** his advancing age was robbing him of the vigor and energy needed in the government of the nation, and the misgovernment of his sons resulted in a general degeneration of all authority; **now make us a king to judge us like all the nations.** All the heathen nations round about had kings to rule over them, and this the petition of the elders, which undoubtedly had in mind Deut. 17, 14, emphasized, especially since Moses virtually had such a contingency in view. **V. 6. But the thing displeased Samuel when they said, Give us a king to judge us.** It was not the reference to the mismanagement of his sons nor to his own advancing age which hurt Samuel, but the fact that their faith was not grounded soundly enough upon Jehovah, who till now had directly managed the affairs of the nation. They wanted an external, visible kingdom as a means of safety and protection against their enemies, whereas the invisible, royal rule of Jehovah had till now been fully sufficient to protect them. **And Samuel prayed unto the Lord,** taking this difficult matter to Jehovah for solution. Instead of simply insisting upon his own wish, this humble, consecrated hero, in this important crisis in the history of his people, proved that his trust in God could not be shaken, that the Lord could be relied upon to give the right decision. **V. 7. And the Lord said unto Samuel, Hearken unto the voice of the people in all that they say unto thee,** the demand of the people agreed with the counsel of God, He was ready to have a temporal kingdom established in Israel; **for they have not rejected thee,**

**but they have rejected Me that I should not reign over them.**
While He was ready to grant their request, He nevertheless
expressed His dissatisfaction with that attitude of mind and
heart on their part which showed that they did not appreciate
the divine-rule, but put themselves in opposition to the royal
majesty of God. **V. 8. According to all the works which they
have done since the day that I brought them up out of Egypt
even unto this day, wherewith they have forsaken Me and
served other gods, so do they also unto thee.** So it was the
disposition of their hearts and minds which displeased the
Lord, the state of mind which had ever caused them to rebel
against Jehovah's rule, to forsake Jehovah for the purpose of
serving other gods. In the person of Samuel they rejected the
Lord and His kingdom, because they foolishly believed that
their interests were not sufficiently safeguarded under the
present arrangement. **V. 9. Now, therefore, hearken unto
their voice,** he was to accede to their demands; **howbeit, yet
protest solemnly unto them and show them the manner of
the king that shall reign over them.** Samuel was to explain
to the people in detail just what they were loading upon their
own shoulders by asking for a king, what the rights of the king
were, and what powers he might arrogate to himself; and he
was to attest and set before them their sin against Jehovah that
they might purify their hearts of their proud and distrustful
temper. In the midst of the Christian Church also men are
found time and again who object to the easy yoke of Christ and
to the beneficent instruction of the divine Word, demanding,
instead, that the honor and pride of this world be introduced
into the Church. Such tendencies are a source of grief to the
Lord and to all sincere Christians.

THE DISADVANTAGES SET FORTH TO THE PEOPLE. —

**V. 10. And Samuel told all the words of the Lord unto the people that asked of him a king,** thereby exhorting them to repentance. **V. 11. And he said, This will be the manner of the king,** the way in which he would probably comport himself, **that shall reign over you: He will take your sons and appoint them for himself,** press them into his own service, **for his chariots,** namely, as drivers, **and to be his horsemen,** to make up the cavalry in his army or in his body-guard; **and some shall run before his chariots,** as runners, or heralds. It is a description of the usual Oriental royal cavalcade on state occasions. **V. 12. And he will appoint him,** simply press into service, **captains over thousands and captains over fifties,** men for every position in his army, from the highest to the lowest; **and will set them to ear his ground,** to till the soil of the royal dominion, **and to reap his harvest, and to make his instruments of war and instruments of his chariots,** the tools, vessels, and vehicles which he used in peace times. **V. 13. And he will take your daughters to be confectionaries,** to prepare fine oils and ointments for perfumery, **and to be cooks, and to be bakers,** for the household of an Oriental prince was organized on a gigantic scale, with a great deal of luxury and pomp. **V. 14. And he will take your fields and your vineyards and your olive yards, even the best of them,** the choicest land for agricultural and horticultural purposes, **and give them to his servants,** to his courtiers. **V. 15. And he will take the tenth of your seed and of your vineyards, and give to his officers,** the eunuchs of the Oriental courts, **and to his servants. v. 16. And he will take your men-servants and your maid-servants,** the very slaves whom they had purchased for their own work, **and your goodliest young men,** rather, your oxen, **and your asses, and put them to**

his work. **V. 17. He will take the tenth of your sheep,** the small cattle, including goats; **and ye shall be his servants,** they would lose all their political and social freedom and place a yoke upon their necks which they would not be able to remove. **V. 18. And ye shall cry out in that day because of your king which ye shall have chosen you;** finding their condition unbearable, they would pray for deliverance; **and the Lord will not hear you in that day,** all their lamentation would be unavailing, as a just punishment of the Lord; the yoke once assumed they must bear forever. The description given by Samuel summarizes the tyranny and despotism of the average Oriental monarch, especially in ancient times, and some of the oppressions mentioned were later experienced by Israel in full measure. **V. 19. Nevertheless the people refused to obey the voice of Samuel,** they would not be dissuaded from their intention; **and they said, Nay; but we will have a king over us, v. 20. that we also may be like all the nations,** like all the heathen people surrounding them; they no longer wanted the proud distinction of being ruled by Jehovah only; **and that our king may judge us,** and go out before us, **and fight our battles.** Those were the duties of the king as they saw them, to be the leader and the governor of the people, in peace and in war. **V. 21. And Samuel heard all the words of the people, and he rehearsed them in the ears of the Lord,** again laying the whole matter before the Lord, after his unsuccessful dealing with the people. **V. 22. And the Lord said to Samuel, Hearken unto their voice and make them a king. And Samuel said unto the men of Israel, Go ye, every man unto his city.** He needed some time to consider, with the Lord's advice, the necessary steps for the selection of a king. Thus the Lord, in yielding to the demand of the people, laid a punishment upon them.  Sinful men cannot be kept in check but by force and oppression; that is a result of man's natural disobedience.

# 1 Samuel 9

**S**aul Entertained by Samuel.

SAUL SEEKS THE LOST ASSES. — **V. 1. Now, there was a man of Benjamin whose name was Kish, the son of Abiel, the son of Zeror, the son of Bechorath, the son of Aphiah, a Benjamite,** literally, "a son of a man of Jemini," **a mighty man of power,** literally, "a man of substance," a man living in comfortable circumstances. We have here, apparently, a case of an abbreviated chronological table, in which less important members are sometimes omitted. Cp. 1 Chron. 8, 29-33; 9, 35-39. **V. 2. And he had a son whose name was Saul, a choice young man and a goodly,** tall, strong, and well-proportioned; **and there was not among the children of Israel a goodlier person than he,** possessed of more manly handsomeness; **from his shoulders and upward he was higher than any of the people,** he excelled in bodily height, corresponding to his other physical development. **V. 3. And the asses of Kish, Saul's father, were lost,** they had strayed away. **And Kish said to Saul, his son, Take now one of the servants with thee, and arise, go seek the asses.** Kish was evidently an energetic man, quick in decision and action. **V. 4. And he, Saul, passed through Mount Ephraim,** the highlands extending down into the territory of Benjamin, moving in a northwesterly direction first, **and passed through the land of Shalisha,** in the foothills toward the west, **but they found them not; then they passed through the land of Shalim,** in a southeasterly direction, **and there they were not; and he passed through the land of the Benjamites,** Its extreme western section, **but they found them not. V. 5. And when they were come to the land of Zuph,** southwest of the territory of Benjamin proper, **Saul said to his servant that was with him, Come, and let us return; lest my father leave caring for the asses and take thought for us.** The tender regard for his father's feelings was a fine trait in Saul's character at that time. **V. 6. And he said unto him, Behold now, there is in this city a man of God, and he is an honorable man,** held in high regard and honor by all men; **all that he saith cometh surely to pass; now let us go thither; peradventure he can show us our way that we should go.** The city to which reference is here made may well have been Ramah or Ramathaim, for this was in the district of Zuph, in the tribe of Benjamin, chap. 1, 1; Josh. 18, 25. **V. 7. Then said Saul to his servant, But, behold, if we go, what shall we bring the man?** He was worried about a possible present or fee. **For the bread is spent in our vessels,** they had consumed all the provisions which they had taken along, **and there is not a present to bring to the man of God; what have we?** Saul had not provided for such a contingency. **V. 8. And the servant answered Saul again, and said, Behold, I have here at hand the fourth part of a shekel of silver,** a piece or coin of determined weight and value (about 16 cents); **that will I give to the man of God to tell us our way. V. 9.**

(**Beforetime in Israel,** as the author here notes in order to have his readers understand the next part of the story, **when a man went to enquire of God, thus he spake, Come, and let us go to the seer; for he that is now called a prophet was beforetime called a seer.**) **V. 10. Then said Saul to his servant, Well said,** that's a good idea; **come, let us go. So they went unto the city where the man of God was.** Saul here appears as a pious, God-fearing man, who valued the word of the servant of God. So the Lord often selects the men through whom He intends to accomplish great things from the lowly among the people. Only he who fears God and His Word is really fit for work in the kingdom of God.

SAUL THE GUEST OF SAMUEL. — **V. 11. And as they went up the hill to the city, they found young maidens going out to draw water,** they met them outside the city gates, as they were on their way to perform the duty still incumbent upon the women of the Orient, **and said unto them, Is the seer here?** that is, Is he at home now? **V. 12. And they answered them and said, He is; behold, he is before you. Make haste now, for he came today to the city,** having returned from one of his periodical trips, chap. 7, 16; **for there is a sacrifice,** a peace-offering with a sacrificial meal, **of the people today in the high place,** the elevation near the city on which the offerings were made; **v. 13. as soon as ye be come into the city,** going directly ahead on the main street, **ye shall straightway find him before he go up to the high place to eat,** to take part in the sacrificial meal; **for the people will not eat,** namely, those invited, **until he come, because he doth bless the sacrifice,** by speaking the prayer of thanksgiving; **and afterwards they eat that be bidden. Now, therefore, get you up; for about this time,** on this very day, **ye shall find him. V. 14. And**

**they went up into the city,** passing in through the gate; **and when they were come into the city, behold, Samuel came out against them,** he met them on the main street, **for to go up to the high place.** Saul was apparently too diffident or bashful to address Samuel at once, but turned around and followed him. **V. 15. Now the Lord had told Samuel in his ear,** literally, "uncovered his ear," revealed to him, **a day before Saul came, saying, v. 16. Tomorrow about this time I will send thee a man out of the land of Benjamin, and thou shalt anoint him to be captain over My people Israel, that he may save My people out of the hand of the Philistines,** for the latter were harassing the Israelites more or less, trying to regain full dominion over them; **for I have looked upon My people, because their cry is come unto Me.** He had looked upon them in mercy, and with the definite intention of bringing them deliverance. **V. 17. And when Samuel saw Saul,** as he met him on the main street of the city, **the Lord said unto him,** Samuel, **Behold the man whom I spake to thee of! This same shall reign over My people,** hold them in restraint by a sharp and strict government. **V. 18. Then Saul,** having followed Samuel down the street, **drew near to Samuel in the gate and said, Tell me, I pray thee, where the seer's house is. V. 19. And Samuel answered Saul and said, I am the seer; go up before me unto the high place,** this invitation being a mark of respect; **for ye shall eat with me today,** the kindness of Samuel causing him to include the servant also, **and tomorrow I will let thee go and will tell thee all that is in thine heart,** revealing to him his innermost thoughts and thus giving evidence of his prophetical ability. **V. 20. And as for thine asses that were lost three days ago,** the search thus having taken since the second day before, **set not thy**

**mind on them,** he should not be worried about them; **for they are found. And on whom is all the desire of Israel? Is it not on thee and on all thy father's house?** The most desirable honor, the noblest possession in all Israel, was to be his, unsought and undesired: the royal dignity. **V. 21. And Saul,** although ignorant of the full import of Samuel's words, **answered and said, Am not I a Benjamite, of the smallest of the tribes of Israel, and my family the least of all the families of the tribe of Benjamin? Wherefore, then, speakest thou so to me?** The warlike tribe of Benjamin had, by the fearful execution carried out upon them, Judg. 20, 20, been reduced to an inconsiderable power, and Saul was conscious of this fact. Besides, his modesty at that time would not permit him to consider himself worthy of any special honor in Israel. **V. 22. And Samuel,** without pursuing the subject further, since he wanted to awaken expectation and hope in the mind of Saul, **took Saul and his servant and brought them into the parlor,** the room where the sacrificial meal was held, **and made them sit in the chiefest place among them that were bidden, which were about thirty persons,** probably the most influential men of the city. Here was another distinction for Saul. **V. 23. And Samuel said unto the cook, Bring the portion which I gave thee,** when the sacrifice had been offered, earlier in the day, **of which I said unto thee, Set it by thee,** reserve it, subject to further orders. **V. 24. And the cook took up the shoulder,** evidently the heave-shoulder, for Samuel exercised the functions of a priest in Israel, **and that which was upon it,** the fat of the flesh, **and set it before Saul**, another distinct honor. **And Samuel said, Behold that which is left,** reserved! **Set it before thee and eat; for unto this time hath it been kept for thee since I said, I have invited the**

**people,** another proof of the prophetic foresight of Samuel. **So Saul did eat with Samuel that day. V. 25. And when they were come down from the high place into the city,** at the close of the sacrificial meal, **Samuel communed with Saul upon the top of the house,** on the flat roof, where they were undisturbed, Deut. 22, 8, the purpose being gradually to prepare Saul for the announcement of the next day. **V. 26. And they arose early; and it came to pass about the spring of the day,** at the rising of the dawn, **that Samuel called Saul to the top of the house,** rather, Samuel called to Saul, who had evidently slept on the roof, by no means unusual in that country, saying, **Up, that I may send thee away. And Saul arose,** made ready for his journey, **and they went out, both of them, he and Samuel, abroad,** out into the open. **V. 27. And as they were going down to the end of the city, Samuel,** who accompanied his guest as another mark of respect, **said to Saul, Bid the servant pass on before us,** for he was not to be a witness of the next act of Samuel, **(and he passed on,) but stand thou still a while that I may show thee the word of God.** All those who are intended for the service of God's people must be instructed in God's Word and truth in order to do their work properly.

# 10

# 1 Samuel 10

**S**aul Becomes king.

SAUL ANOINTED BY SAMUEL. — **V. 1. Then Samuel took a vial,** a flask or small jug, **of oil, and poured it upon his head,** as a mark of consecration to the Lord; for every king was thereby placed in God's service and under His protection, **and kissed him and said, Is it not because the Lord hath anointed thee to be captain over His inheritance?** The question is really an expression of the most vivid assurance, for Samuel was only the instrument in God's hand, the consecration itself being God's act. Saul was now, before God, the king over His inheritance, over the people who were His property. In further confirmation of this fact, Saul was now given three signs. **V.2. When thou art departed from me today, then thou shalt find two men by Rachel's sepulcher,** between Bethel and Bethlehem, Gen. 35, **in the border of Benjamin at Zelzah; and they will say unto thee, The asses which thou wentest to seek are found; and, lo, thy father hath left the care of the asses,** he has put aside all speaking of the lost animals, **and sorroweth**

**for you,** troubled for fear that some misfortune had struck them, **saying, What shall I do for my son?** Thus Saul was not only to be relieved of his anxiety concerning the asses, but his thoughts were to be devoted entirely to the great honor which had been conferred upon him by the Lord. **V. 3. Then shalt thou go on forward from thence, and thou shalt come to the plain of Tabor,** to the well known oak or terebinth at that place, **and there shall meet thee three men going up to God to Bethel,** which was at that time a place of worship, chap. 7, 16, **one carrying three kids, and another carrying three loaves of bread, and another carrying a bottle of wine,** all these being intended for sacrificial offerings; **v. 4. and they will salute thee,** with the customary greeting of peace, **and give thee two loaves of bread, which thou shalt receive of their hands,** as a token of homage. This was the second sign intended to confirm Saul in his conviction that he was chosen by God for the office of king in Israel. **V. 5. After that thou shalt come to the hill of God,** the height of Gibeah, also used for sacrifices, **where is the garrison of the Philistines,** for the enemies had succeeded in maintaining some of their military posts in the midst of Canaan; **and it shall come to pass, when thou art come thither to the city,** near his own home town, **that thou shalt meet a company of prophets,** in a solemn procession, **coming down from the high place with a psaltery,** a zitherlike instrument, **and a tabret,** a form of castanet, **and a pipe,** a flute, **and a harp,** an instrument similar to a guitar, **before them; and they shall prophesy,** sing the praises of God in ecstatic utterances; **v. 6. and the Spirit of the Lord will come upon thee, and thou shalt prophesy with them, and shalt be turned into another man,** be filled with the same ecstasy, his heart being made willing to take the duties of a king of Israel upon himself. This sign was to be the inward seal of his consecration for the office of king. **V. 7. And let it be, when these signs are come unto thee, that thou do as occasion serve thee.** Whatever action the circumstances in Israel would suggest to the mind of Saul, that he should readily perform, without further consultation with anyone, his royal calling, **for God is with thee,** under the guidance of God, had even now begun. **V. 8. And thou shalt go down before me to Gilgal,** in case he should be inclined to go there for the sake of bringing a sacrifice; **and, behold, I will come down unto thee, to offer burnt offerings, and to sacrifice sacrifices of peace-offerings,** for Saul could not do this work, since it pertained to the priestly office; **seven days shalt thou tarry, till I come to thee and show thee what thou shalt do.** The reference is not to a general practice, but to a specific instance, chap. 13, 8, for the Lord still transmitted certain commands through the mouth of Samuel. **V. 9. And it was so,** it so happened, **that, when he had turned his back to go from Samuel, God gave him another heart,** turned his heart and mind, set it firmly upon the work which was expected of him in his office of king; **and all those signs came to pass that day. V. 10. And when they came thither to the hill,** to Gibeah, the home of Saul, **behold, a company of prophets met him; and the Spirit of God came upon him, and he prophesied among them,** just as Samuel had foretold. **V. 11. And it came to pass, when all that knew him beforetime,** and he was surely well known in the entire neighborhood, **saw that, behold, he prophesied among the prophets,** being seized by the Spirit and drawn along into the lofty inspiration which marked their songs of praise, **then the people said one to another,** every man to his neighbor, **What is this that is come unto**

**the son of Kish:** What has happened to him? **Is Saul also among the prophets?** It is a form of mockery directed either against the sons of the prophets in general or against Saul in particular, the idea that he should show such a tendency being absurd. **V. 12. And one of the same place answered and said, But who is their father?** Was it necessary for a person to have a special kind of father, in order to be accepted into the ranks of the prophets; what reason could be offered for excluding Saul from their company? **Therefore it became a proverb, Is Saul also among the prophets?** This proverb received further confirmation by an event in the later life of Saul, chap. 19, 24. **V. 13. And when he had made an end of prophesying,** when the ecstatic mood left him, **he came to the high place,** probably to pray and sacrifice in the holy place after experiencing the divine favor and goodness in so emphatic a way. In Christians the anointing of the Spirit is to them an earnest of the heavenly inheritance and enables them to bear the mockery of the world with quiet patience.

SAUL CHOSEN KING BY LOT. — **V. 14. And Saul's uncle said unto him and to his servant,** upon their return home, **Whither went ye? And he said, To seek the asses; and when we saw that they were no where, we came to Samuel. V. 15. And Saul's uncle said, Tell me, I pray thee, what Samuel said unto you,** he was anxious to have a detailed account of the visit. **V. 16. And Saul said unto his uncle, He told us plainly that the asses were found,** hoping therewith to dispose of this matter. **But of the matter of the kingdom, whereof Samuel spake, he told him not,** for it was evident from Samuel's entire manner that the matter was not yet to be made public. **V. 17. And Samuel called the people together unto the Lord to Mizpeh,** for a great popular assembly; **v. 18.**

**and said unto the children of Israel, Thus saith the Lord God of Israel, I brought up Israel out of Egypt and delivered you out of the hand of the Egyptians and out of the hand of all kingdoms and of them that oppressed you,** these were the mighty deeds performed by God under the old order, when He was still the only acknowledged King of the nation; **v. 19. and ye have this day rejected your God, who Himself saved you out of all your adversities and your tribulations,** all the evils and oppressions which they suffered from the very kingdoms after which they now intended to pattern their state; **and ye have said unto Him, Nay, but set a king over us.** This was a last warning regarding a step the taking of which they might some day bitterly repent. **Now, therefore, present yourselves before the Lord by your tribes and by your thousands,** the divisions of the people by the command of the Lord, Num. 1, 16. This solemn act took place in the presence of Jehovah, before the altar which had been erected in Mizpeh. **V. 20. And when Samuel had caused all the tribes of Israel to come near,** in order that lots might be cast or drawn, **the tribe of Benjamin was taken. V. 21. When he had caused the tribe of Benjamin to come near by their families,** the largest subdivision of the tribe, **the family of Matri was taken, and,** after the father-houses had been treated the same way and the individual heads of families came forward, **Saul, the son of Kish, was taken; and when they sought him, he could not be found,** his shyness having caused him to hide himself, since he knew the outcome of the selection. **V. 22. Therefore they enquired of the Lord further,** through the Urim and Thummim of the high priest, **if the man should yet come thither,** whether they should search for Saul at home or elsewhere. **And the Lord answered, Behold, he hath**

**hid himself among the stuff,** the traveling baggage of the great assembly. **V. 23. And they ran and fetched him thence; and when he stood among the people,** having been obliged to overcome his diffidence, **he was higher than any of the people from his shoulders and upward,** he extended above them, head and shoulders, a magnificent specimen of physical manhood, truly kingly in appearance. **V. 24. And Samuel said to all the people, See ye him whom the Lord hath chosen,** the election being the confirmation of the previous divine choice, **that there is none like him among all the people? And all the people shouted,** in a cry of salutation and homage, **God save the king!** literally, "May the king live!" **V. 25. Then Samuel told the people the manner of the kingdom,** the relation of the temporal monarchy to the theocracy, the rule of God, for it was Jehovah's purpose to rule through Saul as His instrument, cp. Deut. 17, 14-20, **and wrote it in a book, and laid it up before the Lord,** to be preserved for future generations, the Lord Himself being a witness of the act. **And Samuel sent all the people away, every man to his house. V. 26. And Saul also went home to Gibeah; and there went with him a band of men whose hearts God had touched,** of their own free will they constituted themselves his body-guard, his escort of honor. They represented the majority of the people, who were willing to bow under the authority of the man whom God had chosen as their leader. **V. 27. But the children of Belial,** the worthless, vain rabble, **said, How shall this man save us?** They questioned his fitness for the office and declared their unwillingness to submit to his authority. **And they despised him and brought him no presents,** gifts which were a part of the regular income of the princes. **But he held his peace,** literally, "he was as a deaf man," paying no attention to these foolish attacks, and thus showing great foresight and prudence. To this day men in the public office of the Church are subjected to mocking attacks by vain and foolish people. The best way of meeting such a situation is by ignoring attacks of this kind; for the truly faithful, men whose hearts God has touched, will be on the side of right and justice.

# 11

# 1 Samuel 11

Saul's Victory over the Ammonites.

THE SUMMONING OF THE PEOPLE. — **V. 1. Then Nahash, the Ammonite,** the king of the children of Ammon living in the territory east of Jordan, **came up,** undertook a campaign of war, very likely with the object of avenging his people for the defeat administered to them by Jephthah, Judg. 11, 32, **and encamped against Jabesh-gilead,** in the valley east of Jordan, about halfway between the Sea of Galilee and the Dead Sea; **and all the men of Jabesh,** who were apparently suffering with the same lack of courage which caused their fathers to stay away from the campaign against Benjamin, Judg. 21, 8. 9, **said unto Nahash, Make a covenant with us, and we will serve thee.** They wanted to have some reasonable conditions under which they could become tributaries to the Ammonites. This answer is characteristic of Israel's weakness, of the utter lack of a conscious and permanent union between the various tribes. It was a very loose confederacy indeed where such conditions were possible. **V. 2. And Nahash, the Ammonite,** with the arrogant cruelty which was characteristic of heathen conquerors, **answered them, On this condition will I make a covenant with you,** for this price he was willing to accept their complete submission, **that I may thrust out all your right eyes and lay it for a reproach upon all Israel,** to revenge the disgrace which Jephthah had brought upon the Ammonites and to give the entire nation a sample of the treatment awaiting all its members as soon as Nahash should have gained the supremacy. **V. 3. And the elders of Jabesh said unto him, Give us seven days' respite,** so much time of grace he should mercifully grant them, **that we may send messengers unto all the coasts of Israel,** throughout the boundaries, that is, the territory, of the tribes; **and then, if there be no man to save us, we will come out to thee,** forced to submit to his inhuman condition. **V. 4. Then came the messengers to Gibeah of Saul,** the residence of the elected king, who, however, at the time of their arrival, was not in the city, **and told the tidings in the ears of the people,** Saul's fellow-citizens; **and all the people lifted up their voices and wept,** in helpless sorrow over the fate which seemed to be threatening the people of Jabesh. **V. 5. And, behold, Saul came after the herd out of the field,** driving home the yoke of oxen with which he had been engaged on his farm during the day; **and Saul said, What aileth the people that they weep? And they told him the tidings of the men of Jabesh. V. 6. And the Spirit of God came upon Saul when he heard those tidings,** as upon the Judges in the preceding period of Israel's history, **and his anger was kindled greatly,** it flared up in mighty wrath at the reproach inflicted by the enemy of his people. **V. 7. And he took a yoke of oxen, and hewed them in pieces,** according to the manner in which sacrificial animals were dissected, **and sent them throughout**

**all the coasts of Israel by the hands of messengers,** to every tribe, as in Judg. 19, 29. **saying, Whosoever cometh not forth after Saul and after Samuel,** due honor thus being given to the authority of Samuel, **so shall it be done unto his oxen.** This punishment Saul could threaten in the exercise of his judicial power, as a function of his royal office. **And the fear of the Lord fell on the people,** namely, a dread lest they should offend God by refusing to obey the command of the king and of the prophet; **and they came out with one consent,** as one single man, in perfect unity of thought and action. **v. 8. And when he,** Saul, **numbered them in Bezek,** in the Plain of Jezreel, not far from the best northern ford over the Jordan, **the children of Israel were three hundred thousand,** that is, the northern tribes, which afterward formed a nation for themselves, **and the men of Judah thirty thousand.** A holy courage and zeal which knows no fear should be found in all those whom the Lord has called to be the leaders and pastors of His people.

THE UTTER OVERTHROW OF THE AMMONITES. — **V. 9. And they,** the men representing the army of Israel, **said unto the messengers that came, Thus shall ye say unto the men of Jabesh-gilead, Tomorrow, by that time the sun be hot,** before noon, **ye shall have help,** in being delivered from the power of their arrogant enemies. **And the messengers came and showed it to the men of Jabesh,** gave them the joyful information; **and they were glad. V. 10. Therefore the men of Jabesh said,** employing a stratagem which was to make the Ammonites overconfident, **Tomorrow we will come out unto you, and ye shall do with us all that seemeth good unto you,** for this sounded as though they would surrender themselves unconditionally, not having been able to interest the rest of

Israel. **V. 11. And it was so on the morrow that Saul put the people in three companies,** three attacking divisions; **and they came into the midst of the host in the morning watch,** between three o'clock and dawn, when the night is darkest, **and slew the Ammonites,** who were caught and overpowered by surprise, **until the heat of the day; and it came to pass that they which remained were scattered, so that two of them were not left together.** It was an utter rout, a complete overthrow of the invading army. **V. 12. And the people said unto Samuel,** when they had returned from their pursuit of the scattered enemies and were once more encamped, **Who is he that said, Shall Saul reign over us? Bring the men that we may put them to death.** By virtue of his prophetic power, Samuel was to name the children of Belial, chap. 10, 27, who had sneered at Saul. The people were so enthusiastic over the victory gained under the leadership of Saul that they were ready to deal very summarily with men whom they regarded as traitors. **V. 13. And Saul said, There shall not a man be put to death this day; for today the Lord hath wrought salvation in Israel.** This was not only tactful and magnanimous, but showed true piety of heart, which would not permit the sacred joy of the day of victory to be marred by bloodshed, since the victory of the foe was for him nothing but a saving act of God Himself. It was an utterance of royal generosity toward his personal enemies, whose hearts he wanted to win; it was a victory over himself. **V. 14. Then said Samuel to the people, Come and let us go to Gilgal, and renew the kingdom there,** by a solemn confirmation and open acknowledgment of the election as it took place in Mizpeh. **V. 15. And all the people went to Gilgal; and there they made Saul king before the Lord in Gilgal,** the entire nation, as one man, rendering him the homage which made him ruler over Israel in fact as well as in name; **and there they sacrificed sacrifices of peace-offerings,** with which were connected joyful sacrificial meals, **before the Lord; and there Saul and all the men of Israel rejoiced greatly.** So both the happy relation between the covenant God and Israel and the union of the tribes, welded together to form a perfect unit, was here celebrated. For a Christian it is self-evident that for everything which he has managed to perform by the strength and power of God he gives all honor to Jehovah alone.

# 12

# 1 Samuel 12

**S**amuel's Farewell to Israel.

SAMUEL PROTESTS HIS INTEGRITY. — **V. 1. And Samuel said unto all Israel, Behold, I have hearkened unto your voice in all that ye said unto me, and have made a king over you.** "His listening to the voice of the people was based on the repeated divine command and was an act of self-denying obedience to the will of God." (Lange.) These words introduced the farewell speech of Samuel, the climax of the joyful meeting at Gilgal. **V. 2. And now, behold, the king walketh before you,** having charge of the entire government of the people in peace and in war; **and I am old and gray-headed,** cp. chap. 8, 5; **and, behold, my sons are with you,** and the present change in government was evidently necessary, since he himself had felt the need of placing some of his burdens upon the shoulders of his sons; **and I have walked before you from my childhood unto this day,** he had been in public office, and therefore in the eye of the people since his infancy. **V. 3. Behold, here I am; witness against me before the Lord and before His anointed,** the newly-elected king Saul: **Whose ox have I taken, or whose ass have I taken, or whom have I defrauded,** namely, by using his power in a ruthless manner? **Whom have I Oppressed,** by any form of violence, **or of whose hand have I received any bribe to blind mine eyes therewith,** by taking ransom money in order to sell his favor and keep some criminal from the well-deserved punishment? **And I will restore it you.** In case any injustice, any mismanagement of office could be charged against him, he was willing to make public amends. His open challenge showed the serenity of his conscience, his consciousness of being innocent of any flagrant wrongdoing. **V. 4. And they said, Thou hast not defrauded us nor oppressed us, neither hast thou taken ought of any man's hand.** It was a splendid testimonial of the entire people to the honesty and integrity of Samuel. **V. 5. And he said unto them,** his intention being to give to their testimonial the support of a solemn declaration before the Lord, **The Lord is witness against you, and His anointed is witness this day, that ye have not found ought in my hand. And they answered, He is witness.** They accepted the solemn adjuration and supported their declaration by a statement having the force and weight of an oath. **V. 6. And Samuel,** in order to have the people realize still more deeply their ingratitude in rejecting a government which they themselves acknowledged as having been so praiseworthy, **said unto the people, It is the Lord,** He is witness, **that advanced Moses and Aaron,** made them what they were, gave them their place in history, **and that brought your fathers up out of the land of Egypt.** He had heard their declaration. which implied that they had, in the person of Samuel, who represented this covenant God, rejected Jehovah Himself, as Samuel now proceeds to show from their history. **V. 7. Now, therefore, stand still that I may reason with you,** as though he were conducting his own cause before a judge, **before the Lord of all the righteous acts of the Lord,** God's blessings by reason of His covenant faithfulness, in fulfilment of His solemn promises**, which He did to you and to your fathers. V. 8. When Jacob was come into Egypt and your fathers cried unto the Lord,** at the time of the great oppression by the Egyptians, **then the Lord sent Moses and Aaron, which brought forth your fathers out of Egypt and made them dwell in this place.** That was the first great act of God's covenant faithfulness, the deliverance out of the land of Egypt and the introduction into the Land of Promise. **V. 9. And when they forgat the Lord, their God,** in deliberate unfaithfulness and defection to the covenant, **He sold them into the hand of Sisera, captain of the host of Hazor,** Judg. 4, 2, **and into the hand of the Philistines,** Judg. 10, 7; 13, 1, **and into the hand of the king of Moab,** Judg. 3, 12, **and they fought against them. V. 10. And they cried unto the Lord and said, We have sinned because we have forsaken the Lord, and have served Baalim and Ashtaroth,** this had been their confession whenever they had come to the full realization of their helpless plight, as being due to their unfaithfulness, Judg. 10, 10; **but now deliver us out of the hand of our enemies, and we will serve Thee. v. 11. And the Lord sent Jerubbaal,** that is, Gideon, Judg. 6, 14. 32, **and Bedan,** or Barak, Judg. 4, 6, **and Jephthah,** Judg. 11, 1, **and Samuel,** for the speaker could well mention his own name, since he was conscious of his high mission as Judge and deliverer of his people, this fact being generally recognized in Israel, chap. 3, 20, **and delivered you out of the hand of your enemies on every side, and ye dwelled safe,** they were living in quiet and security. **V.**

**12. And when ye saw that Nahash, the king of the children of Ammon, came against you,** who thus had evidently made several raids against the territory of Israel before his bolder campaign against Jabesh, **ye said unto me, Nay; but a king shall reign over us; when the Lord, your God, was your king,** who had, by awaking Judges and saviors, always delivered them out of the hands of their enemies. So their demand for a king had really been a bit of foolish caprice, of sinful rejection of the Lord. **v. 13. Now, therefore, behold the king whom ye have chosen,** in public, popular assembly, **and whom ye have desired! And, behold, the Lord hath set a king over you.** Although their demand was not in accordance with God's plans at this time, Jehovah had granted them the king whom they wanted, who was a gracious gift from His hand. **V. 14. If ye will fear the Lord, and serve Him, and obey His voice, and not rebel against the commandment of the Lord,** for He was still the highest Ruler in the nation and intended to have His government acknowledged without question, **then shall both ye and also the king that reigneth over you continue following after the Lord, your God.** This is really in the nature of a most emphatic wish and prayer, that they might never cease holding to the Lord with all their hearts. **V. 15. But if ye will not obey the voice of the Lord, but rebel against the commandment of the Lord, then shall the hand of the Lord be against you as it was against your fathers,** in spite of the king in whom they were placing so overmuch confidence. The mere fact that they now had a king did not guarantee them freedom from the oppressions with which they had battled in the past, for this could be attained only by an unwavering clinging to Jehovah. The congregation of the Lord is always in need of admonitions to repentance and obedience, If faithful preachers would not continue with rebuking, admonishing, warning, and pleading, disobedience and defection would soon be prevalent everywhere.

SAMUEL ADMONISHES THE PEOPLE TO STEADFASTNESS. — **V. 16. Now, therefore, stand and see this great thing,** a miracle in confirmation of Samuel's reproof and admonition, **which the Lord will do before your eyes.** This they were to experience at once, even now. **v. 17. Is it not wheat-harvest today,** the season at which rain was most unusual? **I will call unto the Lord, and He shall send thunder and rain, that ye may perceive and see,** by this sign, so distinctly at variance with the ordinary weather in Canaan, **that your wickedness is great which ye have done in the sight of the Lord in asking you a king. V. 18. So Samuel called unto the Lord; and the Lord sent thunder and rain that day,** as a manifestation of His anger and of His royal glory, in confirmation of Samuel's words. **And all the people greatly feared the Lord and Samuel,** they were filled with dread at this corroboration of the prophet's statements. **V. 19. And all the people said unto Samuel, Pray for thy servants unto the Lord, thy God, that we die not; for we have added unto all our sins this evil, to ask us a king,** a request which they now finally understood as being an insult to the Lord. **V. 20. And Samuel said unto the people, Fear not; ye have done all this wickedness,** that was indeed not to be denied, and this fact was to keep them in wholesome repentance; **yet turn not aside from following the Lord, but serve the Lord with all your heart,** in undivided, complete devotion; **v. 21. and turn ye not aside,** after idolatrous vanities which were bound to bring harm; **for then should ye go after vain things which cannot profit nor deliver; for they are vain.** The reference is to the idols which had so often been a snare to the children of Israel. **V. 22. For the Lord will not forsake His people for His great name's sake,** since His own glory was at stake; **because it hath pleased the Lord to make you His people,** and He would be careful to guard against every blasphemy of His holy name. **V. 23. Moreover, as for me, God forbid that I should sin against the Lord in ceasing to pray for you; but I will teach you the good and the right way.** There was no personal resentment on the part of Samuel, for he wanted to continue, as heretofore, to serve them in his prophetic office, both by prayer and by instruction. **V. 24. Only fear the Lord and serve Him in truth,** without the slightest hypocrisy, **with all your heart; for consider how great things He hath done for you.** With the remembrance of His great deeds before them always, as they knew them from the history of their people, they would be urged to keep on the right way. **V. 25. But if ye shall still do wickedly,** in spite of all Samuel's admonitions, **ye shall be consumed, both ye and your king,** for the Lord on high is a King of kings and a Lord of lords. If Christians will at all times keep the great deeds of God for their salvation before their eyes, they will find it an easy matter to remain meek and humble in following the Lord's commands in His power.

# 13

## 1 Samuel 13

**S**aul's Disobedience.

THE INVASION OF THE PHILISTINES. — **V. 1. Saul reigned one year,** literally, "A son of [probably forty] years was Saul when he became king"; **and when he had reigned two years over Israel** (he was king, as nearly as can be estimated, twenty-two years), **v. 2. Saul chose him three thousand men of Israel,** evidently from the total number of those who were able to bear arms; **whereof two thousand were with Saul in Michmash,** some eight miles northeast of Jerusalem, **and in Mount Bethel,** the range on which the old Bethel lay, **and a thousand were with Jonathan,** the valiant son of Saul, **in Gibeah of Benjamin; and the rest of the people he sent every man to his tent,** he dismissed them to their homes. **V. 3. And Jonathan smote the garrison of the Philistines that was in Geba,** on the hill near his home town, chap. 10, 5, thereby taking the offensive against the invaders; **and the Philistines heard of it. And Saul blew the trumpet throughout all the land, saying, Let the Hebrews hear;** the Israelites, especially those living west of Jordan, should know of Jonathan's heroic exploit, arouse themselves to action against the oppressors, and fight for their freedom. **V. 4. And all Israel heard say that Saul,** who is named as the chief commander of the military forces of Israel, **had smitten a garrison of the Philistines, and that Israel also was had in abomination with the Philistines**, literally, "was ill-smelling," Gen. 34, 30, said of one who is thoroughly despised and hated. **And the people were called together after Saul to Gilgal,** summoned to the old mustering-place to make ready for the campaign against the Philistines. **V. 5. And the Philistines gathered themselves together,** they quickly mobilized an army, **to fight with Israel, thirty thousand chariots,** or, one thousand, as the text seems originally to have had, **and six thousand horsemen, and people as the sand which is on the seashore in multitude; and they came up,** from the lowlands of Philistia, **and pitched in Michmash,** where Saul had first been stationed, **eastward from Beth-aven,** literally, "over against, in front of, Beth-aven," which itself was east of Michmash, Josh. 7, 2. **V. 6. When the men of Israel saw that they were in a strait,** in a most difficult and dangerous position, **(for the people were distressed,** oppressed by the enemy, who robbed and plundered as they chose,) **then the people did hide themselves in caves, and in thickets,** secluded places in thorny undergrowth, **and in rocks,** in clefts and caves of the hills, **and in high places,** strongly built towers in lonely situations, **and in pits. V. 7. And some of the Hebrews went over Jordan to the land of Gad and Gilead,** the territory of the two and one half tribes. **As for Saul, he was yet in Gilgal,** in the lowlands near Jordan, **and all the people,** the soldiers summoned to duty against the oppressors, **followed him trembling,** literally, "they trembled after him," utterly lacking in the spirit necessary to throw off the yoke of the tyrants. It was a time of trial for Saul and for all Israel, a period such as comes upon all Christians from time to time, to test their faith.

SAUL'S UNAUTHORIZED SACRIFICE. — **V. 8. And he,** Saul, **tarried seven days, according to the set time that Samuel had appointed,** chap. 10, 8; **but Samuel came not to Gilgal,** not even on the morning of the seventh day; **and the people were scattered from him,** fearing that Samuel, after all, would not put in his appearance. **V. 9. And Saul said, Bring hither a burnt offering to me and peace-offerings,** both to atone for the sins of the people and to establish their fellowship with Jehovah once more. **And he offered the burnt offering,** very likely through the priests who were at Gilgal. **V. 10. And it came to pass that, as soon as he had made an end of offering the burnt offering, behold, Samuel came,** evidently still before the close of the seventh day; **and Saul went out to meet him that he might salute him,** with the customary greeting of peace and blessing. **V. 11. And Samuel said,** knowing that Saul had not waited the full length of the appointed time, **What hast thou done? And Saul said,** in a feeble attempt to excuse his overhasty action, **Because I saw that the people were scattered from me, and that thou camest not within the days appointed, and that the Philistines gathered themselves together at Michmash, v. 12. therefore said I, The Philistines will come down now upon me to Gilgal,** in a sudden descent with superior forces, **and I have not made supplication unto the Lord,** literally, "stroked or entreated His face," namely, with the object of gaining His grace and favor. **I forced myself, therefore,** the word used by Saul intimating a strong inward conflict which preceded his resolution to go ahead without the presence of Samuel, **and offered a burnt offering. V. 13. And Samuel said to Saul, Thou hast done foolishly; thou hast not kept the commandment of the Lord, thy God, which He commanded thee,** no excuse could alter the fact of his disobedience; **for now would the Lord have established thy kingdom,** namely, as a hereditary kingdom, **upon Israel forever,** if Saul had only followed His commandment strictly. **V. 14. But now thy kingdom shall not continue,** it would not pass on to his sons, Saul would be the first and last of his line. **The Lord hath sought Him a man after His own heart,** this resolution had already been passed in the counsels of God, **and the Lord hath commanded him to be captain over His people,** as the successor of Saul, **because thou hast not kept that which the Lord commanded thee,** he had not stood the test of absolute faith and trust in Jehovah; for he should have known that the Lord would find ways and means to bring Samuel within the limit of the time set or otherwise to send him word concerning the delay. **V. 15. And Samuel arose,** after having made this statement, **and gat him up from Gilgal unto Gibeah of Benjamin,** the home of Saul. **And Saul,** before continuing his campaign, **numbered the people that were present with him, about six hundred men.** That was all that was left, in spite of his hasty sacrifice; he had indeed acted foolishly, as Samuel had said. **V. 16. And Saul and Jonathan, his son, and the people that were present with them, abode in Gibeah of Benjamin,** or rather, in Geba, at the place where Jonathan had broken up the Philistine garrison; **but the Philistines encamped in Michmash,** v. 5. Disobedience is the consequence of unbelief and doubt. Whenever Christians are put to a test, no matter how long the time of distress and tribulation lasts, they should simply cling to God's Word and promises, for disobedience may quickly be followed by rejection.

THE OPPRESSION OF THE PHILISTINES. — **V. 17. And the spoilers,** soldiers to whom was assigned the task of plundering and devastating the land of Israel, **came out of the camp of the Philistines in three companies. One company turned unto the way that leadeth to Ophrah, unto the land of Shual,** toward the northeast, through the territory of Benjamin and Ephraim; **v. 18. and another company turned the way to Beth-horon,** toward the west; **and another company turned to the way of the border that looketh to the Valley of Zeboim toward the wilderness,** in a southeasterly direction. **V. 19. Now, there was no smith found throughout all the land of Israel; for the Philistines said, Lest the Hebrews make them swords or spears;** so the Philistines had removed all smiths out of the whole country; **v. 20. but all the Israelites went down to the Philistines to sharpen every man his share, and his coulter, and his ax, and his mattock.** So all the agricultural implements which the Israelites used, plowshares, hoes, axes, were sharpened by Philistine smiths, upon whom the subject people were altogether dependent. **V. 21. Yet they had a file for the mattocks, and for the coulters, and for the forks, and for the axes, and to sharpen the goads.** The verses have lately been rendered: "But all the Israelites went down to the Philistines to sharpen every man his plowshare, and his ax, and his adze, and his hoe, and the price was a *pim* for the plowshares, and for the axes, and for the three-tined forks, and for the adzes, and for the setting of the goads." Whenever the implements became dull and needed sharpening, and whenever the ox-goads needed new setting, it was necessary to make the trip to the lowlands occupied by the Philistines, who permitted the Hebrews to carry on the tillage only of the highlands and of the valley of the Jordan, and incidentally charged the Israelites a high price for all the work done by them.3) **V. 22. So it came to pass in the day of battle,** which is described in the next chapter, **that there was neither sword nor spear found in the hand of any of the people that were with Saul and Jonathan,** they were unprovided with real weapons of war, being dependent upon their farm implements for arms against the enemy; **but with Saul and with Jonathan, his son, was there found,** they were the only ones that had real weapons. **V. 23. And the garrison of the Philistines,** a post or vanguard from the main army, **went out to the passage,** or pass, **of Michmash,** as a protection against the Israelites, who might otherwise have slipped up through some of the valleys converging at this point and surprised the Philistine camp. The invariable result of forsaking the Lord is distress and tribulation, the object of such visitations being to cause the backsliders to repent of their sins and to place their full reliance upon the Lord.

# 14

# 1 Samuel 14

**J**onathan's Heroic Feat.

THE PHILISTINES DEFEATED. — **V. 1. Now it came to pass upon a day,** a certain day came along, **that Jonathan, the son of Saul, said unto the young man that bare his armor, Come, and let us go over to the Philistines' garrison,** the advanced post which was to guard against surprise attacks on the part of the Israelites, chap. 13, 23, **that is on the other side. But he told not his father,** who probably would have forbidden the undertaking as too dangerous. **V. 2. And Saul tarried in the uttermost part of Gibeah,** at the extreme northern edge of the city, **under a pomegranate-tree which is in Migron,** the place which he had chosen being apparently well adapted for military purposes, since it was on the edge of a precipice; **and the people that were with him were about six hundred men; v. 3. and Ahiah, the son of Ahitus, Ichabod's brother,** chap. 4, 21, **the son of Phinehas, the son of Ell, the Lord's priest in Shiloh,** where the Tabernacle was still standing, although the ark was near Kirjath-jearim, **wearing an ephod,** performing the functions of the high priest. **And the people knew not that Jonathan was gone,** it was a secret expedition on his part. **V. 4. And between the passages,** the various passes which were made possible by several side valleys at that point, **by which Jonathan sought to go over unto the Philistines' garrison, there was a sharp rock on the one side,** a pillar like rock with steep sides, **and a sharp rock on the other side; and the name of the one was Bozez and the name of the other Seneh,** and these columns guarded the pass. **V. 5. The forefront,** the highest crag, **of the one was situate northward over against Michmash, and the other southward over against Gibeah. V. 6. And Jonathan said to the young man that bare his armor, Come, and let us go over unto the garrison of these uncircumcised,** the name which the Jews usually applied to the heathen that were their enemies; **it may be that the Lord will work for us,** in helping them overcome their enemies; **for there is no restraint to the Lord,** He is at perfect liberty, **to save by many or by few.** Jonathan's resolution was based upon the firm conviction that Israel was the people of God and that Jehovah was its almighty Lord, who would not refuse His children His assistance against the enemies of His kingdom if only they would place their trust firmly in Him. **V. 7. And his armor-bearer said unto him, Do all that is in thine heart,** cheerfully and courageously carrying out his intention. **Turn thee; behold, I am with thee according to thy heart. V. 8. Then said Jonathan,** proposing a sign by which he could tell whether the Lord approved of his undertaking or not, **Behold, we will pass over unto these men, and we will discover ourselves unto them,** purposely letting the Philistines see them as they advanced. **V. 9. If they say thus unto us, Tarry until we come to you,** this showing that they had plenty of courage for attacking; **then we will stand still in our place and will not go up unto them. V. 10. But if they say thus, Come up unto us,** this showing that they did not have the courage to abandon their position, no matter how boastfully they talked, **then we will go up, for the Lord hath delivered them into our hand; and this shall be a sign unto us. V. 11. And both of them discovered themselves unto the garrison of the Philistines,** boldly showed themselves as they advanced; **and the Philistines said,** voicing their scornful contempt for the Israelites in general, **Behold, the Hebrews come forth out of the holes where they had hid themselves,** chap. 13, 6. V. 12. **And the men of the garrison answered Jonathan and his armor-bearer and said, Come up to us, and we will show you a thing,** their very scornful overconfidence making them unfit for battle. **And Jonathan said unto his armor-bearer, Come up after me; for the Lord hath delivered them into the hand of Israel. V. 13. And Jonathan climbed up upon his hands and upon his feet,** scaling the steep cliff, **and his armor-bearer after him; and they,** the enemies, **fell before Jonathan,** he struck them down as he went along; **and his armor-bearer slew after him,** finishing the task left uncompleted by Jonathan. V. 14. **And that first slaughter, which Jonathan and his armor-bearer made, was about twenty men, within as it were an half acre of land, which a yoke of oxen might plow,** literally, "in about a half-furrow of a yoke of land," the ground plowed by a yoke of oxen in half a day. The twenty men, fleeing before Jonathan, were killed and lay in a row of that length along the ridge. V. 15. **And there was trembling in the host,** in the main camp, **in the field, and among all the people,** in the entire army; **the garrison,** the men of the outposts, **and the spoilers,** the companies of plunderers,

**they also trembled,** the panic of fright spreading by quick contagion, **and the earth quaked,** under the confused uproar of the Philistines; **so it was a very great trembling,** a terror of God, sent upon the Philistines for their destruction. **V. 16. And the watchmen of Saul,** the sentinels, **in Gibeah of Benjamin looked; and, behold, the multitude melted away,** thrown into confusion by Jonathan's attack, they dispersed hither and thither, they were disorganized and broken up, **and they went on beating down one another,** they were tossed to and fro and continued to be slain. **V. 17. Then said Saul,** whose attention had been called to the confusion in the enemy's camp, **unto the people that were with him, Number now,** call the roll, **and see who is gone from us. And when they had numbered, behold, Jonathan and his armor-bearer were not there. V. 18. And Saul said unto Ahiah, Bring hither the ark of God. For the ark of God was at that time with the children of Israel;** it was often taken along to war, as being a symbol of God's presence. **V. 19. And it came to pass, while Saul talked unto the priest,** in the effort to get some statement of God, **that the noise,** the confused tumult, **that was in the host of the Philistines went on and increased; and Saul said unto the priest, Withdraw thine hand;** there was no need of a special revelation, the course which he ought to take was obvious. **V. 20. And Saul and all the people that were with him assembled themselves,** raised the battle-cry, **and they came to the battle,** advancing against the enemy; **and, behold, every man's sword was against his fellow, and there was a very great discomfiture,** a headless confusion. **V. 21. Moreover, the Hebrews that were with the Philistines before that time,** either prisoners or levies serving in their army, **which went up with them into the camp from the country**

**round about,** they went over to Israel and turned their arms against their oppressors, **even they also turned to be with the Israelites that were with Saul and Jonathan. V. 22. Likewise all the men of Israel which had hid themselves in Mount Ephraim,** whose ranges extended down to this neighborhood, **when they heard that the Philistines fled, even they also followed hard after them in battle. V. 23. So the Lord saved Israel that day,** it was an obvious display of His power; **and the battle passed over unto Beth-aven,** it continued, at least for a large part of the army, in a northeasterly direction. If in the battles which the Church of the Lord must wage only a few men take the lead with a courageous stand, others will follow, and even the weak and those of little faith are inspired to stand on the Lord's side.

SAUL'S UNWISE ADJURATION. — **V. 24. And the men of Israel were distressed that day,** harassed, thoroughly wearied; **for Saul had adjured the people, saying, Cursed be the man that eateth any food until evening that I may be avenged on mine enemies.** This was an act of false zeal, unauthorized by the Lord, Saul having more regard to his royal power than to the honor of Jehovah. **So none of the people tasted any food,** although they were jaded to the point of exhaustion. **V. 25. And all they of the land,** namely, those who had now joined the forces of Saul, **came to a wood,** into a forested section of the hills; **and there was honey upon the ground,** flowing down in streams from the overloaded hives of wild bees. **V. 26. And when the people were come into the wood, behold, the honey dropped,** running down from the trees where the bees had stored it; **but no man put his hand to his mouth,** to eat any of the honey; **for the people feared the oath. V. 27. But Jonathan heard not when his father charged the people**

**with the oath,** he was not aware of the curse; **wherefore he put forth,** while hastily passing by, **the end of the rod that was in his hand and dipped it in an honeycomb,** one visible in the structure of the bees, **and put his hand,** with which he had removed the honey from the rod, **to his mouth; and his eyes were enlightened,** the slight refreshment revived his strength, and this showed in the glow of his eyes. **V. 28. Then answered one of the people and said, Thy father straitly charged the people with an oath, saying, Cursed be the man that eateth any food this day; and the people were,** rather, are, **faint.** It was a timid protest against Saul's rash order. **V. 29. Then said Jonathan, My father hath troubled the land,** brought disaster to the army of Israel and to all whom they represented; **see, I pray you, how mine eyes have been enlightened because I tasted a little of this honey. V. 30. How much more, if haply,** by any means, **the people had eaten freely today of the spoil of their enemies which they found? For had there not been now a much greater slaughter among the Philistines?** Had the soldiers had nourishing food, they would have been in condition to inflict a much more severe defeat upon the Philistines. **V. 31. And they smote the Philistines that day,** those who had not fled toward Beth-aven, **from Michmash to Aijalon,** far in the western foothills; **and the people were very faint,** weary to the point of utter exhaustion. **V. 32. And the people,** as soon as it was evening, **flew upon the spoil,** in a ravenous desire for food, **and took sheep and oxen and calves,** and slew them on the ground; **and the people did eat them with the blood,** too impatient to let the blood drain out according to God's command, Lev. 19, 26. This was the result of Saul's unwise adjuration. **V. 33. Then they told Saul, saying, Behold the people sin against the Lord, in that they**

eat with the blood. And he said, Ye have transgressed, their conduct being faithlessness to the covenant of Jehovah; roll a great stone unto me this day, right now. V. 34. And Saul said, Disperse yourselves among the people and say unto them, Bring me hither every man his ox and every man his sheep, and slay them here, where the blood could drain off properly, and eat; and sin not against the Lord in eating with the blood. And all the people brought every man his ox with him that night and slew them there. V. 35. And Saul built an altar unto the Lord, apparently as a monument of the great victory; the same was the first altar that he built unto the Lord. V. 36. And Saul said, after the people had once more been strengthened through the food which they ate, Let us go down after the Philistines by night and spoil them, take more booty, until the morning light, and let us not leave a man of them. Saul seems to have been aware of the fact that his rash order had been foolish, and therefore wanted to make up for lost time. And they, his counselors, or the people, said, Do whatsoever seemeth good unto thee. Then said the priest, Ahiah, Let us draw near hither unto God, to consult Him by means of the Urim and Thummim and thus to get His decision. V. 37. And Saul asked counsel of God, Shall I go down after the Philistines? Wilt Thou deliver them into the hand of Israel? But He answered him not that day, at that time, this being an indication that the Lord had turned from the people and withdrawn His assistance. V. 38. And Saul said, pursuing the hint given him by the silence of Jehovah, Draw ye near hither, all the chief of the people, the representatives, probably the elders, Num. 11, 30; and know and see wherein this sin, indicated by the silence of Jehovah, hath been this day. V. 39. For, as the Lord liveth,

**which saveth Israel, though it be in Jonathan, my son, he shall surely die.** This was another rash oath, and just as foolish as the first. **But there was not a man among all the people that answered him,** evidently from terror regarding the consequences. **V. 40. Then said he unto all Israel, Be ye on one side, and I and Jonathan, my son, will be on the other side,** namely, in the casting of lots to determine the guilty one. **And the people said unto Saul, Do what seemeth good unto thee. V. 41. Therefore Saul said unto the Lord God of Israel, Give a perfect lot,** exemption from punishment, establish the truth. **And Saul and Jonathan were taken; but the people escaped,** they went out free, the lot did not accuse them. **V. 42. And Saul said, Cast lots between me and Jonathan, my son. And Jonathan was taken,** discovered as the one on whom, in Saul's opinion, rested the fault. **V. 43. Then Saul said to Jonathan, Tell me what thou hast done. And Jonathan told him and said, I did but taste a little honey with the end of the rod that was in mine hand, and, lo, I must die;** he was ready to pay the penalty, although in this case, since the mere command of a man was concerned, the guilt really fell on him who gave the foolish order. **V. 44. And Saul answered,** with another unwarranted oath, **God do so and more also; for thou shalt surely die, Jonathan. V. 45. And the people,** rousing themselves from their attitude of apparent indifference and silent submission at last, **said unto Saul, Shall Jonathan die, who hath wrought this great salvation in Israel?** They regarded his great victory as a direct evidence of God's favor and assistance. **God forbid! As the Lord liveth, there shall not one hair of his head fall to the ground; for he hath wrought with God this day,** he was obviously a tool in the hand of God. **So the people rescued Jonathan,** from the fate which was threatening him, **that he died not. V. 46. Then Saul went up from following the Philistines,** he did not continue the pursuit; **and the Philistines,** by no means permanently disabled, **went to their own place,** to their own country. The cause of the Lord's silence was evidently not Jonathan's conduct, but Saul's own arbitrary and rash act. If men profess to seek God's glory and honor, but at the same time take His name in vain time and again, the Lord often punishes them by letting them continue in their foolishness.

SAUL'S CAMPAIGNS. — **V. 47. So Saul took the kingdom over Israel,** he was now really established in his royal power, **and fought against all his enemies on every side, against Moab, and against the children of Ammon, and against Edom,** south of the Dead Sea, **and against the kings of Zobah,** a district of Syria between the Euphrates and the Orontes, **and against the Philistines,** whose power was not yet broken; **and whithersoever he turned himself, he vexed them,** he chastised them, he punished them for their attacks on Israel. **V. 48. And he gathered an host,** he increased in strength and made his power felt, **and smote the Amalekites,** the desert tribes in the South, **and delivered Israel out of the hands of them that spoiled them,** making an end to their raids against the territory of Israel. **V. 49. Now, the sons of Saul were Jonathan, and Ishui, and Melchishua; and the names of his two daughters were these: the name of the first-born Merab, and the name of the younger Michal; v. 50. and the name of Saul's wife was Ahinoam, the daughter of Ahimaaz; and the name of the captain of his host was Abner, the son of Ner, Saul's uncle,** and thus his own cousin. **V. 51. And Kish was the father of Saul; and Ner, the father of Abner, was the son of Abiel. V. 52. And there was sore war against the**

88

**Philistines all the days of Saul; and,** for this reason, **when Saul saw any strong man or any valiant man,** who would probably make a good soldier, **he took him unto him.** Even men whom God has rejected as His children are still used by Him in performing His will in the world.

# 15

# 1 Samuel 15

The Campaign against Amalek.

THE UNAUTHORIZED ACTION OF SAUL. — **V. 1. Samuel also said unto Saul,** in delivering to him the Lord's commission, **The Lord sent me to anoint thee to be king over His people, over Israel; now, therefore, hearken thou unto the voice of the words of the Lord.** As the king of Israel by God's direct selection, Saul was bound to carry out the commands of God, the real King of His people. **V. 2. Thus saith the Lord of hosts,** the almighty Ruler of armies, **I remember that which Amalek did to Israel,** during the desert journey, **how he laid wait for him in the way when he came up from Egypt,** Ex. 17, 8. 14. The Amalekites were a roving desert-people, descendants of Esau's grandson, Gen. 36, 12, 16, and very decidedly hostile to Israel. **V. 3. Now go and smite Amalek, and utterly destroy all that they have,** as devoted to the Lord, in a campaign of annihilation, **and spare them not; but slay both man and woman, infant and suckling, ox and sheep, camel and ass.** The entire people with all their possessions were placed under the ban, as being

90

destined for destruction. **V. 4. And Saul gathered the people together,** summoning them for service in war, **and numbered,** mustered, **them in Telaim,** in the southern country, midway between Beersheba and the Dead Sea, **two hundred thousand footmen and ten thousand men of Judah,** for there was need of a mighty army in conquering a strong confederation of Bedouin tribes. **V. 5. And Saul came to a city of Amalek,** evidently their largest camp, **and laid wait in the valley,** set an ambush before venturing an attack. **V. 6. And Saul said unto the Kenites,** a small tribe of nomads friendly to Israel, with whom they had come up from the wilderness under the leadership of Hobab, Judg. 1, 16, **Go, depart, get you down from among the Amalekites, lest I destroy you with them; for ye showed kindness to all the children of Israel when they came up out of Egypt,** Num. 10, 29. **So the Kenites departed from among the Amalekites. V. 7. And Saul smote the Amalekites from Havilah until thou comest to Shur,** all along the southern boundary of Canaan, well into Arabia Petrea, **that is over against,** east of, **Egypt. V. 8. And he took Agag, the king of the Amalekites, alive and utterly destroyed all the people with the edge of the sword,** so that the power of their confederation was broken for many years. **V. 9. But Saul and the people spared Agag and the best of the sheep and of the oxen and of the fatlings,** those of the second brood, commonly considered the best, **and the lambs, and all that was good, and would not utterly destroy them,** taking them, instead, as their booty; **but everything that was vile and refuse,** which had little or no value, **that they destroyed utterly.** Partial obedience is equivalent to total disobedience, and such a course of action inevitably brings upon the transgressors God's punishment.

SAMUEL'S REPROOF. — **V. 10. Then came the word of the Lord unto Samuel, saying, V. 11. It repenteth Me that I have set up Saul to be king,** an expression which denotes that God had found it necessary to change His mode of action into the opposite of what He had determined under the condition of holy and righteous conduct of men; **for he is turned back from following Me and hath not performed My commandments.** Pride and self-will, in the consciousness of his own power in Israel, had caused Saul to disregard the divine charge. **And it grieved Samuel,** it hurt him bitterly to find that Saul had turned away from the Lord, it kindled a holy anger in his heart; **and he cried unto the Lord all night,** probably to obtain for Saul forgiveness for his disobedience. **V. 12. And when Samuel rose early to meet Saul in the morning,** setting out to call Saul to account, as the Lord had commanded, **it was told Samuel, saying, Saul came to Carmel,** southeast of Hebron, **and, behold, he set him up a place,** a monument to commemorate the victory, **and is gone about, and passed on, and gone down to Gilgal,** in the valley of Jordan. **V. 13. And Samuel came to Saul; and Saul said unto him, Blessed be thou of the Lord,** a greeting of hypocritical friendliness; **I have performed the commandment of the Lord,** a calm assurance intended to throw sand into Samuel's eyes. **V. 14. And Samuel,** losing no time in unmasking the hypocrisy of Saul, **said, What meaneth, then, this bleating of the sheep in mine ears and the lowing of the oxen which I hear? V. 15. And Saul said, They have brought them from the Amalekites,** so much he had to concede, though it appears even here that he wants to put the blame on the people; **for the people spared the best of the sheep and of the oxen,** they were the transgressors, while he was blameless, **to sacrifice unto the Lord, thy God; and the**

**rest we have utterly destroyed.** The untruth and hypocrisy of this excuse were evident at once, as well as the selfish interests, for the thank-offerings were always combined with sacrificial meals. **V. 16. Then Samuel said unto Saul, Stay,** he should desist from lying excuses, **and I will tell thee what the Lord hath said to me this night. And he said unto him, Say on. V. 17. And Samuel said, When thou wast little in thine own sight,** for so Saul had described himself when Samuel first met him, chap. 9, 21, **wast thou not made the head of the tribes of Israel, and the Lord anointed thee king over Israel? V. 18. And the Lord sent thee on a journey and said, Go and utterly destroy the sinners, the Amalekites,** who were so persistent in their hostility against Israel and against Jehovah, **and fight against them until they be consumed. V. 19. Wherefore, then,** after this plain command, **didst thou not obey the voice of the Lord, but didst fly upon the spoil,** in eager greed, in passionate craving, **and didst evil in the sight of the Lord? V. 20. And Saul said unto Samuel,** still persisting in his denial of any blame on his part, **Yea, I have obeyed the voice of the Lord, and have gone the way which the Lord sent me, and have brought Agag, the king of Amalek, and have utterly destroyed the Amalekites.** It was a further hypocritical self-justification. **V. 21. But the people,** upon whom Saul again lays all the blame, **took of the spoil, sheep and oxen, the chief of the things which should have been utterly destroyed,** the firstlings of the devoted things, **to sacrifice unto the Lord, thy God, in Gilgal.** Saul evaded the plain words of the Lord that everything was to be put under the ban, and that therefore the animals could no longer be used for burnt offerings. **V. 22. And Samuel saith, Hath the Lord as great delight in burnt offerings and sacrifices as in obeying the voice of the**

**Lord?** A mechanical worship without true loyalty of the heart is not acceptable to Him. **Behold, to obey is better than sacrifice and to hearken than the fat of rams.** This principle, of the utter worthlessness of a dead worship, especially when it goes side by side with a lack of obedience to the Lord, has held in the Church of God at all times, and should be considered most carefully by all those whose churchgoing is a matter of mere routine. **V. 23. For rebellion is as the sin of witchcraft,** or divination, the service of demons in any form, **and stubbornness,** in refusing to obey God's commands, **is as iniquity and idolatry,** in which the living God is denied and rejected. **Because thou hast rejected the word of the Lord, he hath also rejected thee from being king,** Saul was abandoned to his pride, selfishness, and wickedness. He who opposes the Word of the Lord in any way, whether by speaking or by doing, thereby denies the true God and is in danger of being rejected.

SAUL'S HUMILIATION. — **V. 24. And Saul said unto Samuel, I have sinned,** this confession was extorted from him by fear, but was not an expression of true penitence; **for I have transgressed the commandment of the Lord and thy words, because I feared the people and obeyed their voice,** he had loved the honor and favor of men more than the favor and good will of God. **V. 25. Now, therefore, I pray thee, pardon my sin, and turn again with me that I may worship the Lord.** He did not really acknowledge his guilt, but wanted the good will of Samuel again, lest he be publicly rejected and ousted from his position of king, a disgrace which he felt would be all the harder to bear since he had already been told that the position of king would not be hereditary in his family, chap. 13, 14. **V. 26. And Samuel,** who knew that even the repentance of Saul was feigned and insincere, **said unto Saul,**

**I will not return with thee; for thou hast rejected the word of the Lord, and the Lord hath rejected thee from being king over Israel,** in the sight of God he no longer occupied that position. **V. 27. And as Samuel turned about to go away, he,** Saul, **laid hold upon the skirt of his mantle,** evidently with the intention of holding him back by force, **and it rent. V. 28. And Samuel said unto him, The Lord hath rent the kingdom of Israel from thee this day and hath given it to a neighbor of thine that is better than thou.** This much was even now decided in the counsel of the Lord, although even Samuel did not yet know who Saul's successor would be. **V. 29. And also the Strength of Israel,** the Lord, who is the Refuge, the Confidence of Israel, **will not lie nor repent,** He would not change this judicial sentence with the penalty of rejection; **for He is not a man that He should repent,** Num. 23, 19. **V. 30. Then he said, I have sinned,** a hollow sound without true sorrow of heart; **yet honor me now, I pray thee, before the elders of my people and before Israel, and turn again with me that I may worship the Lord, thy God.** Saul was concerned chiefly about his own honor, for he had only one fear, namely, that his authority and influence would be lost in case the people would find out about the open breach between him and Samuel. **V. 31. So Samuel turned again after Saul,** not only for the purpose of maintaining outward order in the nation and of preventing anarchy, but also to carry out the sentence of death upon Agag; **and Saul worshiped the Lord,** he observed this outward formality. **V. 32. Then said Samuel, Bring ye hither to me Agag, the king of the Amalekites. And Agag came unto him delicately,** in a cheerful mood. **And Agag said, Surely the bitterness of death is past,** which may have been an attempt at heroism in the face of death, or a hope that Samuel would spare him. **V. 33. And Samuel said, As thy sword hath made women childless, so shall thy mother be childless among women;** he was but receiving his just reward for his cruelties. **And Samuel hewed Agag in pieces before the Lord in Gilgal,** he carried out Jehovah's sentence of destruction upon him. **V. 34. Then Samuel went to Ramah,** to his home; **and Saul went up to his house to Gibeah of Saul. V. 35. And Samuel came no more to see Saul until the day of his death,** all intercourse with the rejected king on his side ceased from now on; **nevertheless, Samuel mourned for Saul; and the Lord repented that He had made Saul king over Israel.** Although Samuel had loved Saul, yet, since the latter had now been rejected as king, he could do nothing to effect a change of heart in him. A feigned repentance is the climax of hypocrisy and only tends to confirm the Lord's sentence of rejection.

# 16

# 1 Samuel 16

**D**avid Chosen King.

DAVID ANOINTED BY SAMUEL. — **V. 1.** **And the Lord said unto Samuel, How long wilt thou mourn for Saul, seeing I have rejected him from reigning over Israel?** Samuel had yielded to excessive grief over the condition of affairs, for his anxiety concerning the welfare of Israel and his worry over Saul's hardness of heart had put him out of sympathy with God's hidden ways; hence the reproof. **Fill thine horn with oil, and go, I will send thee to Jesse, the Bethlehemite; for I have provided me a king among his sons,** Jehovah had looked them over and chosen one of them. **v. 2. And Samuel said, How can I go? If Saul hear it, he will kill me,** since he would consider the act as treachery and revolt, believing himself still to be the rightful king of Israel. **And the Lord said, Take an heifer with thee, and say, I am come to sacrifice to the Lord,** for apparently it was nothing unusual for the prophet to hold divine services in various parts of Israel, especially now that Shiloh was desecrated. **V. 3. And call Jesse to the sacrifice,** inviting him to take part in the sacrificial meal as his own special guest, **and I will show thee what thou shalt do,** give him immediate directions, reveal His will at the time; **and thou shalt anoint unto Me him whom I name unto thee.** This involved no falsehood, but its chief object was to conceal the main reason of Samuel's coming from such as had no authority to know of it. **V. 4. And Samuel did that which the Lord spake, and came to Bethlehem. And the elders of the town trembled at his coming, and said, Comest thou peaceably?** Samuel had evidently held visitations from time to time and earnestly rebuked any wrongs and evil conditions which he found. **V. 5. And he said, Peaceably,** he had no special occasion to rebuke them; **I am come to sacrifice unto the Lord; sanctify yourselves, and come with me to the sacrifice,** the celebration being intended to strengthen the people's fellowship with Jehovah. **And he sanctified Jesse and his sons,** addressing this admonition to them in particular, so they would be sure to wash themselves and put on clean garments, **and called them to the sacrifice,** as his own special guests. **V. 6. And it came to pass, when they were come, that he looked on Eliab,** the first-born, **and,** being impressed by his appearance and bearing, **said, Surely the Lord's anointed is before Him,** this thought immediately arose in his heart. **V. 7. But the Lord said unto Samuel,** giving an answer to his spirit, **Look not on his countenance or on the height of his stature,** on the fact that he was a handsome, stalwart young man; **because I have refused him; for the Lord seeth not as man seeth,** He has different standards of judgment; **for man looketh on the outward appearance,** judging from what he can see, **but the Lord looketh on the heart,** judging by the disposition of the soul, proving the heart and the reins. This is a general truth which applies to the relation of God to men at all times. God, knowing the inward thoughts of men, is unfailing in His judgment. **V. 8. Then Jesse called Abinadab and made him pass before Samuel,** for the purpose of careful inspection. **And he said, Neither hath the Lord chosen this. V. 9. Then Jesse made Shammah to pass by. And he said, Neither hath the Lord chosen this. V. 10. Again, Jesse made seven of his sons to pass before Samuel,** that is, a total of seven, including the three oldest. **And Samuel said unto Jesse, The Lord hath not chosen these. V. 11. And Samuel said unto Jesse, Are here all thy children? And he said, There remaineth yet the youngest, and, behold, he keepeth the sheep.** As the youngest he had to stand back and take charge of the chores, while his older brothers made ready to go to the sacrificial feast. **And Samuel said unto Jesse, Send and fetch him; for we will not sit down,** literally, "surround," namely, the table, to partake of the meal, **till he come hither. V. 12. And he sent and brought him in. Now, he was ruddy,** said of the red color of his hair, which is unusual in the Orient, **and withal of a beautiful countenance,** with bright eyes and a clear look, **and goodly to look to,** handsome and stalwart of body as well. **And the Lord said,** announcing His decision to the thoughts of Samuel, **Arise, anoint him; for this is he,** chosen by the Lord in spite of his youth. **V. 13. Then Samuel took the horn of oil and anointed him in the midst of his brethren,** they were witnesses of the solemn act; **and the Spirit of the Lord came upon David from that day forward,** he received a special endowment with gifts and powers for his royal calling, so that he was gradually led forward to full development, to complete fitness for his life's work. **So Samuel rose up and went to Ramah,** back to his home. It is probable that the significance of the ceremony was not made known to the other sons of Jesse, who may have been under the impression that David was simply to be regarded as a pupil of the great prophet. But the Lord's will went forward in due time. It happens quite often that the Lord chooses men for His work who are without honor before men. But just such instruments He fills with His Spirit, making them fit to perform the work of their high calling.

DAVID PLAYS FOR SAUL. — **V. 14. But the Spirit of the Lord departed from Saul,** now that his rejection was an established fact, **and an evil spirit from the Lord,** having been given permission to that effect by the Lord, **troubled him,** fell upon him and terrified him, filled him with anxious worry and a nameless dread. It was a wicked power, which had a strange control over him. **V. 15. And Saul's servants said unto him, Behold now, an evil spirit from God,** sent as a punishment from God, **troubleth thee. V. 16. Let our lord now command thy servants which are before thee to seek out a man who is a cunning player on an harp,** a skilful harpist; **and it shall come to pass, when the evil spirit from God is upon thee, that he shall play with his hand, and thou shalt be well,** for the soothing influence of music was known even at that time. **V. 17. And Saul said unto his servants, Provide me now a man that can play well, and bring him to me,** for he was glad to try this method of alleviating his trouble. **V. 18. Then answered one of the servants and said, Behold, I have seen a son of Jesse, the Bethlehemite, that is cunning in playing,** a skilful harpist, **and a mighty, valiant man,** full of bravery and of a warlike spirit, **and a man of war,** apparently fit to be a good soldier, **and prudent in matters,** eloquent of speech, **and a comely person,** strong and handsome, **and the Lord is with him.** The recommendation shows all the characteristics which later appeared in the history of David. **V. 19. Wherefore Saul sent messengers unto Jesse and said, Send me David, thy son, which is with the sheep,** Saul thus making use of his kingly prerogative in pressing men into his personal service. **V. 20. And Jesse took an ass laden with bread, and a bottle,** a skin, **of wine, and a kid,** as presents to the king, **and sent them by David, his son, unto Saul,** presents of this kind being a sign of obedience and subjection. **V. 21. And David came to Saul and stood before him,** as his servant; **and he,** Saul, **loved him greatly; and he became his armorbearer,** being trained for military service. **V. 22. And Saul sent to Jesse, saying, Let David, I pray thee, stand before me,** continue in the king's service; **for he hath found favor in my sight. V. 23. And it came to pass, when the evil spirit from God was upon Saul,** when he had special attacks of his affliction, when the gloomy moods were upon him, **that David took an harp and played with his hand; so Saul was refreshed and was well,** he found relief, **and the evil spirit departed from him.** David's story shows that the Lord leads His children in marvelous ways. Those who are intended for servants in His kingdom are so guided by Him that all they see, hear, learn, and experience is of value to them for their future calling.

# 1 Samuel 17

**D**avid's Victory over Goliath.
    GOLIATH'S DEFIANCE OF ISRAEL. — **V. 1. Now, the Philistines,** the federation of the five city states, **gathered together their armies to battle, and were gathered together at Shochoh, which belongeth to Judah,** some ten miles southwest of Jerusalem, **and pitched between Shochoh and Azekah, in Ephesdammim,** in a range of hills which gave their camp a good strategic position. **V. 2. And Saul and the men of Israel were gathered together and pitched by the Valley of Elah,** in the Terebinth Valley, northeast of the Philistine position, **and set the battle in array against the Philistines. V. 3. And the Philistines stood on a mountain on the one side,** literally, "towards the mountain," on the higher slopes, **and Israel stood on a mountain on the other side; and there was a valley between them,** the deeper bed of the brook. **V. 4. And there went out a champion out of the camp of the philistines,** one of the few descendants of the giant race left by Joshua, Josh. 11, 22, **named Goliath, of Gath, whose height was six cubits and a span** (about nine feet and

nine inches). **V. 5. And he had an helmet of brass upon his head, and he was armed,** clothed, **with a coat of mail,** a scale-corselet made of overlapping metal plates; **and the weight of the coat was five thousand shekels of brass** (a copper shekel being a little less than half an ounce, the total weight probably some 150 pounds). **V. 6. And he had greaves of brass upon his legs,** where his coat of mail did not extend, **and a target of brass,** a copper lance, or javelin, **between his shoulders. V. 7. And the staff of his spear was like a weaver's beam; and his spear's head weighed six hundred shekels of iron** (about seventeen pounds); **and one bearing a shield went before him,** for the great shield was needed only when the soldier was on the defensive. **V. 8. And he stood and cried unto the armies of Israel,** the divisions and companies as they were set up in battle array, **and said unto them, Why are ye come out to set your battle in array? Am not I a Philistine and ye servants to Saul? Choose you a man for you, and let him come down to me,** to the valley beneath the hillside where the Israelites were standing in battle-line. **V. 9. If he be able to fight with me and to kill me, then will we be your servants; but if I prevail against him and kill him, then shall ye be our servants and serve us.** So Goliath's proposal was to have the entire matter decided by single combat, since he felt sure that the outcome would be in favor of the Philistines. **V. 10. And the Philistine said, I defy the armies of Israel this day,** by issuing his challenge in this manner; **give me a man that we may fight together.** The contempt lay in the expression "slaves of Saul" and was expressed with all the greater boldness, since there was no answer on the part of Israel. **V. 11. When Saul and all Israel heard those words of the Philistine, they were dismayed,** cast down, terrified, **and greatly afraid.** "Israel is afraid because its king is. They dare not in childlike spirit appropriate the promises of Jehovah. The wings that should bear them up in trustful upsoaring to the Lord of hosts are crippled."

DAVID SENT TO THE CAMP. — V. 12. **Now, David was the son of that Ephrathite of Bethlehem-judah whose name was Jesse; and he had eight sons; and the man went among men for an old man in the days of Saul,** he was advanced in years and consequently felt the weakness of old age. **V. 13. And the three eldest sons of Jesse went and followed Saul to the battle,** they were in the army which had been summoned to repel the invaders; **and the names of his three sons that went to battle were Eliab, the first-born, and next unto him Abinadab, and the third Shammah,** chap. 16, 6-9. **V. 14. And David was the youngest; and the three eldest followed Saul. V. 15. But David went and returned from Saul,** he went back and forth between his home and the king's court, just as Saul had need of him, **to feed his father's sheep at Bethlehem,** he helped out at home as much as possible, especially now that Saul had gone forth on the campaign against the Philistines. He had indeed been enrolled among Saul's armor-bearers, but he had not yet been drilled in the art of warfare as it was then practiced. **V. 16. And the Philistine drew near morning and evening and presented himself forty days. V. 17. And Jesse said unto David, his son,** during these forty days, **Take now for thy brethren an ephah** (about 26 quarts) **of this parched corn,** roasted peas or grain, **and these ten loaves, and run to the camp to thy brethren; v. 18. and carry these ten cheeses,** portions of curds, probably on the order of cottage-cheese, **unto the captain of their thousand,** under whose command his brothers were, **and look how thy**

**brethren fare,** inquiring after their welfare; **and take their pledge,** some personal. token which would assure the father that they were indeed well. **V. 19. Now, Saul and they,** the eons of Jesse, **and all the men of Israel were in the Valley of Elah, fighting with the Philistines.** This remark belongs to the instructions which Jesse addressed to David. **V. 20. And David rose up early in the morning, and left the sheep with a keeper,** faithful to his charge also in this, **and took, and went as Jesse had commanded him; and be came to the trench,** the wagon rampart which served for a fortification of the camp, **as the host was going forth to the fight,** to be set up in battle array, **and shouted for the battle,** raised their war-cry, to encourage their own ranks and to terrify the enemies in case they should contemplate an attack. **V. 21. For Israel and the Philistines had put the battle in array, army against army,** in readiness for the battle which was expected every day. **V. 22. And David left his carriage,** the load which he had come to deliver, **in the hand of the keeper of the carriage,** the officer in charge of the army's baggage, **and ran into the army, and came and saluted his brethren,** asking for his brothers, inquiring after their well-being. **V. 23. And as he talked with them, behold, there came up the champion, the Philistine of Gath, Goliath by name, out of the armies of the Philistines, and spake according to the same words,** as he usually did; **and David heard them. V. 24. And all the men of Israel, when they saw the man, fled from him, and were sore afraid,** the very sight of the man filled them with such fear and trembling that they were unable to give battle. **V. 25. And the men of Israel said,** after the manner of men discussing a great calamity, **Have ye seen this man that is come up? Surely to defy Israel is he come up,** to challenge them to single combat with a contemptuous sneer; **and it shall be that the man who killeth him, the king will enrich him with great riches, and will give him his daughter, and make his father's house free in Israel,** exempt from taxes and every form of public service. This was the promise of Saul in a public proclamation, intended to inspire some man with the courage to risk his life in battle. **V. 26. And David spake to the men that stood by him, saying, What shall be done to the man that killeth this Philistine and taketh away the reproach from Israel,** which was daily heaped upon the entire people by this contemptuous challenge? **For who is this uncircumcised Philistine,** a man outside of the covenant with Jehovah, **that he should defy the armies of the living God?** The main thought in David's mind was this, that the insult offered to Israel, the people of Jehovah, must be wiped out at all costs. **V. 27. And the people answered him after this manner,** in agreement with the proclamation of the king, as before, **saying, So shall it be done to the man that killeth him. V. 28. And Eliab, his eldest brother, heard when he spake unto the men, and Eliab's anger was kindled against David, and he said, Why camest thou down hither,** from the higher ranges near Bethlehem? **And with whom hast thou left those few sheep in the wilderness?** He intimated that their family could ill afford to lose the few heads of small cattle which they owned. His zeal was blinded by envy and jealousy. **I know thy pride and the naughtiness of thine heart; for thou art come down that thou mightest see the battle.** The intimation was that David was not satisfied with his lowly calling, that he wished to rise above his station and take part in the war, since his wickedness enjoyed the brutality of the battle. Eliab's is a type of a small soul, incapable of great thoughts and deeds.

**V. 29. And David said,** in a quiet, but very decided denial of the wrong charged to him, **What have I now done? Is there not a cause?** He surely had a right to ask a simple question. **V. 30. And he turned from him,** letting his oldest brother stand in his pitiful smallness, **toward another and spake after the same manner; and the people answered him again after the former manner. V. 31. And when the words were heard which David spake, they rehearsed them before Saul,** in a respectful announcement; **and he sent for him,** he had David brought before him. David is a type of a simple believer, who performs his work in all simplicity, showing himself faithful even in the smallest details which are entrusted to him.

DAVID SLAYS GOLIATH. — **V. 32. And David said to Saul, Let no man's heart fail because of him,** Goliath, no man's courage must fail on his account, the entire army should lay aside its fear; **thy servant will go and fight with this Philistine.** It was a simple, modest offer to undertake that single combat to which Goliath had been challenging. **V. 33. And Saul,** who was decidedly lacking in the divine courage needed for Jehovah's battles, **said to David, Thou art not able to go against this Philistine to fight with him; for thou art but a youth,** a young man, and not versed in the arts of war, **and he a man of war from his youth,** trained in the use of arms from early childhood. **V. 34. And David said unto Saul, Thy servant kept his father's sheep, and there came a lion and a bear,** the reference being to two different occasions, **and took a lamb out of the flock; v. 35. and I went out after him,** in either case, **and smote him, and delivered it out of his mouth; and when he arose against me, I caught him by his beard,** this applying to the lion, **and smote him,** probably with his shepherd's staff, **and slew him. V. 36. Thy servant**

**slew both the lion and the bear; and this uncircumcised Philistine shall be as one of them,** shall share the fate of these two ravenous beasts, **seeing he hath defied the armies of the living God,** that being David's chief reason for believing that the covenant God would not abandon His people's cause, since it was really His honor which was at stake. **V. 37. David said, moreover, The Lord, that delivered me out of the paw of the lion and out of the paw of the bear, He will deliver me out of the hand of this Philistine.** David's courage thus rested on his faith and trust in the mighty help of the Lord, for whose honor he intended to battle. **And Saul said unto David, Go, and the Lord be with thee. V. 38. And Saul armed David with his armor,** had him try on special garments intended to be worn with the armor, **and he put an helmet of brass upon his head; also he armed him with a coat of mail. V. 39. And David girded his sword upon his armor, and he assayed to go; for he had not proved it,** he had never made an attempt to move about in heavy armor of this kind, but found it too unwieldy for his inexperienced arms and body. **And David said unto Saul, I cannot go with these, for I have not proved them,** he did not possess the skill to handle them. **And David put them off him. V. 40. And he took his staff in his hand, and chose him five smooth stones out of the brook,** down in the valley, **and put them in a shepherd's bag which he had,** in a special kit which he carried with him, **even in a scrip,** a pouch or pocket; **and his sling was in his hand; and he drew near to the Philistine,** equipped only with his shepherd's implements. **V. 41. And the Philistine came on and drew near unto David; and the man that bare the shield went before him. V. 42. And when the Philistine looked about and saw David,** took note of him for the first time, **he disdained him,** gave him only a contemptuous glance; **for he was but a youth,** still a young man, **and ruddy, and of a fair countenance. V. 43. And the Philistine said unto David, Am I a dog that thou comest to me with staves?** the exaggeration purposely expressing his contempt. **And the Philistine cursed David by his gods,** adding blasphemy to his contempt. **V. 44. And the Philistine said to David, Come to me,** let him but dare to undertake an attack, **and I will give thy flesh unto the fowls of the air and to the beasts of the field.** To his scornful defiance he added a bloodthirsty threat. **V. 45. Then said David to the Philistine, Thou comest to me with a sword and with a spear and with a shield,** on these the Philistine relied to give him the victory; **but I come to thee in the name of the Lord of hosts, the God of the armies of Israel, whom thou hast defied.** David's courage was based entirely upon his faith in the covenant God and His almighty power. **V. 46. This day will the Lord deliver thee into mine hand,** in an utterly helpless state; **and I will smite thee, and take thine head from thee; and I will give the carcasses of the host of the Philistines this day unto the fowls of the air and to the wild beasts of the earth, that all the earth may know that there is a God in Israel,** namely, the one true God, Jehovah, who alone has the outcome of the battle in His hand. **V. 47. And all this assembly,** the entire army of Israel, **shall know that the Lord saveth not with sword and spear,** that He is not dependent upon external mighty means to gain the victory; **for the battle is the Lord's,** the decision rests with Him alone, **and He will give you into our hands. V. 48. And it came to pass, when the Philistine arose and came and drew nigh to meet David, that David hasted and ran toward the army,** where it was drawn up in battle-line, **to meet the Philistine. V. 49. And David put** his hand in his bag, and took thence a stone, and slang it, and smote the Philistine in his forehead that the stone sunk into his forehead, breaking open the strong frontal bone; and he fell upon his face to the earth, stunned, if not killed, by the missile. V. 50. So David prevailed over the Philistine with a sling and with a stone, and smote the Philistine and slew him; but there was no sword in the hand of David, he had no regular weapons of war. V. 51. Therefore David ran and stood upon the Philistine, stepping on the trunk of the fallen giant, and took his sword, and drew it out of the sheath thereof, and slew him, and cut off his head therewith, thus making sure of his death. And when the Philistines saw their champion was dead, they fled. V. 52. And the men of Israel and of Judah arose, suddenly inspired with a mighty courage by the deed of David, and shouted, and pursued the Philistines until thou come to the valley, into the lowlands, and to the gates of Ekron, one of the chief Philistine cities. And the wounded of the Philistines fell down by the way to Shaaraim, a city in the western lowlands of Judah, even unto Gath and unto Ekron. V. 53. And the children of Israel returned from chasing after the Philistines, and they spoiled their tents, taking all the booty in the form of food, clothing, and money out of their abandoned camp. V. 54. And David took the head of the Philistine, and brought it to Jerusalem, for the city itself was in the hands of the Israelites, only the fortress of Jebus on Mount Zion had not yet been conquered; but he put his armor in his tent, as his own part of the spoil. V. 55. And when Saul saw David go forth against the Philistine, he said unto Abner, the captain of the host, Abner, whose son is this youth? He wanted to know about his parentage, where he hailed from. And Abner said, As

**thy soul liveth, O king, I cannot tell. V. 56. And the king said, Inquire thou whose son the stripling is.** So far as this strange question is concerned, there are two explanations. Either Saul was seeking information about the family of David, in order to carry out his promise of freeing the family from taxation, or Saul's memory had been affected by his affliction, especially since he rarely saw David except at the times when the madness was upon him. **V. 57. And as David returned from the slaughter of the Philistine, Abner took him and brought him before Saul, with the head of the Philistine in his hand. V. 58. And Saul said to him, Whose son art thou, thou young man? And David answered, I am the son of thy servant Jesse, the Bethlehemite.** With this information Saul could now carry out his promise of which the soldiers had spoken. David's battle with Goliath is a picture of the battle which is the lot of all Christians in overcoming the attacks of Satan and of the sneering unbelievers. Although the odds often seem decidedly unfavorable to the Christians, they always have the Lord of hosts on their side and therefore must finally obtain the victory. At the same time we are here reminded of the great Son of David, who also, in a most singular manner, conquered the prince of this world and has given us the victory.

# 18

# 1 Samuel 18

The Consequences of David's Victory.

SAUL'S REGARD CHANGES TO HATRED. — **V. 1. And it came to pass, when he had made an end of speaking unto Saul,** when David had given the king the information which he desired concerning his family, **that the soul of Jonathan,** the heroic son of Saul, **was knit with the soul of David,** chained to his in a firm and inseparable union, bound by the band of love; **and Jonathan loved him as his own soul,** with a total absence of selfishness, in an ideal friendship. **V. 2. And Saul took him that day, and would let him go no more home to his father's house;** he was now permanently in the king's service, and could no more, as he formerly did, chap. 17, 15, return home from time to time to assist in the work and to perform his shepherd's duties. **V. 3. Then Jonathan and David made a covenant,** a formal sealing of their mutual love and friendship, **because he loved him as his own soul;** they promised each other perpetual friendship. **V. 4. And Jonathan,** as a testimony and token of his love and friendship, **stripped himself of the robe that was upon him,**

**and gave it to David, and his garments, even to his sword and to his bow and to his girdle.** Thus the barrier of rank and position was completely set aside; for Jonathan's object was not only to have David appear at court in proper dress, but also to honor David as a military hero, the conqueror of the terrible Philistine, who should therefore appear in a dress befitting his station. **V. 5. And David went out whithersoever Saul sent him,** on any campaign for which the king thought his military ability fitted him, **and behaved himself wisely,** being both prudent and prosperous; **and Saul set him over the men of war,** made him commander of a body of soldiers, **and he was accepted in the sight of all the people,** regarded very highly, **and also in the sight of Saul's servants,** the officials at Saul's court, who might have been jealous of his success. **V. 6. And it came to pass, as they came,** when the army returned from the pursuit of the Philistines to celebrate the victory, **when David was returned from the slaughter of the Philistine, that the women came out of all cities of Israel,** to celebrate the victory in the proper manner, **singing and dancing, to meet King Saul, with tabrets,** castanets, **with joy,** with joyful outcry, **and with instruments of music,** with triangles. **V. 7. And the women answered one another as they played, and said, Saul hath slain his thousands and David his ten thousands.** They not only performed choral dances, but also alternate dances intended to interpret the battle and the victory, while, at the same time, they raised their voices in antiphonal singing, their song showing the high regard in which David was held on account of his heroic deed. **V. 8. And Saul was very wroth,** his jealousy immediately flared up, **and the saying displeased him; and he said, They have ascribed unto David ten thousands and to me they have ascribed but**

**thousands; and what can he have more but the kingdom?** All that was missing in David's case was the royal dignity and position, this being a presentiment which may almost have amounted to a suspicion, since Samuel had distinctly stated that the royal power would pass into another family. **V. 9. And Saul eyed David from that day and forward,** he looked upon him with envious suspicion. **V. 10. And it came to pass on the morrow that the evil spirit from God,** chap. 16, 13-16, **came upon Saul, and he prophesied in the midst of the house,** he raged and raved in madness; **and David played with his hand,** performed on the harp, **as at other times; and there was a javelin,** a small spear used as a scepter, **in Saul's hand. V. 11. And Saul cast the javelin,** made a lunge at him; **for he said, I will smite David even to the wall with it,** pass it through David into the wall. **And David avoided out of his presence twice,** he dodged the attack, but remained at his post in the attempt to soothe the king, to drive away his madness. **V. 12. And Saul was afraid of David, because the Lord was with him,** as all the evidence plainly showed, **and was departed from Saul;** the king felt more and more that he had been forsaken and rejected by the Lord in favor of David. **V. 13. Therefore Saul removed him from him,** from his position at court, where he was sheltered, **and made him his captain over a thousand,** probably promoted him to a higher position in the army; **and he went out and came in before the people,** in various military campaigns. **V. 14. And David behaved himself wisely in all his ways,** he used good judgment in all his undertakings and was correspondingly successful; **and the Lord was with him,** crowning his work with blessing. **V. 15. Wherefore, when Saul saw that he behaved himself very wisely, he was afraid of him,** every new incident showing the trend of affairs added new fuel to the fire of his jealousy and anger, as well as to his fear. **V. 16. But all Israel and Judah loved David because he went out and came in before them;** their regard for him increased as they noted that he went about his business quietly and effectively, and that all his military undertakings were successful. All believers are bound to expect hatred on the part of the godless world, especially since the infidels cannot help but note that God is on the side of His children. But in the measure that they show their hatred in works of enmity God holds His protecting hand over those that trust in Him.

SAUL PLANS TO HAVE DAVID REMOVED. — **V. 17. And Saul said to David, Behold my elder daughter Merab, her will I give thee to wife,** in fufilling the promise which was well known to all the soldiers of the army, chap. 17,25; **only be thou valiant for me,** distinguished for courage, **and fight the Lord's battles.** This was not a condition, but an obligation laid upon David, Saul taking this opportunity to impress the younger man with his zeal for the people of God and with the necessity of thwarting the evil intentions of the heathen neighbors. "But behind this proper language of Canaan was hid Saul's cunning and wickedness towards David." (Lange.) **For Saul said,** namely, within himself, this was the thought which urged him on, **Let not mine hand be upon him,** it would have been a dangerous matter for him to take the life of David outright, **but let the hand of the Philistines be upon him;** Saul hoped that David would at some time fall in battle, and that the desired end would thus be obtained. **V. 18. And David said unto Saul,** in true modesty, without the least suspicion of Saul's guile, **Who am I? and what is my life or my father's family in Israel that I should be son-in-law to the king?**

115

David implied that neither his own person nor his position in life, nor his family connections made him worthy of the honor offered him by the king. **V. 19. But it came to pass at the time when Merab, Saul's daughter, should have been given to David that she was given unto Adriel, the Meholathite, to wife.** It was simply a whim of Saul's which caused him to break his promise to David, for he grew more capricious as the years went by. **V. 20. And Michal, Saul's daughter, loved David; and they told Saul, and the thing pleased him,** this turn of affairs promised to fit well with his plans. **V. 21. And Saul said, I will give him her that she may be a snare to him,** serve as a bait or lure to him, **and that the hand of the Philistines may be against him;** he had a scheme in mind which would surely be successful. **Wherefore Saul said to David, Thou shalt this day be my son-in-law in the one of the twain,** literally, "The second time thou shalt become my son-in-law," namely, first by the betrothal to Merab, the second time by the actual marriage to Michal. **V. 22. And Saul commanded his servants, saying, Commune with David secretly,** as if they did it without the king's knowledge, **and say, Behold, the king hath delight in thee, and all his servants love thee; now, therefore, be the king's son-in-law.** The offer was pure hypocrisy, and all the more revolting since it was a part of the king's scheme to destroy David through Michal's love. **V. 23. And Saul's servants spake those words in the ears of David. And David,** remembering his first experience with Saul, **said, Seemeth it to you a light thing,** a small matter, **to be a king's son-in-law, seeing that I am a poor man and lightly esteemed?** His experience in the matter of Merab had impressed upon him once more the great distance between his station and the honored position for which he was supposed to strive, and being a poor man, it was hardly possible for him to pay the dowry or morning gift expected of a suitor. **V. 24. And the servants of Saul told him, saying, On this manner spake David,** stating the objections advanced by David. **V. 25. And Saul said,** still with the same anxiety to attain his object, **Thus shall ye say to David, The king desireth not any dowry, but an hundred foreskins of the Philistines,** taken, of course, from their dead bodies, **to be avenged of the king's enemies. But Saul thought to make David fall by the hand of the Philistines;** he was sure that this scheme to put David out of the way could not fail. **V. 26. And when his servants told David these words, it pleased David well to be the king's son-in-law,** especially since he was to win Michal by a heroic achievement; **and the days were not expired,** that is, the period set by Saul for obtaining the morning-gift. **V. 27. Wherefore David arose and went, he and his men,** the thousand of whom he was commander, **and slew of the Philistines two hundred men; and David brought their foreskins, and they gave them in full tale to the king,** counted them out in full number, not only those required, but the hundred extra ones as a free gift, **that he might be the king's son-in-law. And Saul gave him Michal,** his daughter, **to wife.** His hostile schemes being thwarted once more, he was obliged to fulfil his promise. **V. 28. And Saul saw and knew that the Lord was with David,** it was so obvious that he could not close his eyes against the fact, **and that Michal, Saul's daughter, loved him;** even the fact of her love for David was a thorn in the king's side. **V. 29. And Saul was yet the more afraid of David,** for it was evident that God shielded the young man against his wicked designs; **and Saul became David's enemy continually,** all the days of his life. **V. 30.**

**Then the princes of the Philistines went forth,** in campaigns to overthrow the power of Israel; **and it came to pass, after they went forth, that David behaved himself more wisely than all the servants of Saul,** he always exercised prudent judgment and thus had success in his undertakings, **so that his name was much set by,** he was highly thought of by all the people. All the upright in heart honor and love the faithful servants of God and acknowledge the blessings which the Lord gives to His people through them.

# 19

# 1 Samuel 19

**S**aul's Persecution of David.

JONATHAN PROVES HIS FRIENDSHIP FOR DAVID. — **V. 1. And Saul spake to Jonathan, his son, and to all his servants that they should kill David;** he openly announced his intention of putting David out of the way, for he could no longer control his deadly hate. **V. 2. But Jonathan, Saul's son, delighted much in David,** his great love for his friend was unchanged; **and Jonathan told David, saying, Saul, my father, seeketh to kill thee,** his loyalty for his friend urged him to warn David, even at the risk of offending his father. **Now, therefore, I pray thee, take heed to thyself until the morning, and abide in a secret place, and hide thyself; v. 3. and I will go out and stand beside my father in the field where thou art,** probably a place where Saul often talked over private matters with his son, **and I will commune with my father of thee; and what I see, that I will tell thee;** he would immediately make known to David just what he would find out from his father, and it was for this reason that he had David hide near by, lest his going to some distant place after the conversation with his father awaken suspicion of an understanding with David. **V. 4. And Jonathan,** in the interview which he obtained, **spake good of David unto Saul, his father,** pointing out all his excellent qualities and his fine services to the entire nation, **and said unto him, Let not the king sin against his servant,** for David had always occupied this position with great cheerfulness, **against David, because he hath not sinned against thee, and because his works have been to thee-ward very good;** far from doing the king any harm, he had always and in all things done him great service by his feats of arms and by his attendance at court. **V. 5. For he did put his life in his hand,** risking his most precious possession, **and slew the Philistine, and the Lord wrought a great salvation for all Israel,** in delivering the people from the danger threatened by the Philistines; **thou sawest it and didst rejoice. Wherefore, then, wilt thou sin against innocent blood to slay David without a cause?** It was an urgent, yet modest appeal to whatever nobility was still left in Saul's character; a fine example to all men of how to speak the best of their neighbors. **V. 6. And Saul hearkened unto the voice of Jonathan,** he was persuaded by his son's noble intercession. **And Saul sware,** going to the other extreme, as usual, **As the Lord liveth, he shall not be slain. V. 7. And Jonathan called David, and Jonathan showed him all those things,** giving him the joyful information that he was reinstated in Saul's favor. **And Jonathan brought David to Saul, and he was in his presence,** resumed his place at court, **as in times past.** True love and friendship to our neighbor demands of us that we defend him against all evil suspicions, put the best construction on everything, and calm down the anger of the jealous.

MICHAL SAVES DAVID'S LIFE. — **V. 8. And there was war again,** for the Philistines would not remain quiet; **and David went out,** marched forth to battle, **and fought with the Philistines, and slew them with a great slaughter,** administered a decisive defeat; **and they fled from him. V. 9. And the evil spirit from the Lord was upon Saul;** a judgment of the covenant God upon the reprobate king, **as he sat in his house with his javelin in his hand; and David played with his hand,** for he had again taken his position as harpist. **V. 10. And Saul,** apparently in a fit of jealousy on account of the latest success of David, **sought to smite David even to the wall with the javelin,** by driving the spear through his body; **but he slipped away out of Saul's presence,** dodging the threatened blow once more, **and he smote the javelin into the wall. And David fled, and escaped that night. V. 11. Saul also sent messengers unto David's house,** which he had reached before nightfall, **to watch him, and to slay him in the morning; and Michal, David's wife, told him, saying, If thou save not thy life tonight, tomorrow thou shalt be slain.** The description given by David in Ps. 59, where he tells of this event, shows that there were jealous courtiers in attendance upon Saul, who were anxious to remove their powerful rival and therefore even added fuel to Saul's jealousy. **V. 12. So Michal let David down through a window. And he went, and fled, and escaped,** for Saul's watchmen were guarding only the door. **V. 13. And Michal took an image,** a picture of a household god, such as the Israelites still retained as the remnant of the idolatrous practices brought from their Chaldean home, Gen. 31, 19. 34, **and laid it in the bed, and put a pillow of goats' hair for his bolster,** a braided or woven quilt, **and covered it with a cloth.** Thus the figure, covered with the upper garment which served as a covering at night, looked very much like that of a human being. **V. 14. And when Saul sent messengers to take David,** in the morning, **she said, He is sick,** for she probably thought, by telling this falsehood, to gain time for David, in order that he might have a longer start on his pursuers. **V. 15. And Saul sent the messengers again to see David, saying, Bring him up to me in the bed that I may slay him;** he was determined to carry out his purpose this time. **V. 16. And when the messengers were come in, behold, there was an image in the bed, with a pillow of goats' hair for his bolster.** So the deceit was discovered. **V. 17. And Saul,** angry because he had been duped, **said unto Michal, Why hast thou deceived me so and sent away mine enemy,** the expression implying that the enemy of the father should be the enemy of the daughter as well, **that he is escaped? And Michal answered Saul,** her fear of her father and her anxiety to save her own life causing her to tell another falsehood, **He said unto me, Let me go; why should I kill thee?** There is no wrong in throwing raging, ravening, murderous pursuers off the track, for such murderers are the instruments of Satan, who seeks to destroy the children of God in every possible manner.

SAUL IN RAMAH. — **V. 18. So David fled, and escaped, and came to Samuel to Ramah,** he turned to the prophet, his fatherly friend, first of all, **and told him all that Saul had done to him. And he and Samuel went and dwelt in Naioth,** the place where the children of the prophets lived, with Samuel at their head. **V. 19. And it was told Saul, saying, Behold, David is at Naioth in Ramah,** where there was a complex of buildings enclosed with a fence or wall. **V. 20. And Saul sent messengers to take David; and when they saw the company of the prophets prophesying,** praising God in a state of ecstasy, **and Samuel standing as appointed over them,** for he was the head of this prophets' seminary, **the Spirit of God was upon the messengers of Saul, and they also prophesied,** singing divine praises under the direction of an influence which they could not resist. **V. 21. And when it was told Saul, he sent other messengers, and they prophesied likewise. And Saul sent messengers again the third time, and they prophesied also.** All this was to be a hint, on the part of Divine Providence, that God was hindering the messengers from carrying out Saul's command; it was He who was protecting David against willful murder. **V. 22. Then went he,** Saul, **also to Ramah,** in a stubborn determination to carry out his will, **and came to a great well that is in Sechu,** a large cistern not far from Ramah; **and he asked and said, Where are Samuel and David? And one said, Behold, they be at Naioth in Ramah. V. 23. And he went thither to Naioth in Ramah; and the Spirit of God was upon him also,** He took hold of him and held him in His power; **and he went on and prophesied until he came to Naioth in Ramah.** "The difference between Saul and his messengers was that the inspiration came on him as he was approaching the residence of the prophet, and that it attained a higher grade and lasted longer, completely suppressing his self-consciousness." **V. 24. And he stripped off his clothes also,** either by removing all his clothes or at least his outer garment, leaving only the inner shirt of linen or cotton, **and prophesied before Samuel in like manner, and lay down,** literally, "fell," **naked all that day and all that night.** The length and the vehemence of the attack of ecstasy which Saul experienced was to indicate to him and others that his persecution of David was a battling against Jehovah and His Spirit, which should therefore not be persisted in, lest more serious effects follow. **Wherefore they say, Is Saul also among the prophets?** The proverbial saying, which had first gone the rounds when Saul returned from Ramah after meeting Samuel, was now given new nourishment. Unfortunately the heart of Saul remained unchanged, just as the hearts and minds of unbelievers in our days are sometimes drawn into a wave of religious excitement, without a subsequent change of life. Nevertheless, God has even the hearts of His enemies in His power, and they sometimes confess the truth against their will, thus serving the interests of the Lord's kingdom.

# 20

# 1 Samuel 20

**T**he Proof of Jonathan's Friendship.
CONFERENCE BETWEEN DAVID AND JONATHAN.
— **V. 1. And David fled from Naioth in Ramah,** from the enclosure in which the seminary of the prophets was located, **and came and said before Jonathan,** with whom he was united in the closest and firmest friendship, chap. 18, 1-4, **What have I done? What is mine iniquity? and what is my sin before thy father that he seeketh my life?** The threefold question by which he appealed to the personal knowledge of Jonathan was a threefold denial of any fault on his part. **V. 2. And he,** Jonathan, **said unto him, God forbid,** that is, By no means; **thou shalt not die,** this is not only the assurance of a friend, but of a prince. **Behold, my father will do nothing, either great or small,** absolutely nothing, **but that he will show it me,** he uncovered or revealed, talked over, all his plans with Jonathan as the heir apparent to the throne. **And why should my father hide this thing from me? It is not so;** he was sure that Saul had not again determined upon the destruction of David at any cost. **V.**

**3. And David,** whose experience with Saul had taught him to estimate the true state of affairs more correctly, **sware moreover,** in addition to what he had said to Jonathan, **and said, Thy father certainly knoweth that I have found grace in thine eyes,** the kindly feeling of his son for David could not have escaped his observation; **and he saith, Let not Jonathan know this lest he be grieved; but truly, as the Lord liveth, and as thy soul liveth,** the double oath expressing the gravity of the situation as he saw it, **there is but a step,** hardly as much as a step, **between me and death.** "The picture is of a precipice, from which he is only a step removed, over which he may any moment be plunged." (Lange.) **V. 4. Then said Jonathan unto David, Whatsoever thy soul desireth, I will even do it for thee,** he would be glad to fulfill David's every wish, every thought. **V. 5. And David said unto Jonathan, Behold, tomorrow is the new moon,** a minor, but joyful festival of the Jewish church-year, connected with a cheerful meal, Num. 10, 10; 28, 11-15, **and I should not fail to sit with the king at meat,** as custom required it; **but let me go,** Jonathan should consent to his remaining away deliberately, **that I may hide myself in the field unto the third day at even,** for according to David's plan so much time was required to find out the disposition of the king. **V. 6. If thy father at all miss me, then say, David earnestly asked leave of me that he might run to Bethlehem, his city; for there is a yearly sacrifice there for all the family,** a celebration with a sacrificial meal, for such celebrations at that time, when the Tabernacle had been desecrated by the removal of the ark, were held in various parts of the country. **V. 7. If he say thus, It is well; thy servant shall have peace,** it would be evident that Saul's hostile disposition showed itself only during his attacks of rage; **but if he be very wroth, then**

**be sure that evil is determined by him,** that the destruction of David was a settled thing in Saul's mind. **V. 8. Therefore thou shalt deal kindly with thy servant,** show him merciful kindness; **for thou hast brought thy servant into a covenant of the Lord with thee;** it was on the basis of this covenant of friendship that David appealed to Jonathan. **Notwithstanding, if there be in me iniquity, slay me thyself,** in case of a trespass on his part, he would rather die by the hand of his friend; **for why shouldest thou bring me to thy father? V. 9. And Jonathan said, Far be it from thee,** there was no sin for which David was bound to atone by death; **for if I knew certainly that evil were determined by my father to come upon thee, then would not I tell it thee?** It is a solemn protestation, with the force of an oath. **V. 10. Then said David to Jonathan, Who shall tell me?** He wondered how he could get the information about Saul's decree concerning himself, for the matter was too delicate to be entrusted to a servant. **Or what if thy father answer thee roughly?** There was great danger that Saul would deal harshly with Jonathan in case he would make known his evil plans to David and this fact come to the knowledge of the king. **V. 11. And Jonathan said unto David, Come, and let us go out into the field,** where they would be away from observation, not in danger of being overheard, and where Jonathan might point out to David a hiding place which he had in mind for his own plan. **And they went out, both of them, into the field. V. 12. And Jonathan said unto David,** in a solemn invocation and vow before Jehovah, **O Lord God of Israel, when I have sounded,** searched out, gotten the information from, **my father about tomorrow any time or the third day, and, behold, if there be good toward David, and I then send not unto thee, and show it thee, v. 13. the Lord**

**do so and much more to Jonathan.** Jonathan most. solemnly promised that he would immediately inform David in case Saul was favorably disposed toward him. **But if it please my father to do thee evil, then I will show it thee and send thee away, that thou mayest go in peace,** he would not even entrust the message to a servant, but would come in person to impress his warning upon his friend's mind and to make arrangements for his escape; **and the Lord be with thee, as he hath been with my father,** a wish which indicates that Jonathan may have guessed the true situation of affairs. **V. 14. And thou shalt not only while yet I live show me the kindness of the Lord, that I die not,** in case he should enter upon his royal office before Jonathan's death; **v. 15. but also thou shalt not cut off thy kindness from my house forever,** kindness of the nature shown by Jehovah, the covenant God, to His people; **no, not when the Lord hath cut off the enemies of David, every one, from the face of the earth.** Although Jonathan was a member of Saul's house, who was an enemy of David, he himself was united with David by the bonds of the truest friendship, and therefore wanted both himself and his children spared when David's time of revenge would come. **V. 16. So Jonathan made a covenant with the house of David, saying, Let the Lord even require it at the hand of David's enemies,** namely, by punishing all those who opposed him, for this Jonathan foresaw. **V. 17. And Jonathan caused David to swear again,** adjuring David to fulfill this last request, **because he loved him,** making his love toward David the ground of his request; **for he loved him as he loved his own soul,** chap. 18, 1. **V. 18. Then Jonathan said to David, Tomorrow is the new moon; and thou shalt be missed, because thy seat,** at the table of the king, **will be empty. V. 19. And when thou hast stayed**

**three days,** on the third day, **then thou shalt go down quickly,** on account of the danger of being observed, **and come to the place where thou didst hide thyself when the business was in hand,** when Jonathan, near that spot, had changed the murderous intention of Saul, chap. 19, 2, **and shalt remain by the stone Ezel,** evidently a well-known landmark. **V. 20. And I will shoot three arrows on the side thereof, as though I shot at a mark,** three arrows being taken because some other archer might shoot just one. or two by chance, but surely not three. **V. 21. And, behold, I will send a lad, saying, Go find out,** fetch, **the arrows. If I expressly say unto the lad, Behold, the arrows are on this side of thee, take them; then come thou; for there is peace to thee, and no hurt, as the Lord liveth.** Just as the boy would come nearer to Jonathan, so David would be able to return without danger. **V. 22. But if I say thus unto the young man, Behold, the arrows are beyond thee,** on the farther side, (then) **go thy way; for the Lord hath sent thee away,** bids him flee. The sign was simple and easily remembered. **V. 23. And as touching the matter which thou and I have spoken of,** everything pertaining to their covenant, **behold, the Lord be between thee and me forever,** for it was in His fear that they should feel bound to keep their promises of mutual faithfulness. True friendship and mercy requires us to take as eager and real an interest in the weal and woe of another as if it concerned ourselves, to stand by him in danger, and to show kindness even to the children of one who has bestowed kindness upon us.

JONATHAN'S INFORMATION TO DAVID. — **V. 24. So David hid himself in the field; and when the new moon was come, the king sat him down to eat meat,** at the head of the table, the place of honor. **V. 25. And the king sat upon his seat, as**

129

**at other times, even upon a seat by the wall; and Jonathan arose, and Abner sat by Saul's side, and David's place was empty.** It seems that Jonathan arose from his place next to Saul and gave his seat to Abner, his uncle, while he himself took the place ordinarily occupied by David, in order to avert suspicion. **V. 26. Nevertheless Saul spake not anything that day,** made no remark concerning the peculiar absence of David; **for he thought, Something hath befallen him, he is not clean; surely he is not clean,** that is, Levitically clean, a condition which kept a person away from sacrificial meals, Lev. 15, 16 ff.; Deut. 23, 11. **V. 27. And it came to pass on the morrow, which was the second day of the month, that David's place was empty,** literally, "on the morrow after the new moon," the second day; **and Saul said unto Jonathan, his son, Wherefore cometh not the son of Jesse to meat, neither yesterday nor today? V. 28. And Jonathan answered Saul, David earnestly asked leave of me to go to Bethlehem; v. 29. and he said, Let me go, I pray thee; for our family hath a sacrifice in the city; and my brother,** the oldest brother, as the head of the family, **he hath commanded me to be there; and now, if I have found favor in thine eyes, let me get away,** take myself off, **I pray thee, and see my brethren. Therefore he cometh not unto the king's table.** The report of Jonathan is entirely in keeping with the cordial relation existing between friends. **V. 30. Then Saul's anger was kindled against Jonathan, and he said unto him, Thou son of the perverse, rebellious woman,** literally, "of perversity, of rebelliousness," a common expression for a man of obstinate and unruly disposition, **do not I know that thou hast chosen the son of Jesse to thine own confusion,** disgrace, **and unto the confusion of thy mother's nakedness,** to thy shame and to the shame of thy mother's nakedness, who would be ashamed of having given birth to such a rebellious son? **V. 3l. For as long as the son of Jesse liveth upon the ground,** as long as David was alive and was, in the opinion of Saul, making rebellious attempts to possess the royal throne, **thou shalt not be established, nor thy kingdom;** David was standing in the way of making the kingdom hereditary in Saul's family. **Wherefore, now, send and fetch him unto me, for he shall surely die;** Saul considered him a son, a candidate, of death. **V. 32. And Jonathan,** by way of gentle remonstrance, in order to set forth David's innocence, **answered Saul, his father, and said unto him, Wherefore shall he be slain? What hath he done? V. 33. And Saul cast a javelin at him to smite him,** he brandished and probably even hurled the small spear which he used as a scepter; **whereby Jonathan knew that it was determined, firmly settled, of his father to slay David. V. 34. So Jonathan arose from the table in fierce anger and did eat no meat,** did not partake of food, **the second day of the month; for he was grieved for David,** on account of the shame heaped upon his friend by Saul, which his generous nature deeply resented, while he overlooked the insult offered to himself, **because his father had done him shame. V. 35. And it came to pass in the morning that Jonathan went out into the field at the time appointed with David, and a little lad with him.** He was careful to keep the agreement with David in every detail. **V. 36. And he said unto his lad, Run, find out now the arrows which I shoot,** gathering them up from the ground as Jonathan practiced with his bow. **And as the lad ran, he shot an arrow beyond him,** farther than the boy had passed on. **V. 37. And when the lad was come to the place of the arrow which Jonathan had shot,** where it had flown, **Jonathan cried after the lad and said, Is not the arrow beyond thee? V. 38. And Jonathan cried after the lad, Make speed, haste, stay not,** lest in looking about in a leisurely fashion he might espy David behind the rock. **And Jonathan's lad gathered up the arrows and came to his master,** bringing the arrow, as he probably did in the next two cases. **V. 39. But the lad knew not anything; only Jonathan and David knew the matter. V. 40. And Jonathan gave his artillery,** bow, quiver, and arrows, **unto his lad and said unto him, Go, carry them to the city,** this giving him an opportunity to be alone with David. **V. 41. And as soon as the lad was gone, David arose out of a place toward the south,** for on that side of the rock he had concealed himself, **and fell on his face to the ground, and bowed himself three times,** both to do Jonathan honor and gratefully to acknowledge his efforts in his behalf; **and they kissed one another, and wept one with another, until David exceeded,** until David broke out in loud weeping. **V. 42. And Jonathan said to David, Go in peace, forasmuch as we have sworn, both of us, in the name of the Lord, saying, The Lord be between me and thee, and between my seed and thy seed forever.** This oath they wanted to keep with all firmness; nothing should ever persuade them to break it. **And he,** David, **arose and departed; and Jonathan went into the city.** Thus true love and friendship demonstrates its sincerity when one friend warns the other against harm and danger. And it is true in general that we should weep with those who mourn and comfort those who are in trouble, encouraging them with reference to Jehovah's mercy.

# 21

# 1 Samuel 21

**T**he First Movements of David on His Flight.
DAVID AT NOB. — **V. 1. Then came David to Nob,** a city of priests between Gibeah and Jerusalem, on a hill in whose neighborhood the Tabernacle seems to have been located for some years, at least temporarily,4) **to Ahimelech, the priest,** either he or his father or his son also bearing the name Abiathar, Mark 2, 26; **and Ahimelech was afraid at the meeting of David,** full of apprehension, since he may have known of Saul's hatred of David, **and said unto him, Why art thou alone, and no man with thee?** For David had left the few companions who had joined him in a safe place, since he wanted to talk to the high priest alone. **V. 2. And David said unto Ahimelech, the priest, The king hath commanded me a business, and hath said unto me, Let no man know anything of the business whereabout I send thee, and what I have commanded thee,** he was to reveal neither the reason for, nor the contents of, his commission; **and I have appointed my servants to such and such a place.** The glib falsehood which David here told had evil results, and was not even justified

by the fact that Ahimelech might have refused to assist him in case he had known that he was fleeing from the wrath of the king. **V. 3. Now, therefore, what is under thine hand?** David wanted anything in the line of food upon which the priest could quickly lay his hand. **Give me five loaves of bread in mine hand, or what there is present,** whatever he could find in a hurry. **V. 4. And the priest answered David and said, There is, no common bread under mine hand,** no kind of ordinary bread, such as was commonly used for food, **but there is hallowed bread,** for apparently the cakes of showbread had just been replaced by a fresh set, Lev. 24, 8, the ordinance requiring that the bread which had been removed be eaten by the priests in the Holy Place; **if the young men have kept themselves at least from women,** Lev. 15, 18. The high priest was willing to make an exception in this case, but felt that he must insist upon ceremonial, Levitical purity. **V. 5. And David answered the priest and said unto him, Of a truth women have been kept from us about these three days,** the time since they had started on this expedition, **since I came out, and the vessels**, the gear and baggage of the soldiers, which might also become Levitically unclean, Lev. 11, 32. 33; 13, 47. 48, **of the young men are holy, and the bread is in a manner common, yea, though it were sanctified this day in the vessel,** literally, "Though it is a profane way or procedure, yet it is sanctified today by the vessel," namely, by David himself as a chosen, anointed servant of the Lord; that fact set aside the ceremonial impurity of the act, particularly since it was a work of mercy which the high priest performed. **V. 6. So the priest gave him hallowed bread; for there was no bread there but the showbread, that was taken from before the Lord, to put hot bread in the day when it was taken away;** the cakes having been standing on the golden table for seven days, they had just been renewed or replaced by a new set, Lev. 24, 6-9. **V. 7. Now, a certain man of the servants of Saul was there that day, detained before the Lord,** either as a proselyte, expecting to be received into the congregation of the Lord, or for the sake of some purification, or under suspicion as a leper; **and his name was Doeg, an Edomite, the chiefest of the herdmen that belonged to Saul.** This remark is here inserted on account of the subsequent history of Ahimelech. Note: Love is the fulfillment of the Law; love is the queen of all commandments, since all our works should be done in love. Even the outward ordinances of the Church are intended to serve the ends of love and peace. **V. 8. And David said unto Ahimelech, And is there not here under thine hand,** in his charge, **spear or sword? For I have neither brought my sword nor my weapons with me, because the king's business required haste,** literally, "it was pressed," David had to be on his way without a moment's delay. **V. 9. And the priest said, The sword of Goliath, the Philistine, whom thou slewest in the Valley of Elah,** chap. 17, 2. 50, **behold, it is here wrapped in a cloth behind the ephod,** deposited for safe-keeping in the national Sanctuary, as a thanksgiving offering to the Lord and as a constant reminder of His merciful help in overcoming the enemies; **if thou wilt take that, take it; for there is no other save that here. And David said, There is none like that; give it me.** It was valuable not only on account of its great size and good workmanship, but also on account of its associations. David may have felt that it was a holy weapon, promising him victory. He who goes forth to the battles of life with the blessing of God, with the weapons sanctified by His presence, may rest assured that no danger can really harm him.

DAVID AT GATH. — **V. 10. And David arose, and fled that day for fear of Saul, and went to Achish,** whose official title was Abimelech, Ps. 34, **the king of Gath,** in the Philistine country. **V. 11. And the servants of Achish said unto him, Is not this David the king of the land,** for as such they designate him on account of his victorious campaigns, which entirely overshadowed those of Saul? **Did they not sing one to another of him in dances, saying, Saul hath slain his thousands, and David his ten thousands?** Cp. chap. 18, 7. **V. 12. And David,** who may have hoped to remain in the country of the Philistines unrecognized, **laid up these words in his heart,** he was worried about what they might lead to, **and was sore afraid of Achish, the king of Gath,** since the Philistines might, in a fit of revenge, fall on him and kill him. **V. 13. And he changed his behavior before them,** he perverted his understanding, **and feigned himself mad in their hands,** he played the madman as they tried to get hold of him, **and scrabbled on the doors of the gate,** pounded on them with his fists, **and let his spittle,** the foam at the mouth which he produced after the manner of madmen, **fall down upon his beard. V. 14. Then said Achish unto his servants, Lo, ye see the man is mad,** he has gone insane; **wherefore, then, have ye brought him to me? V. 15. Have I need of madmen that ye have brought this fellow to play the madman in my presence?** The king evidently feared personal harm from David, who, as he thought, had gone insane. While David's plan to remain unrecognized among the Philistines did not succeed, the presence of mind which caused him to simulate an attack of insanity undoubtedly saved his life. Thus God is able to protect and to deliver His children in the midst of the enemies. Without His will not one hair of our heads falls to the ground.

# 22

# 1 Samuel 22

**S**aul's Murder of the Priests.

DAVID A FUGITIVE IN JUDAH AND MOAB. — **V. 1. David, therefore,** because he could find no refuge in the land of the Philistines, **departed thence and escaped to the cave Adullam,** in the foothills of the Judean mountains, about sixteen miles southwest of Jerusalem; **and when his brethren and all his father's house heard it, they went down thither to him,** all his nearest relatives joined him, evidently because they feared the revenge of Saul upon their entire family; for it was nothing unusual for an Oriental prince to destroy a whole family for the fault of one person. **V. 2. And everyone that was in distress,** feeling that the government of Saul was an arbitrary misrule, **and everyone that was in debt,** oppressed by his creditors and having failed to receive from the government that protection against the violation of the law of loan and interest which he might expect, Ex. 22, 25; Lev. 25, 36; Deut. 23, 19, **and everyone that was discontented,** bitter or embittered of soul, whose anxiety of soul over the condition of the kingdom, as it grew worse from day to day, drove them to a leader from whom they might, for the future, hope for better things, **gathered themselves unto him; and he became a captain over them,** their leader; **and there were with him about four hundred men,** the number afterward rising to six hundred, chap. 23, 13. It was not a wild and lawless band, hut a well organized company, who were here trained in warfare, so that many of them afterwards became heroes in the nation. **V. 3. And David went thence to Mizpeh of Moab,** southeast of the Dead Sea, the country of his great-grandmother; **and he said unto the king of: Moab, Let my father and my mother, I pray thee, come forth, and be with you, till I know what God will do for me.** He wanted his aged parents to have some protection, to live in some degree of security, until the present uncertain period. of his own life would come to an end. **V. 4. And he brought them before the king of Moab,** to remain under the latter's protection; **and they dwelt with him all the while that David was in the hold,** in his fortified position, in his mountain fastness near Mizpeh. **V. 5. And the Prophet Gad said unto David,** in a direct message which shows the loving care of God, **Abide not in the hold; depart, and get thee into the land of Judah.** The Prophet Gad may have been one of the band which lived near Ramah, where David became acquainted with him, chap. 19, 18. **Then David departed,** out of the land of Moab, **and came into the forest of Hareth,** an unknown region, probably in the southwestern part of the territory of Judah. Like David, his great descendant, Jesus, accompanied by only a small band of faithful men, befriended by publicans and sinners, journeyed about in this country, in Palestine, entering into His glory through suffering and persecution.

SAUL TAKES REVENGE UPON THE PRIESTS OF NOB. — **V. 6. When Saul heard that David was discovered,** when the place of his concealment was known at court, **and the men that were with him, (now Saul abode in Gibeah under a tree in Ramah,** under the tamarisk on the height, where this session took place, **having his spear in his hand, and all his servants were standing about him,) v. 7. then Saul said unto his servants that stood about him,** it was a full assembly of all the members of the court, **Hear now, ye Benjamites, will the son of Jesse give everyone of you fields and vineyards, and make you all captains of thousands and captains of hundreds,** the intimation being that David had given them rich promises in order to bribe them, **v. 8. that all of you have conspired against me, and there is none that showeth me that my son,** namely, Jonathan, **hath made a league with the son of Jesse, and there is none of you that is sorry for me,** showing the sympathy which true loyalty demands, **or showeth unto me that my son hath stirred up my servant,** David, **against me, to lie in wait,** as an enemy seeking the king's life, **as at this day?** Both suspicions, that David was intriguing to take his throne And life, and that Jonathan was stirring up David to this conduct, were false. "Saul fancies himself in the meshes of a conspiracy against his person and kingdom organized by his own son, and accuses his courtiers of knowledge thereof and active participation therein. To such a pitch had the darkening And wasting of his inner life grown through hate and suspicion." (Lange.) **V. 9. Then answered Doeg, the Edomite, which was set over the servants of Saul,** chap. 21, 7, **and said, I saw the son of Jesse coming to Nob, to Ahimelech, the son of Ahitub. V. 10. And he enquired of the Lord for him, and gave him victuals,** food on the way, **and gave him the sword of Goliath, the Philistine.** Doeg was actuated by wickedness, falsehood, calumny, and deceit, as Ps. 52, 2-5 shows. **V. 11. Then the king sent to call Ahimelech, the priest, the son of Ahltub, and all his father's house, the priests that were in Nob,** for they all belonged to the one family of Aaron; **and they came all of them to the king. V. 12. And Saul said, Hear now, thou son of Ahitub,** a formal and solemn address, to impress upon Ahimelech the greatness of his supposed transgression. **And he,** possessed, as he was, of a good conscience, **answered, Here I am, my lord. V. 13. And Saul said unto him, Why have ye conspired against me, thou and the son of Jesse, in that thou hast given him bread and a sword, and hast enquired of God for him that he should rise against me, to lie in wait, as at this day?** The same false and unjust suspicions and accusations are here repeated by Saul, who assumed at once that Ahimelech was guilty of conspiracy and treason. **V. 14. Then Ahimelech answered the king and said, And who is so faithful,** in whom so much confidence has always been reposed, **among all thy servants as David, which is the king's son-in-law, and goeth at thy bidding,** having access to the inner council of the king as one of his privy counselors, **and is honorable in thine house?** These three facts surely justified any person in considering David a true friend of the king. **V. 15. Did I then begin to enquire of God for him?** That day had not been the first time that he had obtained the divine answer for David, for that had often occurred before. **Be it far from me,** namely, any conspiracy or treason against the king; **let not the king impute anything unto his servant nor to all the house of my father,** they were not guilty of any wrong-doing; **for thy servant knew nothing of all this, less or more,** he was absolutely unaware of any conspiracy against the king and had not been guilty of any act of treason. **V. 16. And the king,** insane with suspicions which caused him to mistrust all men, **said, Thou shalt surely die, Ahimelech, thou and all thy father's house. V. 17. And the king said unto the footmen that stood about him,** the runners, the members of the guard, who acted also as executioners, **Turn, and slay the priests of the Lord, because their hand also is with David,** he considered them as taking the part of David against the rightful authority, **and because they knew when he fled, and did not show it to me,** made no immediate report of the matter. **But the servants of the king,** possessing more sanity and also more reverence for the servants of the Lord than Saul, **would not put forth their hand to fall upon the priests of the Lord.** Their refusal makes the heinousness. of Saul's sin all the more conspicuous. **V. 18. And the king said to Doeg, Turn thou and fall upon the priests. And Doeg the Edomite turned, and he fell upon the priests, and slew on that day fourscore and five persons that did wear a linen ephod,** a white cape like shoulder-dress patterned after the fine ephod of the high priest. It was a cold-blooded, bloodthirsty deed, a murderous slaughter. **V. 19. And Nob, the city of the priests, smote he with the edge of the sword,** in an insane fury of destruction, **both men and women, children and sucklings, and oxen, and asses, and sheep, with the edge of the sword,** his action indicating that he considered the whole city under the ban of Jehovah for harboring David. **V. 20. And one of the sons of Ahimelech, the son of Ahitub, named Abiathar, escaped, and fled after David,** he came to David, the fugitive. **V. 21. And Abiathar showed David that Saul had slain the Lord's priests,** in a most cruel and bloody revenge. **V. 22. And David said unto Abiathar, I knew it that day,** he had felt it, he had had a premonition, **when Doeg the Edomite was there, that he would surely tell Saul. I have occasioned the death**

**of all the persons of thy father's house.** He was very strict in his self-judgment and self-condemnation on account of his heedlessness. **V. 23. Abide thou with me, fear not; for he that seeketh my life,** chiefly Saul and his henchmen, **seeketh thy life; but with me thou shalt be in safeguard.** While a fugitive from the insane wrath of Saul, David felt that he stood under the protection of Jehovah, and that Abiathar, therefore, sought by Saul in the same manner, could cheerfully and safely cast his lot with the king's son-in-law. Saul's horrible deed merely indicated that his obduracy had reached a point from which there would be no return. So the high priest of God and the Urim and Thummim were now with David. In like manner the small, persecuted band of Christians has the best protection and consolation, the Word and truth of God, in its midst.

# 1 Samuel 23

**D**avid in the Wilderness.

DAVID'S RESCUE OF KEILAH. — **V. 1. Then they told David,** he received information, **saying, Behold, the Philistines,** a strong band of their raiders, **fight against Keilah,** a city evidently in the lowland of Judah, near the Philistine frontier, **and they rob the threshing-floors,** where the grain was stacked ready for threshing. **V. 2. Therefore David enquired of the Lord, saying, Shall I go and smite these Philistines?** He seems to have had reasons for considering himself the champion of the oppressed. **And the Lord said unto David,** through the Urim and Thummim of the high priest, v. 6, **Go, and smite the Philistines, and save Keilah.** The command, "Rescue Keilah," included the promise that success would crown his efforts. **V. 3. And David's men,** who at that time did not share his simple trust in Jehovah, **said unto him, Behold, we be afraid here in Judah,** they were apprehensive of the persecution of Saul; **how much more, then, if we come to Keilah against the armies of the Philistines,** where they would have enemies before and behind? **V. 4. Then David inquired of the Lord yet again,** in the same manner. **And the Lord answered him and said, Arise, go down to Keilah; for I will deliver the Philistines into thine hand.** This definite promise was intended to allay the fears of David's men. **V. 5. So David and his men. went to Keilah, and fought with the Philistines, and brought away their cattle, and smote them with a great slaughter.** The Philistines, instead of gaining booty, were themselves spoiled, losing their flocks and herds and suffering a very severe defeat. **So David saved the inhabitants of Keilah. V. 6. And it came to pass,** as is here noted in explanation, **when Abiathar, the son of Ahimelech, fled to David to Keilah,** joining him just when the campaign to rescue the city was planned, **that he came down with an ephod,** the shoulder-dress of the high priest with the Urim and Thummim, **in his hand.** This was in David's favor, for he could now at any time ask the will of the Lord. **V. 7. And it was told Saul,** who had his spies watching all the movements of David, **that David was come to Keilah. And Saul said, God hath delivered him into mine hand,** for he tried to deceive himself into believing that David, and not himself, had been rejected by God; **for he is shut in, by entering into a town that hath gates and bars.** Saul thought that David had prepared a trap for himself by making a fortified city his headquarters, since escape would there be more difficult, once the city was surrounded. **V. 8. And Saul called all the people together to war,** formally summoned all the soldiers of his army, **to go down to Keilah, to besiege David and his men,** and thus to get him into his power. **V. 9. And David,** who also had his spies in the field, **knew that Saul secretly practised mischief against him,** he found out about this plan to destroy him; **and he said to Abiathar, the**

**priest, Bring hither the ephod,** for the purpose of getting information from the Lord. **V. 10. Then said David,** in a prayer showing his trust in Jehovah, **O Lord God of Israel, Thy servant hath certainly heard that Saul seeketh to come to Keilah, to destroy the city for my sake. V. 11. Will the men of Keilah deliver me up into his hand? Will Saul come down, as Thy servant hath heard? O Lord God of Israel, I beseech Thee, tell Thy servant.** The questions are not given in the wrong order, due to David's excitement, as has been said, but David feared that the men of Keilah would deliver him into Saul's hands as soon as they found out that the king had planned to come. **And the Lord said,** answering the last question first, **He will come down. V. 12. Then said David,** repeating his first question, **Will the men,** the citizens, **of Keilah deliver me and my men into the hand of Saul? And the Lord said, They will deliver thee up.** Instead of taking the part of the man who had rescued them from their enemies, the men of Keilah would have been guided by policy. **V. 13. Then David and his men, which were about six hundred,** since new men were being added to his band constantly, **arose and departed out of Keilah, and went whithersoever they could go,** without a definite plan, as chance and circumstance led them. **And it was told Saul that David was escaped from Keilah; and he forbare to go forth,** he abandoned his campaign. In this story also David is a type of the Son of God. For He also, while engaged in rescuing His people from the hand of their most terrible enemies, was betrayed into the hands of the unjust. Moreover, such is the lot of all those who openly take the part of the Lord.

IN THE WILDERNESS OF ZIPH. — **V. 14. And David abode in the wilderness in strongholds,** on sheltering heights in the great semiarid region of Southern Judah, whose several parts were named after the cities in the neighborhood, **and remained in a mountain in the Wilderness of Ziph,** establishing his camp there for some time. **And Saul sought him every day,** all the days of his life, continually, **but God delivered him not into his hand.** This remark serves as an introduction to the entire next section. **V. 15. And David saw that Saul was come out to seek his life,** he received information to that effect, it was impressed upon his consciousness more and more; **and David was in the Wilderness of Ziph in a wood,** a thick forest, which offered him the best form of concealment. **V. 16. And Jonathan, Saul's son, arose, and went to David into the wood,** in proof of the continued faithfulness of his friendship, **and strengthened his hand in God,** encouraged him by reminding him of God's promises of His divine presence and protection. **V. l7. And he said unto him, Fear not; for the hand of Saul, my father, shall not find thee,** he was convinced that David was sheltered by God's special protection; **and thou shalt be king over Israel,** a conviction which had been forced upon him by the trend of events, **and I shall be next unto thee,** he was perfectly willing to resign all claim to the throne; **and that also Saul, my father, knoweth,** he was aware that David was to be his successor. **V. 18. And they two made a covenant before the Lord,** renewing the covenant which united their hearts, chap. 20, 16.17. 42; **and David abode in the wood,** remaining in concealment with his men, **and Jonathan went to his house. V. 19. Then came up the Ziphites,** whose behavior furnishes a most glaring contrast to that of Jonathan, **to Saul to Gibeah, saying, Doth not David hide himself with us,** in our neighborhood, **in strongholds in the wood,** where they could note his every movement, **in the hill of Hachilah, which is on the south side of Jeshimon?** This wooded, rocky mountain lay on the south side of a waste region which stretched out on the west side of the Dead Sea, within the steppes of Judah. **V. 20. Now, therefore, O king, come down according to all the desire of thy soul to come down; and our part shall be to deliver him into the king's hand.** So passionate were they in their adherence to Saul that they would do all in their power to deliver David into his hand. **V. 21. And Saul said,** with the blindness of an evil conscience, **Blessed be ye of the Lord; for ye have compassion on me,** praising them in this respect, just as he had rebuked his servants for their lack of sympathy for him, chap. 22, 8. **V. 22. Go, I pray you, prepare yet, and know and see his place where his haunt is,** where his foot will be, every retreat of David in his constant shifting about; **for it is told me that he dealeth very subtilly,** that was a prominent trait in David's character. **V. 23. See, therefore, and take knowledge of all the lurking-places where he hideth himself, and come ye again to me with the certainty,** literally, "what is certain," that is with sure information, **and I will go with you; and it shall come to pass, if he be in the land, that I will search him out throughout all the thousands of Judah,** the larger division of the tribe, Num. 1, 16, that is, in their territory. Thus Saul still showed his fixed idea that David was attempting to take his throne and life, and thus committing a great crime against God. **V. 24. And they arose and went to Ziph before Saul,** who was soon to follow with his men; **but David and his men were in the Wilderness of Maon,** south of the mountain of Hachilah, in the plain **on the south of Jeshimon,** on or near a conical hill which still bears a very similar name. **V. 25. Saul also and his men went**

**to seek him. And they told David; wherefore he came down into a rock,** descended the rock, the mountain where he had been, in order to reach the lowland and a new hiding-place, **and abode in the Wilderness of Maon. And when Saul heard that, he pursued after David in the Wilderness of Maon. V. 26. And Saul went on this side of the mountain, and David and his men on that side of the mountain,** the mountain thus separating the two armies; **and David made haste to get away for fear of Saul,** he was very anxious to escape; **for Saul and his men compassed David and his men round about to take them,** they were at the point of surrounding them. **V. 27. But there came a messenger unto Saul, saying, Haste thee and come; for the Philistines have invaded the land,** they had undertaken a raid on a large scale, their object being to obtain booty. **V. 28. Wherefore Saul returned from pursuing after David, and went against the Philistines; therefore they called that place Sela-hammahlekoth** (rock of divisions, rock of escapes), because it was undoubtedly due to its upthrust that David escaped with his men. **V. 29. And David went up from thence, and dwelt in strongholds at En-gedi,** about the middle of the western shore of, the Dead Sea. The Lord, who governs all things, protected His servant in this extremity. And the same God has ways and means to help us in all our troubles and difficulties. if we but commit our way to Him.

# 1 Samuel 24

David Spares Saul in the Cave.

SAUL IN THE CAVE. — **V. 1. And it came to pass, when Saul had returned from following the Philistines,** just as soon as he had repulsed the invaders, made them desist from their raid, **that it was told him, saying, Behold, David is in the Wilderness of Engedi,** where the many caves in the limestone hills offered excellent places for concealment. **V. 2. Then Saul,** still filled with the same bloodthirstiness which had brought him to the Wilderness of Maon, **took three thousand chosen men out of all Israel, and went to seek David and his men upon the rocks of the wild goats,** for, due to the wildness and steepness of the hills in this neighborhood, it was a favorite haunt of ibexes, or wild goats. **V. 3. And he came to the sheepcotes by the way,** a locality with large caves which had been fitted up to house sheep, where was a cave; **and Saul went in to cover his feet,** to do his easement; **and David and his men remained in the sides of the cave,** they were in the rear of the cave or in some of its side passages. **V. 4. And the men of David said unto**

**him,** for they could plainly see Saul, as they looked toward the light, while Saul's eyes could not penetrate the darkness in the rear, Behold the day of which the Lord said unto thee, **Behold, I will deliver thine enemy into thine hand, that thou mayest do to him as it shall seem good unto thee.** Their reference seems to be only to what they considered a divine ordering of this favorable opportunity to take revenge upon Saul. **Then David arose, and cut off the skirt of Saul's robe privily,** a corner of his upper garment, which Saul had evidently laid aside. **V. 5. And it came to pass afterward that David's heart smote him,** his conscience bothered him, **because he had cut off Saul's skirt,** for since he regarded the person of Saul as sacred, he feared that Saul might consider his act a violation of his royal majesty. **V. 6. And he said unto his men, The Lord forbid that I should do this thing unto my master, the Lord's anointed, to stretch forth mine hand against him, seeing he is the anointed of the Lord.** Saul still held the office and had the dignity of a king in Israel, and for that reason his person, in the eyes of David, was inviolable. **V. 7. So David stayed his servants with these words,** literally, "rent to pieces, cut down," said of a solemn rebuke, **and suffered them not to rise against Saul,** for the purpose of taking bloody revenge upon the oppressor. **But Saul rose up out of the cave and went on his way.** David's act was one of true magnanimity. Christians should always remember to leave vengeance to God, for He will requite in an adequate and just manner.

DAVID PROTESTS HIS INNOCENCE. — **V. 8. David also arose afterward, and went out of the cave,** boldly taking this opportunity to defend himself against the slanders which filled Saul's heart with mistrust against him, Ps. 7, **and cried after Saul, saying, My lord the king!** In these words he confesses himself bound to Saul as his subject and acknowledges him as the anointed of the Lord, who occupied his office by divine right. **And when Saul looked behind him, David stooped with his face to the earth, and bowed himself,** his behavior thus corresponding to his address of Saul. **V. 9. And David said to Saul, Wherefore hearest thou men's words,** such as those of the men of Ziph and of Cush, the Benjamite, **saying, Behold, David seeketh thy hurt?** David thus represented the entire situation as due to intriguing tongues. **V. 10. Behold, this day thine eyes have seen how the Lord had delivered thee today into mine hand in the cave,** for so the incident clearly appeared; **and some bade me kill thee,** the temptation to kill Saul had been presented to David; **but mine eye spared thee, and I said, I will not put forth mine hand against my lord; for he is the Lord's anointed.** This fact David urged in his favor, first of all. **V. 11. Moreover, my father,** as David calls Saul in pious reverence, **see, yea, see the skirt of thy robe in my hand,** a bit of evidence which demonstrated how absolutely Saul had been in his power; **for in that I cut off the skirt of thy robe and killed thee not know thou and see that there is neither evil nor transgression,** deliberate crime and wickedness, **in mine hand, and I have not sinned against thee,** he could rightly protest his innocence; **yet thou hunts my soul to take it,** pursuing him like a dangerous animal through forests and over mountains. **V. 12. The Lord judge between me and thee,** for to His decision David left the entire matter, **and the Lord avenge me of thee,** for this unwarranted persecution of David would not go unpunished, as he firmly believed; **but mine hand shall not be upon thee,** he would not seek or take his own revenge. **V. 13. As saith the proverb of the ancients, Wickedness proceeded from the wicked; but mine**

**hand shall not be upon thee.** A wicked and godless person might have embraced the opportunity to take revenge, but David had purposely refrained from doing so. And David finally urged that Saul's conduct was foolish and inconsistent with royal dignity. **V. 14. After whom is the king of Israel come out? After whom dost thou pursue? After a dead dog,** who could no longer bite and bother people, **after a flea,** at best poor game for a royal hunter. David stressed his insignificance and harmlessness, for he neither had the desire nor was he in a position to work the king harm. **V. 15. The Lord, therefore,** because David was innocent and because Saul's persecution was foolish, **be judge,** and judge **between me and thee, and see, and plead my cause, and deliver me out of thine hand,** to be freed from the persecution of Saul by the justice of God. David here is an example to all children of God, showing what love of the enemy means. Like him, Christians should spare their enemies and reward them good for evil.

SAUL ACKNOWLEDGES HIS FAULT. — **V. 16. And it came to pass, when David had made an end of speaking these words unto Saul, that Saul said, Is this thy voice, my son David?** Saul was deeply affected by the fervor of David, by the justice of his plea, by the pious reverence shown by him. **And Saul lifted up his voice and wept,** momentarily overcome by emotion. **V. 17. And he said to David, Thou art more righteous than I; for thou hast rewarded me good, whereas I have rewarded thee evil.** The evidence before his eyes forced Saul to make at least this acknowledgment. **V. 18. And thou hast showed this day how that thou hast dealt well with me, forasmuch as when the Lord had delivered me into thine hand, thou killedst me not,** David had not taken the opportunity offered by God's providence. **V. 19. For if a man find his enemy,**

**will he let him go well away?** It was a most unusual way of dealing with an enemy, to let him go scot-free when such a fine chance to dispose of him offered. **Wherefore the Lord reward thee good for that thou hast done unto me this day.** For the time being, Saul permitted the nobler sentiments to come into his heart, but there was no true conversion. **V. 20. And now, behold, I know well that thou shalt surely be king, and that the kingdom of Israel shall be established in thine hand.** This conclusion was forced upon Saul by the evident protection of the Lord which David enjoyed, and he still remembered what Samuel had told him regarding his own rejection. **V. 21. Swear now, therefore, unto me by the Lord that thou wilt not cut off my seed,** his children, **after me, and that thou wilt not destroy my name out of my father's house.** It was not unusual in the Orient for the king of a new dynasty to exterminate the entire family of the former king, down to the most remote relatives, and this Saul wanted to avoid. **V. 22. And David sware unto Saul. And Saul went home,** returned to his royal residence; **but David and his men gat them up unto the hold,** for they knew better than to expect Saul to retain the kind disposition and bearing which he had last shown. Saul's emotion was no true repentance, his heart had not been changed. Such a person is and remains a child of wrath, whether he rages and raves against the Lord or whether he is more quiet.

# 25

# 1 Samuel 25

David, Nabal, and Abigail.

NABAL'S FOOLISHNESS. — **V. 1. And Samuel died,** his death taking place at about this critical time in the history of Israel; **and all the Israelites were gathered together, and lamented him, and buried him in his house at Ramah,** the entire nation thus honoring him as a great prophet, whose rule had been a blessing for Israel. **And David arose, and went down to the Wilderness of Paran,** the northern end of the Arabian desert. **V. 2. And there was a man in Maon,** chap. 23, 24, a city southeast of Hebron, **whose possessions were in Carmel,** he had his herds and flocks on the mountain-meadows near the city, in the elevated plain of Judah; **and the man was very great,** rich and influential, **and he had three thousand sheep and a thousand goats; and he was shearing his sheep in Carmel,** usually an occasion of great festivities. **V. 3. Now, the name of the man was Nabal and the name of his wife Abigail; and she was a woman of good understanding,** sensible, well versed in genteel conduct, **and of a beautiful countenance,** well formed; **but the man** was churlish and evil in his doings; and he was of the house of Caleb, to whom this entire region near Hebron had been given, Judg. 1, 10-15. **V. 4. And David heard in the wilderness that Nabal did shear his sheep,** and therefore would probably have an abundance of food on hand for the joyful meal. **V. 5. And David sent out ten young men,** as on an important and solemn embassy, **and David said unto the young men, Get you up to Carmel, and go to Nabal, and greet him in my name,** with the customary greeting of peace; **v. 6. and thus shall ye say to him that liveth in prosperity,** rather, May good fortune attend thee for a long and happy life! **Peace be both to thee, and peace be to thine house, and peace be unto all that thou hast.** This comprehensive greeting was intended to render Nabal well-disposed toward the messengers. **V. 7. And now, I have heard that thou hast shearers,** with all that this implied; now, **thy shepherds which were with us,** with whom David's men lived on terms of good fellowship, protecting them against wild animals and against robbers, **we hurt them not,** by any form of injury, **neither was there ought missing unto them all the while they were in Carmel.** Even during his exile David proved himself the champion of the people. **V. 8. Ask thy young men,** his sheep-herders, **and they will show thee,** testifying to the splendid fellowship which existed between David's men and them. **Wherefore let the young men find favor in thine eyes; for we come in a good day,** for such a festivity should be an auspicious occasion; **give, I pray thee, whatsoever cometh to thine hand,** as much as he could afford at this time, **unto thy servants and to thy son David. V. 9. And when David's young men came, they spake to Nabal according to all those words,** making their request in his very words, **in the name of David, and ceased,** they sat down, awaiting the fulfillment of their request. **V. 10. And Nabal answered David's servants and said, Who is David? and who is the son of Jesse?** What was David and his concerns to him? Why should he bother about his troubles? **There be many servants nowadays that break away every man from his master;** these words insulted David as a common runaway and renegade, who had maliciously severed his relation with Saul. **V. 11. Shall I, then, take my bread and my water and my flesh that I have killed for my shearers, and give it unto men whom I know not whence they be?** Both the necessities of life and the luxuries he denied them; the very idea of sharing these with David and his men he represented as preposterous. **V. 12. So David's young men turned their way, and went again, and came and told him all those sayings,** gave him the report of this contemptuous and insulting rebuff. **V. 13. And David said unto his men, Gird ye on every man his sword,** to take revenge for this insult. **And they girded on every man his sword, and David also girded on his sword; and there went up after David about four hundred men, and two hundred abode by the stuff,** guarding the camp. Nabal is a type of a covetous fool, whose heart has been hardened against every form of distress and want, who is willing enough to accept services at the hand of others, but wants to know nothing of services on his part.

ABIGAIL'S TACT AND PRUDENCE. — **V. 14. But one of the young men,** of the servants of Nabal, **told Abigail, Nabal's wife, saying, Behold, David sent messengers out of the wilderness to salute our master; and he railed on them,** drove over them, flew on them in a rage. **v. 15. But the men,** namely, those of David, **were very good unto us, and we were not hurt,** injured, made subjects of shame and contempt,

**neither missed we anything as long as we were conversant with them,** during all the time of their fellowship with them, **when we were in the fields; v. 16. they were a wall unto us both by night and day, all the while we were with them keeping the sheep,** their presence had proved a powerful protection against the wild beasts as well as against the robbers of the desert. **V. 17. Now, therefore, know and consider what thou wilt do,** Abigail was to find some way to avert a probable calamity; **for evil is determined against our master and against all his household,** this they might count on as firmly settled; **for he,** Nabal, **is such a son of Belial,** bad, foolish, and profitless, **that a man cannot speak to him.** That was the estimate in which Nabal was held by his household and by his servants. **V. 18. Then Abigail made haste, and took two hundred loaves, and two bottles of wine,** the skins used for this purpose in the Orient, **and five sheep ready dressed, and five measures of parched corn,** more than forty quarts of roasted gram, **and an hundred clusters of raisins,** in the form of cakes made of pressed raisins, **and two hundred cakes of figs,** also in the pressed form, **and laid them on asses. V. 19. And she said unto her servants, Go on before me; behold, I come after you.** Like Jacob, Gen. 32, 13-20, she sent the presents of reconciliation ahead of her. **But she told not her husband Nabal,** who would probably have interfered very decidedly. **V. 20. And it was so, as she rode on the ass, that she came down by the covert of the hill,** probably a depression or pass between two peaks, hidden from sight at any distance, **and, behold, David and his men came down against her; and she met them. V. 21. Now, David had said, Surely in vain have I kept all that this fellow hath in the wilderness,** in protecting his wealth in flocks, **so that nothing was missed of all that pertained unto him; and he hath requited me evil for good.** David had been bitterly disappointed in his expectation of receiving any recognition whatever on the part of Nabal and had now flared up in passionate anger, which was not right. **V. 22. So and more also do God unto the enemies of David if I leave of all that pertain to him by the morning light any that pisseth against the wall,** so much as a single person. David wrongly considered the act of Nabal a manifestation of enmity against the cause of Jehovah. **V. 23. And when Abigail saw David, she hasted, and lighted off the ass, and fell before David on her face,** in an attitude of supplication and subjection, **and bowed herself to the ground, v. 24. and fell at his feet,** humbling herself more and more before him, **and said, Upon me, my lord, upon me, let this iniquity be,** the blame or guilt for this unfortunate affair; **and let thine handmaid, I pray thee, speak in thine audience, and hear the words of thine handmaid.** He was to consider her alone as the foolish and guilty person with whom he was to deal. **V. 25. Let not my lord, I pray thee, regard this man of Belial, even Nabal,** he should not take his behavior to heart; **for as his name is, so is he; Nabal** (fool) **is his name, and folly is with him; but I, thine handmaid, saw not the young men of my lord whom thou didst send.** Having drawn attention to her own person, she proceeds with her arguments. **V. 26. Now, therefore, my lord, as the Lord liveth, and as thy soul liveth, seeing the Lord hath withholden thee from coming to shed blood,** literally, "into blood-guiltiness," **and from avenging thyself with thine own hand,** by saving or procuring help for himself, thus making himself guilty of a serious crime, **now let thine enemies, and they that seek evil to my lord, be**

**as Nabal,** sons of folly, the correlate of godlessness, which invariably brings the punishment of God upon the sinner. To these two points Abigail now adds the third argument, in offering her gift. **V. 27. And now this blessing,** the present which she had sent before her, **which thine handmaid hath brought unto my lord, let it even be given unto the young men that follow my lord,** these words showing that she was a skilful diplomat. It is only now that she asks for pardon and forbearance. **V. 28. I pray thee, forgive the trespass of thine handmaid,** the guilt which she had taken upon herself by her own confession; **for the Lord will certainly make my lord a sure house,** as a reward of his magnanimity in this case, **because my lord fighteth the battles of the Lord, and evil hath not been found in thee all thy days,** that is, bad luck, misfortune. **V. 29. Yet a man is risen to pursue thee and to seek thy soul,** or, "Should a man arise and pursue," for she delicately omits a direct reference to Saul; **but the soul of my lord shall be bound in the bundle of life with the Lord, thy God,** said of the sure protection which the children of God enjoy in the merciful fellowship of the Lord here on earth; **and the souls of thine enemies, them shall He sling out, as out of the middle of a sling,** the pan of the sling where the missile is placed before it is shot. It is a strong expression for the total rejection which should strike the enemies of David by the divine punishment. **V. 30. And it shall come to pass, when the Lord shall have done to my lord according to all the good that He hath spoken concerning thee,** for she knew that God had chosen and called David to be king of Israel, **and shall have appointed thee ruler over Israel, v. 31. that this shall be no grief unto thee nor offense of heart unto my lord,** a stumbling-block or vexation, **either that thou hast**

**shed blood causeless, or that my lord hath avenged himself,** bloodshed and self-help being the double sin that he would have been guilty of; **but when the Lord shall have dealt well with my lord, then remember thine handmaid,** not to forget her entirely in his own prosperity. **V. 32. And David said to Abigail, Blessed be the Lord God of Israel, which sent thee this day to meet me,** for David ever acknowledged himself to be under divine guidance; **v. 33. and blessed be thy advice,** her tactful wisdom, **and blessed be thou, which hast kept me this day from coming to shed blood, and from avenging myself with mine own hand,** thus accepting the correction in the two points which she made. **V. 34. For in very deed, as the Lord God of Israel liveth, which hath kept me back from hurting thee, except thou hadst hasted and come to meet me, surely there had not been left unto Nabal by the morning light,** by tomorrow morning, **any that pisseth against the wall. V. 35. So David received of her hand that which she had brought him**, the presents in food, **and said unto her, Go up in peace to thine house,** without anxiety; **see, I have hearkened to thy voice, and have accepted thy person,** her petition had been favorably regarded by him. Like David, all believers will find many an occasion for thanking the Lord for mercifully keeping them from some severe transgression, often in the very nick of time.

DAVID MARRIES ABIGAIL. — V. 36. **And Abigail came to Nabal; and, behold,** although he had been too stingy to share with David and his men, **he held a feast in his house, like the feast of a king,** with all its luxury and sumptuousness; **and Nabal's heart was merry within him,** on account of the rich feast, **for he was very drunken,** intoxicated to such a point that he was not aware of anything outside of his own pleasure;

**wherefore she told him nothing, less or more,** not a word, **until the morning light.** V. 37. **But it came to pass in the morning, when the wine was gone out of Nabal,** when he had become sober once more, **and his wife had told him these things, that his heart died within him, and he became as a stone,** struck with apoplexy, probably due to violent anger because his wife had presumed to deal with the hated David without consulting his authority. V. 38. **And it came to pass about ten days after that the Lord smote Nabal that he died,** his death being a punishment for his ungodliness. V. 39. **And when David heard that Nabal was dead, he said, Blessed be the Lord, that hath pleaded the cause of my reproach from the hand of Nabal, and hath kept His servant from evil;** it was clearly God's judgment upon the insult offered him by Nabal and ever so much better than the revenge which he himself would have taken; **for the Lord hath returned the wickedness of Nabal upon his own head.** To David it was like a case in law, in which the Lord had rendered the judicial decision. **And David sent and communed with Abigail, to take her to him to wife.** V. 40. **And when the servants of David were come to Abigail to Carmel, they spake unto her, saying, David sent us unto thee to take thee to him to wife.** It was the usual formal proposal. V. 41. **And she arose, and bowed herself on her face to the earth,** in the Oriental manner of deepest devotion, **and said,** with the same extreme formal humility, **Behold, let thine handmaid be a servant to wash the feet of the servants of my lord,** thus declaring herself willing, in consenting to the proposal, to perform the lowest service of the house-slaves. V. 42. **And Abigail hasted, and arose, and rode upon an ass, with five damsels of hers that went after her,** her usual train of servants; **and she went after the**

**messengers of David, and became his wife.** The author now immediately supplies further information concerning David's other domestic relations. V. 43. **David also took Ahinoam of Jezreel,** a city in the mountains of Judah; **and they were also both of them his wives,** in addition to Michal, chap. 18, 28. V. 44. **But Saul had given Michal, his daughter, David's wife, to Phalti, the son of Laish, which was of Gallim,** a town between Gibeah and Jerusalem. Cp. 2 Sam. 3, 14 ff. Note: What the believers do good to either friends or enemies is rewarded by God, both in time and in eternity.

# 1 Samuel 26

**D**avid Again Spares Saul.
DAVID IN SAUL'S CAMP. — **V. 1. And the Ziphites,** who had once before played traitors against David, **came unto Saul to Gibeah, saying, Doth not David hide himself in the hill Hachilah, which is before Jeshimon,** south of the wilderness? **V. 2. Then Saul arose, and went down to the wilderness of Ziph,** having forgotten, apparently, that he owed his life to the magnanimity of David, chap. 24, 18, **having three thousand chosen men of Israel with him,** evidently his permanent guard and the nucleus of his standing army, chap. 13, 2, **to seek David in the Wilderness of Ziph. V. 3. And Saul pitched in the hill of Hachilah,** for the entire neighborhood bore this name, the mountain with its foothills and lower slopes, **which is before Jeshimon, by the way,** on the well-known highroad which passed along near the mountain. **But David abode in the wilderness,** having withdrawn from the mountain Hachilah, **and,** or for, **he saw,** he found out through his scouts, **that Saul came after him into the wilderness. V. 4. David, therefore, sent out spies,**

**and understood that Saul was come in very deed,** he received definite information to that effect, the matter was beyond a doubt. **V. 5. And David arose and came to the place where Saul had pitched,** he himself made a scouting trip by night, accompanied by at least a few of his faithful men; **and David,** having reached a spot where he could overlook the entire camp of Saul, **beheld the place where Saul lay, and Abner, the son of Ner, the captain of his host; and Saul lay in the trench,** inside the wagon fortification, or rampart, **and the people pitched round about him. V. 6. Then answered David and said to Ahimelech, the Hittite,** for parts of this heathen nation had remained and were gradually merged with the Israelites, **and to Abishai, the son of Zeruiah, brother to Joab,** the son of David's sister and afterwards one of David's captains, 1 Chron. 2, 16; 2 Sam. 18, 2; 20, 6; 23, 19, **saying, Who will go down with me to Saul to the camp?** It was a very dangerous trip for the purpose of reconnoitering the king's camp. **And Abishai said, I will go down with thee. V. 7. So David and Abishai came to the people by night; and, behold, Saul lay sleeping within the trench,** probably considering the bulwark of the wagons a sufficient safeguard, **and his spear**, the sign of royal authority, **stuck in the ground at his bolster,** near his head, to be ready for any emergency; **but Abner and the people lay round about him,** all soundly asleep. **V. 8. Then said Abishai to David, God hath delivered thine enemy into thine hand this day;** for so, according to the usage of war, he regarded Saul; **now, therefore, let me smite him, I pray thee, with the spear even to the earth at once, and I will not smite him the second time.** This grim remark, that there would be no need of a second blow, shows how David's men felt about Saul's searching expedition. **V. 9. And David said**

to Abishai, **Destroy him not; for who can stretch forth his hand against the Lord's anointed and be guiltless?** David had not changed his position toward Saul's person, as being sacred and inviolable by virtue of his kingship, chap. 24, 6. **V. 10. And David said furthermore, As the Lord liveth, the Lord shall smite him,** or, unless the Lord smite him, for David's oath put the revenge entirely in God's hand, **or his day shall come to die, or he shall descend into battle and perish,** these three being the contingencies which David took into account: sudden death by a stroke, a normal death, and death in battle. **V. 11 The Lord forbid that I should stretch forth mine hand against the Lord's anointed;** he would not, on the part of the Lord, on the Lord's account, take vengeance into his own hand; **but, I pray thee, take thou now the spear that is at his bolster,** at his head, **and the cruse of water,** the water-pitcher, **and let us go. V. 12. So David,** Abishai acting for him, **took the spear and the cruse of water from Saul's bolster; and they gat them away; and no man saw it, nor knew it, neither awaked; for they were all asleep, because a deep sleep from the Lord was fallen upon them,** Jehovah thus expressing His approval of David's expedition. That is the disposition of the children of God, not to seek their own revenge, but to place their matter into the hands of the Lord, for He has said, "Vengeance is Mine, I will repay."

SAUL OVERCOME BY DAVID'S PLEA. — **V. 13. Then David went over to the other side, and stood on the top of an hill afar off;** having crossed the valley, he climbed back to the very top of the hill from which he had probably come down in the evening; **a great space being between them,** for David trusted Saul so little that he preferred to have a great distance between himself and the king. **V. 14. And David cried to the**

**people and to Abner, the son of Ner, saying, Answerest thou not, Abner?** This is much like our expression, Heigh-ho! or, Halloo! **Then Abner answered and said, Who art thou that criest to the king?** Abner resented this calling toward the king, by which his rest was disturbed. **V. 15. And David said to Abner, Art not thou a valiant man,** a warrior entrusted with the protection and security of the king? **And who is like to thee in Israel? Wherefore, then, hast thou not kept the lord, thy king?** It was the general's special duty to watch over the king's life. **For there came one of the people in to destroy the king, thy lord;** Saul had been in real peril of life. **V. 16. This thing is not good that thou hast done. As the Lord liveth, ye are worthy to die,** literally, "Sons of death are ye," **because ye have not kept your master, the Lord's anointed;** they deserved death for their neglect of duty. **And now see where the king's spear is, and the cruse of water that was at his bolster. V. 17. And Saul knew David's voice and said, Is this thy voice, my son David?** Since David was so far away and it was not yet light, Saul could recognize him only by his voice. **And David said, It is my voice, my lord, O king! V. 18. And he said,** once more urging his innocence, which stood out all the more strongly in view of the fact that he had spared Saul's life once more, **Wherefore doth my lord thus pursue after his servant? For what have I done? or what evil is in mine hand?** His manner of addressing Saul is as humble, as gentle, and as reverent as ever. **V. 19. Now, therefore, I pray thee, let my lord the king hear the words of his servant. If the Lord have stirred thee up against me, let Him accept an offering,** literally, "If Jehovah incited thee against me, let Him smell a peace-offering," the idea being that Saul should reconcile God to himself by an offering which had the purpose of restoring the right relationship between Jehovah and His children; **but if they,** the ones that incited the king, **be the children of men, cursed be they before the Lord; for they have driven me out this day from abiding in the inheritance of the Lord, saying, Go, serve other gods.** Their enmity had the object of making David flee out of the country where the Lord lived among His people in His Sanctuary and thus tempting him to commit idolatry, because he could not worship Jehovah at the altars erected to His honor. **V. 20. Now, therefore, let not my blood fall to the earth before the face of the Lord,** Saul was not to continue his enmity to the point where he would force David to die in a strange land; **for the king of Israel is come out to seek a flea,** for by this name David emphasizes his own insignificance in the country, cp. chap. 24, 14, **as when one doth hunt a partridge in the mountains,** for a. single straying partridge in the mountains is not worth hunting, since the birds may easily be found in flocks in the fields. **V. 2l. Then said Saul,** with the same momentary emotion which he had shown before, chap. 24, 16, **I have sinned; return, my son David; for I will no more do thee harm because my soul was precious in thine eyes this day. Behold, I have played the fool, and have erred exceedingly.** Instead of turning to the Lord in true repentance and asking Him for grace and power to overcome the evil of his heart, he makes a promise which was no more sincere than that of the same kind made on the previous occasion. **V. 22. And David answered and said, Behold the king's spear! And let one of the young men come over and fetch it. V. 23. The Lord render to every man his righteousness and his faithfulness,** this being said with special references to himself; **for the Lord delivered thee into my hand today, but I would not stretch forth mine hand**

**against the Lord's anointed.** He had stood the test when he spared the life of Saul, and exhibited his righteousness and faithfulness. **V. 24. And, behold, as thy life was much set by this day in mine eyes,** literally, "made large," esteemed highly, **so let my life be much set by in the eyes of the Lord,** into whose hands David confidently committed himself, **and let Him deliver me out of all tribulation,** all the misery and distress which the hostility of Saul would still prepare for him. **V. 25. Then Saul said to David, Blessed be thou, my son David,** still speaking under the influence of the fleeting better feeling which David's noble conduct awakened in him; **thou shalt both do great things, and also shalt still prevail,** both undertake and also fully perform, for Saul could not shut his eyes to the fact that the blessing of Jehovah was resting upon David. **So David went on his way,** not accepting Saul's invitation to return with him, **and Saul returned to his place.** Thus these two men parted forever, for Saul's enmity continued and forced David to flee into heathen territory. When a person has so hardened his heart that all kindness leaves no lasting impression, his final condemnation is only a matter of time.

# 27

# 1 Samuel 27

**D**avid in the Land of the Philistines.
DAVID IN GATH AND ZIKLAG. — **V. 1.** **And David said in his heart,** taking counsel with himself, expressing the inmost conviction of his heart, **I shall now perish,** be cut down, snatched away, swept off, one day by the hand of Saul; **there is nothing better for me,** literally, "There is nothing good for me," there was no advantage, no sense in his staying in the territory of Israel, **than that I should speedily escape into the land of the Philistines,** that was his one place of refuge; **and Saul shall despair of me to seek me any more in any coast of Israel,** desist from the pursuit as a hopeless undertaking; **so shall I escape out of his hand. V. 2. And David arose, and he passed over with the six hundred men that were with him,** whose number had remained unchanged in recent years, **unto Achish, the son of Maoch, king of Gath,** evidently the same man with whom he sought refuge a number of years before, chap. 21, 10, who by this time, however, must have been convinced that David was no longer an ally of Saul. **V. 3. And David dwelt with Achish**

at Gath, he and his men, every man with his household, with his family, even David with his two wives, Ahinoam, the Jezreelitess, and Abigail, the Carmelitess, Nabal's wife, chap. 25, 42. 43. V. 4. And it was told Saul that David was fled to Gath, where the latter had some leisure to devote to music and poetry, Ps. 8; and he sought no more again for him, David thus gaining his object. V. 5. And David said unto Achish, If I have now found grace in thine eyes, let them give me a place in some town in the country, one of the suburbs or country-cities, that I may dwell there; for why should thy servant dwell in the royal city with thee? David's plea and suggestion was that his men were overcrowding the city and that their expenses were very large, but his real motive undoubtedly was to get away from the idolatrous customs of the Philistines, which surely must have brought him, as the guest of the king, into unpleasant situations at times. V. 6. Then Achish gave him Ziklag that day, a city which had been apportioned to the tribe of Simeon, Josh. 19, 5, but had evidently been taken by the Philistines only recently and was still deserted; wherefore Ziklag pertaineth unto the kings of Judah unto this day, having been given to David as an outright present. V. 7. And the time that David dwelt in the country of the Philistines was a full year and four months. It was undoubtedly weakness of faith which caused David to leave the territory of Judah, for he had expressly been told by the Prophet Gad to remain there. It happens time and again that even staunch servants of the Lord become weak under continued suffering, forgetting entirely that God's merciful power is able to keep them in all dangers. But the Lord has compassion with the weakness of His children.

DAVID'S CAMPAIGN AGAINST THE HEATHEN. — V. 8. And

**David and his men,** no longer under the direct observation of the Philistines, **went up and invaded the Geshurites and the Gezrites,** small nations living south of the Philistine territory, **and the Amalekites,** the nomadic tribes whom Saul had almost destroyed, chap. 15, 7; **for those nations were of old the inhabitants of the land, as thou goest to Shur, even unto the land of Egypt,** on the Egyptian border. **V. 9. And David smote the land, and left neither man nor woman alive,** since they would naturally inform against him, **and took away the sheep, and the oxen, and the asses, and the camels, and the apparel, and returned and came to Achish,** bringing this rich booty along. **V. 10. And Achish said,** it was his custom to ask, **Whither have ye made a road today?** referring to their latest raid. **And David said, Against the south of Judah and against the south of the Jerahmeelites and against the south of the Kenites,** his geographical references being purposely vague and indefinite, in order to make Achish think that his expeditions were directed against some tribe of Israel or against their allies on the southern border. **V. 11. And David saved neither man nor woman alive to bring tidings to Gath**, saying, Lest they should tell on us, David and his men, **saying, So did David, and so will be his manner all the while he dwelleth in the country of the Philistines,** that is, such was David's custom while nominally under the jurisdiction of the Philistine king. V. 12. And Achish believed David, saying, He hath made his people Israel utterly to abhor him, making himself a stench, a loathing, completely alienating himself from the Israelites; **therefore he shall be my servant forever.** Thus Achish was deceived, while David continued to harass and destroy the desert tribes which were a menace to Israel. Thus he, while receiving evil at the hand of Saul, rewarded good to the entire people of Israel, a fine example of love toward one's enemies.

# 28

# 1 Samuel 28

Saul at Endor.
THE CONSULTATION WITH THE WITCH. — **V. 1. And it came to pass in those days,** while David was still living in their country, **that the Philistines gathered their armies together for warfare to fight with Israel.** It was a mustering of all the soldiers of the Philistine city-states that were fit for military duty; for the purpose was not a mere raid, but a campaign of conquest. **And Achish said unto David, Know thou assuredly,** since the circumstances were such as David saw before his eyes, **that thou shalt go out with me to battle, thou and thy men,** as a part of the Philistine army. This was the predicament, the danger, into which David had brought himself by his flight into the land of the Philistines. **V. 2. And David said to Achish, Surely,** since circumstances were of such a nature, **thou shalt know what thy servant can do.** David's answer was purposely evasive and ambiguous, but Achish took it to promise the action which he required, whereas David's answer really said, Conditions will determine what thy servant will do. **And Achish said to David, Therefore**

will I make thee keeper of mine head forever, captain of his body-guard. **V. 3. Now, Samuel was dead,** chap. 25, 1, **and all Israel had lamented him,** observing the customary mourning, **and buried him in Ramah, even in his own city,** in the garden or court of his house, **And Saul,** in accordance with the very strict provisions of the Law, Ex. 22, 18; Lev. 19, 31; 20, 27; Deut. 18, 10. 11, **had put away those that had familiar spirits,** the conjurers of the dead, **and the wizards,** the necromancers or speaking soothsayers, **out of the land,** in order to show himself jealous for God's honor and thus to win Jehovah's favor. **V. 4. And the Philistines gathered themselves together,** they mustered their armies, **and came and pitched in Shunem,** on the western border of the Plain of Jezreel; **and Saul gathered all Israel together, and they pitched in Gilboa,** the mountain range in the territory of Issachar, in the southeastern part of the same plain, only a few miles from the Philistine camp. **V. 5. And when Saul saw the host of the Philistines,** for their camp was plainly visible from his own, **he was afraid, and his heart greatly trembled,** due probably to a strong feeling which suddenly came upon him that he was forsaken of God. **V. 6. And when Saul inquired of the Lord, the Lord answered him not, neither by dreams nor by Urim,** that is, the Urim and Thummim of the high priest's ephod, for Saul had either had a new ephod made after the escape of .Abiathar, chap. 23, 6, or there were, for a while, two high priests, cp. 2 Sam. 8, 17; 15, 24. 29. 35; 1 Chron. 15, 11, **nor by prophets,** to whom Saul now once more turned. It was no true inquiry, made with a humble heart, and therefore was ignored by the Lord. **V. 7. Then said Saul unto his servants,** his hardened heart prompting him to turn to superstitious means forbidden by the Law, **Seek me a woman that hath a**

**familiar spirit,** one in possession of an Ob, or spirit, one able to conjure up the dead, **that I may go to her and inquire of her,** to have the future disclosed to him. **And his servants said to him, Behold, there is a woman that hath a familiar spirit at Endor,** a town about twelve miles north of Gilboa, on the northern slopes of the Little Hermon, almost ten miles southeast of Nazareth. **V. 8. And Saul disguised himself,** by taking off all the garments and insignia indicating his rank, **and put on other raiment; and he went, and two men with him,** as his guides and his body-guard. **And they came to the woman by night,** partly to escape the notice of the Israelites themselves, partly that of the Philistine outposts. **And he said,** when they had reached the woman's house, **I pray thee, divine unto me by the familiar spirit,** she was to uncover the future for him by making use of necromancy, **and bring me him up whom I shall name unto thee. V. 9. And the woman said unto him,** since she suspected that this was a test, a trap to catch her and convict her, **Behold, thou knowest what Saul hath done, how he hath cut off those that have familiar spirits,** the order for their extirpation having been carried out with great rigor, **and the wizards, out of the land; wherefore, then, layest thou a snare for my life to cause me to die?** Cp. Lev. 20, 27. Evidently this was the manner in which necromancers were caught, when they agreed to a request as here made by Saul. **V. 10. And Saul sware to her by the Lord,** this oath by the name of Jehovah again showing the hardening of his heart, **saying, As the Lord liveth, there shall no punishment happen to thee for this thing,** no harm would strike her. **V. 11. Then said the woman,** satisfied that she was now safe, **Whom shall I bring up unto thee? And he said, Bring me up Samuel,** the words indicating the common belief that the dead were in a place somewhere beneath the earth, under the ground, and that their souls could be summoned from there. **V. 12. And when the woman,** after setting into operation her hellish arts, **saw Samuel,** for it was his form which the evil spirit in whose service she was, assumed, **she cried with a loud voice,** since she now saw clearly that her visitor must be the king himself; **and the woman spake to Saul, saying, Why hast thou deceived me? For thou art Saul. V. 13. And the king said unto her, Be not afraid; for what sawest thou?** Up till that time the vision was still hidden from Saul. **And the woman said unto Saul, I saw gods,** a supernatural being, a spicitual form, **ascending out of the earth. V. 14. And he said unto her, What form is he of?** He wanted a more exact description of the apparition. **And she said, An old man cometh up; and he is covered with a mantle. And Saul perceived that it was Samuel,** the long prophet's mantle having given him the information, as the apparition showed it. **And he stooped with his face to the ground, and bowed himself,** in awe and reverence. Note : That this apparition could not have been the real Samuel is evident from the fact that those who die in the Lord are blessed, their souls are in the bliss of heaven, from henceforth, from the moment of death, and the devil has no jurisdiction over those who have fallen asleep in the Lord. One of Satan's own evil spirits here had to serve the Lord as a messenger proclaiming to Saul his early destruction. Witchcraft, Spiritism, and other forms of superstition are still found in the world, and just as prominently as ever. Many a person who has left the true God seeks counsel and assistance in the dens of Spiritists, mediums, and other soothsayers. As faith goes out, superstition comes in. But what the diviners or clairvoyants state is not all falsehood and deception; for the devil is able, with God's permission, to perform works which, to all appearances, are identical with miracles, and to uncover the future. Christians, therefore, will take the greatest care in fleeing from the temptation of consulting such soothsayers.

THE ANSWER RECEIVED BY SAUL. — **V. 15. And Samuel,** the apparition of the evil spirit which had the form of Samuel, **said to Saul, Why hast thou disquieted me, to bring me up? And Saul answered, I am sore distressed,** in great straits; **for the Philistines make war against me, and God is departed from me, and answereth me no more, neither by prophets nor by dreams; therefore I have called thee,** have caused thee to be called, **that thou mayest make known unto me what I shall do.** There was a contradiction in Saul's appeal, which shows that he knew himself to be asking counsel of the devil, for if God would not answer him by the living prophets, what satisfaction could he have gotten from the dead? This is also brought out by the spirit. **V. 16. Then said Samuel, Wherefore, then, dost thou ask of me, seeing the Lord is departed from thee and is become thine enemy?** And now the apparition, evidently even now invisible to the eyes of Saul, announces his fate to him. **V. 17. And the Lord bath done to Him,** for Himself, according to His own counsel, **as He spake by me; for the Lord hath rent the kingdom out of thine hand, and given it to thy neighbor, even to David.** So the complete realization and definite fulfillment of the divine sentence of rejection was now at hand. **V. 18. Because thou obeyedst not the voice of the Lord, nor executedst His fierce wrath upon Amalek, therefore hath the Lord done this thing unto thee this day,** His judgment would now be carried out. **V. 19. Moreover, the Lord will also deliver Israel with thee into the hand of the Philistines,** for the people were guilty with their king; **and tomorrow shalt thou and thy sons be with me,** in the kingdom of death; **the Lord also shall deliver the host of Israel into the hand of the Philistines.** The defeat of Israel, the death of Saul and his sons, and the complete destruction of the camp of Israel were the three decisive blows which would fall on Saul. **V. 20. Then Saul,** overcome by the horror of the revelation, **fell straightway all along on the earth,** he suddenly, from his kneeling position, pitched forward at full length on the floor, **and was sore afraid because of the words of Samuel; and there was no strength in him, for he had eaten no bread,** partaken of no food, **all the day nor all the night. V. 21. And the woman came unto Saul,** hurried to his side, **and saw that he was sore troubled,** greatly terrified, **and said unto him, Behold, thine handmaid hath obeyed thy voice, and I have put my life in my hand,** in exercising her powers of conjuring against the Law of Jehovah and the land, **and have hearkened unto thy words which thou spakest unto me.** She exhibited natural sympathy with the king, worn out by excitement and abstinence from food as he was, this being the consideration which prompted her to offer him her hospitality. **V. 22. Now, therefore, I pray thee, hearken thou also unto the voice of thine handmaid, and let me set a morsel of bread before thee,** urging him, as we would say, to have at least a bite; **and eat that thou mayest have strength when thou goeston thy way. V. 23. But he,** still lying on the floor, **refused and said, I will not eat. But his servants, together with the woman, compelled him,** they urged him so long until he was persuaded; **and he hearkened unto their voice. So he arose from the earth, and sat upon the bed,** the divan, or sofa. **V. 24. And the woman had a fat calf in the house; and she hasted and killed it, and took fiour, and**

**kneaded it, and did bake unleavened bread thereof,** for there was no time to set yeast; **v. 25. and she brought it before Saul and before his servants; and they did eat. Then they rose up and went away that night.** Thus Saul, in dull despair, ran into his destruction, an example of warning to all who harden their hearts to the influence of the Lord.

# 29

# 1 Samuel 29

**D**avid Dismissed by Achish.
THE OBJECTIONS OF THE PHILISTINE PRINCES.
— **V. 1. Now, the Philistines gathered together all their armies to Aphek,** not far from Shunem, in the Plain of Jezreel; **and the Israelites pitched by a fountain which is in Jezreel,** on the northwest slope of Gilboa. **V. 2. And the lords of the Philistines passed on by hundreds and by thousands,** crossing the valley in full battle array, with their officers and princes at their head; **but David and his men passed on in the rearward with Achish,** the Philistines of Gath forming the rear-guard. **V. 3. Then said the princes of the Philistines, What do these Hebrews here?** They may have remembered, from an earlier campaign, that the Israelites in their own army had turned against them and helped to destroy them, chap. 14, 21, or they may have been particularly suspicious of David. **And Achish said unto the princes of the Philistines, Is not this David, the servant of Saul, the king of Israel,** thereby alluding to Saul's enmity toward him, **which hath been with me these days, or these years,** our expression being "a year

and a day," **and I have found no fault in him since he fell unto me unto this day?** He had found nothing which would cause him to suspect his loyalty to the Philistine cause. **V. 4. And the princes of the Philistines were wroth with him,** that is, the rulers of the four other city-states; **and the princes of the Philistines said unto him, Make this fellow return that he may go again to his place which thou hast appointed him,** to Ziklag, **and let him not go down with us to battle,** lest in the battle **he be an adversary to us; for wherewith should he reconcile himself unto his master? Should it not be with the heads of these men?** They felt that it would be the best opportunity for David and his men to reinstate themselves in the favor of Saul by defeating apart of the Philistine army. **V. 5. Is not this David of whom they sang one to another in dances, saying, Saul slew his thousands, and David his ten thousands?** Cp. chap. 18, 7; 21, 11. The defeat which they had suffered at the time when Goliath had been slain still rankled in their memory, and their recollection of this achievement proved the means of rescuing David from the unpleasant necessity of going into battle on their side, although their fears would probably have been realized in that event. It was an act of grace and mercy on God's part which took him out of the battle.

DAVID'S RETURN TO THE LAND OF THE PHILISTINES. — **V. 6. Then Achish called David and said unto him, Surely, as the Lord liveth,** for he swore by the Lord of Israel, in order to emphasize the sincerity of his statement, **thou hast been upright, and thy going out and thy coming in with me in the host is good in my sight,** his entire behavior at all times had met with the approval of the Philistine king; **for I have not found evil in thee since the day of thy coming unto me unto** this day; nevertheless, the lords favor thee not, they refused to drop their suspicions against him. **V. 7. Wherefore, now, return and go in peace, that thou displease not the lords of the Philistines. V. 8. And David said unto Achish, But what have I done? And what hast thou found in thy servant so long as I have been with thee,** literally, "before thee," in thy presence, **unto this day, that I may not go fight against the enemies of my lord the king?** This was again ambiguous, and purposely so, for David would most assuredly not have fought against his own countrymen. **V. 9. And Achish,** accepting David's words as referring to himself, **answered and said to David, I know that thou art good in my sight, as an angel of God,** that was his impression and conviction, that David's behavior would have done credit to an angel; **notwithstanding the princes of the Philistines have said, He shall not go up with us to the battle. V. 10. Wherefore, now, rise up early in the morning with thy master's servants,** the subjects of Saul, **that are come with thee, and as soon as ye be up early in the morning, and have light, depart. V. 11. So David and his men rose up early to depart in the morning,** as soon as it was light enough to see, **to return into the land of the Philistines,** to Ziklag. **And the Philistines went up to Jezreel,** advancing to attack the army of Israel. God's faithfulness in turning aside the evil results of David's foolish move is a source of comfort also to us. He does not let us be tempted above that we are able; He spares us tests and temptations which would be too severe for us, which would endanger our faith. Moreover, the very children of the world who hate us are often instrumental, by God's providence, in having God's good and gracious will fulfilled in us.

# 1 Samuel 30

**D**avid's Revenge upon the Amalekites.
DAVID'S RETURN TO ZIKLAG. — **V 1. And it came to pass, when David and his men were come to Ziklag on the third day,** after leaving the army of Achish in this Plain of Jezreel, **that the Amalekites,** evidently as a reprisal for David's raids upon them, chap. 27, 8, **had invaded the south,** the south country of Judah, **and Ziklag, and smitten Ziklag,** defenseless as the city was, **and burned it with fire; v. 2. and had taken the women captives that were therein,** intending to make slaves of them and of their children; **they slew not any, either great or small, but carried them away and went on their way,** back to their own country. **V. 3. So David and his men came to the city, and, behold, it was burned with fire; and their wives, and their sons, and their daughters were taken captives. V. 4. Then David and the people that were with him lifted up their voice and wept until they had no more power to weep.** The blow was so sudden, so unexpected, that their sorrow was correspondingly great and their grief bitter. **V. 5 And David's two wives**

were taken captives, Ahinoam, the Jezreelitess, and Abigail, the wife of Nabal, the Carmelite. V. 6. And David was greatly distressed, deeply oppressed and anxious in spirit; for the people spake of stoning him, evidently putting all the blame upon him for joining Achish on his campaign against Israel, because the soul of all the people was grieved, full of bitterness, which has a tendency to be unreasonable, every man for his sons and for his daughters. But David encouraged himself in the Lord, his God, seeking strength and comfort in prayer and in firm confidence in the Lord, also by a direct inquiry of the Lord. V. 7. And David said to Abiathar, the priest, Ahimelech's son, chap. 23, 6. 9, I pray thee, bring me hither the ephod, which contained the Urim and Thummim. And Abiathar brought thither the ephod to David. V. 8. And David inquired at the Lord, by means of the Urim, Shall I pursue after this troop, the raiders who had taken away the women and children? Shall I overtake them? And He answered him, Pursue; for thou shalt surely over take them and without fail recover all, most certainly deliver all the captives from the slavery which threatened them. V. 9. So David went, he and the six hundred men that were with him, without taking time to rest, and came to the brook Besor, which flowed down from the hilly section of Judah and down through the country of the Philistines, "Where those that were left behind stayed, unable to proceed on account of exhaustion. V. 10. But David pursued, he and four hundred men; for two hundred abode behind, which were so faint that they could not go over the brook Besor, the crossing of which seems to have been connected with great difficulties. These men were left behind with the baggage, while their more stalwart brethren followed the enemy. Like

David, every Christian, though beset with anxiety and distress, may cheerfully and courageously take up the work assigned to him, after he has strengthened himself with prayer and the Word of God.

DAVID RECOVERS THE SPOIL. — **V. 11 And they,** the men with David, **found an Egyptian in the field,** for the Amalekites could easily obtain Egyptian slaves, **and brought him to David, and gave him bread, and he did eat; and they made him drink water,** in order to revive him from his utter exhaustion, for he was almost famished; **v. 12 and they gave him a piece of a cake of figs,** a slice of pressed figs, **and two clusters,** pressed cakes, **of raisins; and when he had eaten, his spirit came again to him,** he recovered, he was filled with new life; **for he had eaten no bread nor drunk any water three days and three nights. V. 13. And David said unto him,** when he was strong enough to talk, **To whom belongest thou? And whence are thou? And he said, I am a young man of Egypt, servant,** slave, **to an Amalekite; and my master left me because three days agone I fell sick.** He had simply been abandoned because his master could not bother with him on their hasty flight. **V. 14. We made an invasion upon the south of the Cherethites,** a Philistine tribe of the south country, **and upon the coast which belongeth to Judah, and upon the south of Caleb,** the neighborhood of Hebron; **and we burned Ziklag with fire. V. 15. And David said to him, Canst thou bring me down to this company,** to the place where the raiding troop had its permanent camp? **And he said, Swear unto me by God that thou wilt neither kill me nor deliver me into the hands of my master, and I will bring thee down to this company.** The caution of the Egyptian was due to the fact that informers and guides were often put to death by those whom they had served, while the hatred of those whom they had betrayed may well be understood. **V. 16. And when he,** the Egyptian, **had brought him,** David with his men, **down, behold, they,** the Amalekites, **were spread abroad upon all the earth,** having abandoned themselves entirely to the enjoyment of their successful raid, not dreaming of the nearness of any enemy, **eating, and drinking, and dancing, because of all the great spoil that they had taken out of the land of the Philistines and out of the land of Judah,** celebrating the event with rejoicing. **V. 17. And David,** finding them so utterly unprepared, **smote them from the twilight,** from the break of day, **even unto the evening of the next day,** literally, "of their morrow," for the Israelites began their day at sundown; it was an all day battle. **And there escaped not a man of them, save four hundred young men, which rode upon camels and fled. V. 18. And David recovered all that the Amalekites had carried away; and David rescued his two wives.** The pursuit was a complete success. **V. 19. And there was nothing lacking to them, neither small nor great, neither sons nor daughters, neither spoil, nor anything that they had taken to them; David recovered all,** all the booty from the entire raided district. **V. 20. And David took all the flocks and the herds,** those captured from the Amalekites in addition to the recovered property of the raided territory, **which they drave before those other cattle,** at the head of David's little band, **and said, This is David's spoil.** If matters are only begun with the Lord, then He will give His blessing and success in due season.

THE DISTRIBUTION OF THE SPOIL. — **V. 21. And David came to the two hundred men, which were so faint that they could not follow David, whom they had made also to abide**

187

**at the brook Besor,** David having given this order on account of their great exhaustion; **and they went forth to meet David, and to meet the people that were with him; and when David came near to the people, he saluted them,** giving them a friendly greeting, wishing them peace and happiness. **V. 22. Then answered all the wicked men and men of Belial,** vain and profitless fools, **of those that went with David,** for even in that band there were such, **and said, Because they went not with us, we will not give them ought of the spoil that we have recovered, save to every man his wife and his children, that they may lead them away and depart,** literally, "But every man his wife and his children; these let them lead away and go." They held the selfish idea that, because the two hundred had not shared in the danger, they should neither share the spoil. **V. 23. Then said David,** his tactful gentleness averting a rupture in the ranks which might have become a calamity, **Ye shall not do so, my brethren, with that which the Lord hath given us, who hath preserved us, and delivered the company that came against us into our hand.** The success of their venture had been due entirely to Jehovah and His blessing and could, therefore, in no way be regarded as their own achievement. **V. 24. For who will hearken unto you in this matter?** The majority would certainly not share their selfish sentiments. **But as his part is that goeth down to the battle, so shall his part be that tarrieth by the stuff,** who remains behind to watch the baggage; **they shall part alike,** share according to the same division. **V. 25. And it was so from that day forward, that he,** David, **made it a statute and an ordinance for Israel unto this day.** It was a rule which held as late as the time of the Maccabees, being considered just and fair to all. **V. 26. And when David came to Ziklag, he**

**sent of the spoil,** after everyone of his men had recovered what had been taken from him and other booty besides, **unto the elders of Judah, even to his friends, saying, Behold a present for you,** a gift of blessing, **of the spoil of the enemies of the Lord; v. 27. to them which were in Bethel, and to them which were in South Ramoth,** the city of this name in the south country, **and to them which were in Jattir, v. 28. and to them which were in Aroer, and to them which were in Siphmoth, and to them which were in Eshtemoa, v. 29. and to them which were in Rachal, and to them which were in the cities of the Jerahmeelites, and to them which were in the cities of the Kenites, v. 30. and to them which were in Hormah, and to them which were in Chorashan, and to them which were in Athach, v. 31. and to them which were in Hebron, and to all the places where David himself and his men were wont to haunt,** who had shown kindness to him when he was a fugitive. All the cities here mentioned, some of which have been identified quite certainly, are in the southern and southwestern part of the territory of Judah. Note: If the Lord lays His blessing upon our endeavors, it behooves us to share it with others as there is need or occasion.

# 31

# 1 Samuel 31

**D**eath and Burial of Saul and His Sons.

DEATH OF SAUL AND HIS SONS. — **V. 1. Now, the Philistines,** whose armies had been placed in battle array in the Plain of Jezreel, chap. 29, 1.2, **fought against Israel; and the men of Israel fled from before the Philistines,** as Saul had been told, **and fell down slain in Mount Gilboa,** where they fled from the valley upon the attack of the Philistine forces. **V. 2. And the Philistines followed hard upon Saul and upon his sons,** they pursued him with great tenacity, they hung closely at his feet, they strove to overtake him; **and the Philistines slew Jonathan, and Abinadab, and Melchishua, Saul's sons,** chap. 14, 49. **V. 3. And the battle went sore against Saul,** literally, "toward" him, for the whole weight of the battle turned in his direction, **and the archers hit him,** striking him from all sides with arrows; **and he was sore wounded of the archers,** rather, he was much frightened, for he saw no way of escaping the enemy's superior forces, since the battle had apparently resolved itself into individual combats on the part of Israel. **V. 4. Then said Saul unto** his armor-bearer, **Draw thy sword, and thrust me through therewith, lest these uncircumcised,** the Philistines, **come and thrust me through, and abuse me,** torture him cruelly before putting him to death. **But his armor-bearer would not; for he was sore afraid,** he was responsible for the king's life and felt too much awe for his person. **Therefore Saul took a sword, and,** turning the point toward his own body, **fell upon it,** committed suicide. **V. 5. And when his armor-bearer saw that Saul was dead, he fell likewise upon his sword and died with him. V. 6. So Saul died, and his three sons, and his armor-bearer, and all his men,** those of his immediate neighborhood, his body-guard, **that same day together.** That was the end of the man who had once had the Spirit of God and had been filled with power from above. Those who forsake the Lord are truly forsaken, and therefore in the end have no comfort, no help in the hour of death, but go their way into eternal destruction.

BURIAL OF SAUL AT JABESH-GILEAD. — **V. 7. And when the men of Israel that were on the other side of the valley,** in the hill-country toward the north and northeast, **and they that were on the other side Jordan,** apparently such as had not been mustered in the army, **saw that the men of Israel fled, and that Saul and his sons were dead, they forsook the cities,** for fear that they could not hold them anyway, **and fled; and the Philistines,** eventually, at the end of the campaign, **came and dwelt in them. V. 8. And it came to pass on the morrow, when the Philistines came to strip the slain,** to take their garments, jewelry, and weapons as booty, **that they found Saul and his three sons fallen in Mount Gilboa. V. 9. And they cut off his,** Saul's, **head, and stripped off his armor, and sent into the land of the Philistines round**

**about,** evidently using these grim trophies to announce their victory, **to publish it in the house of their idols and among the people,** for they ascribed their victory to their idols. **V. 10. And they put his armor in the house of Ashtaroth,** their chief female goddess, whose largest temple was at Askelon; **and they fastened his body to the wall of Beth-shan,** a city in the valley of the Jordan which had been occupied by the Philistines as a result of the battle. **V. 11. And when the inhabitants of Jabesh-gilead,** the city in the country east of Jordan which had been saved from the Ammonites by Saul's timely intervention, chap. 11, **heard of that which the Philistines had done to Saul; v. 12. all the valiant men arose, and went all night, and took the body of Saul and the bodies of his sons from the wall of Beth-shan,** under cover of night, **and came to Jabesh, and burned them there,** their mutilation probably rendering them unfit for burial. **V. 13. And they took their bones,** the charred remains after the flesh had burned off, **and buried them under a tree,** a well-known tamarisk, **at Jabesh, and fasted seven days,** in deep mourning over the death of their benefactor, a touching and rare example of gratitude. Saul, although rejected by God, had been in fact king of Israel until his death. We also should honor those in authority, even if they are godless rascals, for the sake of the office given to them by God, which makes them His representatives.

# II

# 2 Samuel

# 32

# Introduction

This book is merely a continuation of the First Book of Samuel, having originally formed a single book with it. So far, then, as authorship, probable date of writing, and other questions pertaining to the general understanding of the book are concerned, the remarks in the introduction to the first book apply. The Second Book of Samuel contains the history of David's rule over Judah and Israel, seven years in Hebron over Judah only, thirty-three years in Jerusalem over the entire nation, during which time the Golden Age of the Old Testament was ushered in. There is also a full account of David's transgression and of his subsequent repentance, while the last chapters tell of the end of his reign.

The Second Book of Samuel, like the First, is full of special interest to us believers of the New Testament, because it pictures to us the frailty of the human heart, even in the case of men who stood high in the estimate of the Lord. The sins of David were not overlooked or condoned by God, but received the sharpest reprimand. But, on the other hand, as soon as

David's repentance was evident, the Lord most graciously forgave his sins, even where He did not absolve him of their effects. The book should be studied with these facts in mind.

# 33

# 2 Samuel 1

**D**avid's Lament over Saul and Jonathan.
THE MESSAGE OF THE AMALEKITE. — V.1. **Now it came to pass after the death of Saul,** as related in the last chapter, **when David was returned from the slaughter of the Amalekites,** 1 Sam. 30, **and David had abode two days in Ziklag,** v.2. **it came even to pass on the third day that, behold, a man came out of the camp from Saul,** a man who had fought in the Israelitish army, **with his clothes rent and earth upon his head,** as a sign of the deepest grief; **and so it was, when he came to David, that he fell to the earth and did obeisance,** giving homage to David as the future king. V.3. **And David said unto him, from whence comest thou? And he said unto him, Out of the camp of Israel,** out of the army in the field, **am I escaped,** indicating, even here, that a great calamity had befallen the host. V.4. **And David said unto him, how went the matter? I pray thee, tell me.** The question, How was the affair, How did things go? is at the same time an exclamation of dismay. **And he answered, that the people are fled from the battle,** the army being broken up in wild confusion, **and many**

**of the people also are fallen and dead,** in addition to Saul's body-guard, which had been cut down to the last man, 1 Sam. 31, 6; **and Saul and Jonathan, his son, are dead also.** This was the climax of his sad message. V.5. **And David said unto the young man that told him, How knowest thou that Saul and Jonathan, his son, be dead?** V.6. **And the young man that told him said, As I happened by chance upon Mount Gilboa,** in the confusion of the battle and of the flight, **behold, Saul leaned upon his spear,** apparently so exhausted and weak that he found it difficult to stand up alone; **and, lo, the chariots and horsemen followed hard after him.** It is here that the messenger's falsehoods begin, for it was out of the question for the chariots of the Philistines to follow the fleeing army into the hills. V.7. **And when he,** Saul, **looked behind him, he saw me and called unto me. And I answered, here am I.** V.8. **And he said unto me, who art thou? And I answered him, I am an Amalekite.** Here again the improbability of the report is apparent, since Saul would hardly have been standing alone, with not a single Israelite, not even an armor-bearer, to come to his assistance. V.9. **He said unto me again, Stand, I pray thee, upon me,** by stepping up very closely to him, **and slay me; for anguish is come upon me,** he had been seized with a cramp and found himself unable to wield his weapons, **because my life is yet whole in me,** and he was afraid lest, in his defenseless condition, he would suffer the indignity of falling into the hands of the Philistines. V.10. **So I stood upon him,** went closely up to him, **and slew him, because I was sure that he could not live after he was fallen,** he would not survive this defeat; **and I took the crown that was upon his head and the bracelet that was on his arm,** for men, especially army officers, wore arm-bands as a mark of their rank, **and**

**have brought them,** the symbols of the royal dignity, **hither unto my lord.** The man's idea was to secure the favor of David by his action and obtain a rich reward. V.11. **Then David took hold on his clothes and rent them,** as a sign of uncontrollable grief, **and like wise all the men that were with him,** not only out of deference to David, but because they were aware of the significance of this defeat for the whole nation; v.12. **and they mourned, and wept, and fasted until even,** abandoning themselves to their grief as it swept over them, **for Saul, and for Jonathan, his son, and for the people of the Lord, and for the house of Israel,** the king, the prince, the army, and the entire nation all coming in to make their grief very great, **because they were fallen by the sword.** The people of the Lord, by a holy covenant, had in this battle been abandoned by Jehovah; the house of Israel, all descendants of the same patriarch, was overthrown. V.13. **And David said unto the young man that told him,** who had distorted the facts and lied in order to gain the favor of David, as though he had killed a dangerous enemy, **Whence art thou? And he answered, I am the son of a stranger, an Amalekite,** of a man who had settled in Israel, but had not yet been acknowledged as a member. V.14. **And David said unto him, How wast thou not afraid to stretch forth thine hand to destroy the Lord's anointed?** What David had not dared to do, out of respect for the king's position and person, this stranger, by his own confession, had profanely done, and evidently in hopes of a reward. V.15. **And David called one of the young men and said, Go near and fall upon him.** David here spoke the sentence of death by virtue of his position as Saul's successor, upon a self-confessed murderer. **And he smote him that he died.** V.16. **And David said unto him, Thy blood be upon thy head,** this bloody punishment was in agreement with the crime which he had confessed to; **for thy mouth hath testified against thee, saying, I have slain the Lord's anointed**. David thus avenged a notorious and shocking political crime. If a person accuses himself of some transgression and glories in a crime which he did not commit, he shows a disposition which is guilty before God, and need not be astonished if he is judged according to his own words.

DAVID'S LAMENT. — V.17. **And David lamented with this lamentation over Saul and over Jonathan, his son;** he composed this elegy, or song of mourning, as an expression of his deep and sincere grief over the death of the king and of his dearest friend v.18. **(also he bade them teach the children of Judah the use of the bow,** he commanded that this song be practiced, learned by heart; **behold, it is written in the Book of Jasher,** it was a battle-song recorded in the Book of the Upright, and the bow was afterwards a very important weapon in Israel): v.19. **The beauty,** the glory, **of Israel is slain upon thy high places,** namely, by the death of Saul and Jonathan on Mount Gilboa. **Now are the mighty fallen!** V.20. **Tell it not in Gath, publish,** announce, **it not in the streets of Askelon,** these being two of the five large Philistine cities, **lest the daughters of the Philistines rejoice, lest the daughters of the uncircumcised triumph.** If Philistia should learn of the death of the heroes of Israel, there would be, and there undoubtedly was, a scornful joy over the victory. V.21. **Ye mountains of Gilboa, let there be no dew, neither let there be rain upon you nor fields of offerings,** of first-fruits; the heavens should withhold their moisture, and the earth should refuse to give her increase, as a sign of mourning over the defeat; **for there the shield of the mighty is vilely cast away,** defiled with dust and blood, **the shield of Saul, as though he had not been anointed with oil;** no one was there to take the shield, the emblem of the leader of the army, out of the dirt to clean and to polish its surface anew. V.22. **From the blood of the slain, from the fat of the mighty,** considered a sign of great strength, **the bow of Jonathan turned not back, and the sword of Saul returned not empty;** both heroes were accustomed to gain complete victories, to destroy every opposing enemy, their bravery, their prowess, was known far and wide. V.23. **Saul and Jonathan were lovely and pleasant,** worthy of lore, beloved, and amiable, **in their lives, and in their death they were not divided.** United by love in life, they were bound together in death, together they gave their lives for Israel. **They were swifter than eagles,** distinguished for quickness and agility; **they were stronger than lions,** of lionlike courage and strength. V.24. **Ye daughters of Israel, weep over Saul, who clothed you in scarlet,** in crimson or purple garments from the booty of war, **with other delights,** adornments that pleased them; **who put on ornaments of gold upon your apparel,** as a proof of his kingly largess. V.25. **How are the mighty fallen in the midst of the battle! O Jonathan, thou wast slain in thine high places!** Here the key-note of the entire lament is once more sounded, with special reference to Jonathan. V.26. **I am distressed for thee,** filled with anxious thoughts by reason of grief and mourning, **my brother Jonathan; very pleasant,** beloved, **hast thou been unto me; thy love to me was wonderful, passing the love of women,** known for the depth of their affection and devotion. V.27. **How are the mighty fallen, and the weapons of war,** the heroes of Israel, as the instruments of battle, **perished!** The elegy was a national song and preserved the names of Saul and Jonathan in Israel. True lore and friendship requites that a person mourn the loss of a friend and always keep him in fond remembrance.

# 34

## 2 Samuel 2

**D**avid King over Judah.

DAVID AT HEBRON. — V.1. **And it came to pass after this that David enquired of the Lord,** by means of the Urim and Thummim of the high priest. 1 Sam. 23, 2. 10. 11; 30, 7-9, **saying, Shall I go up,** namely, from the low lands of Philistia, **into any of the cities of Judah,** this being his own tribe? **And the Lord said unto him, Go up. And David said, Whither shall I go up,** that is, to which special city or district? **And He said, Unto Hebron,** about twenty miles south of Jerusalem and near the center of the territory of Judah. V.2. **So David went up thither, and his two wives also, Ahinoam, the Jezreelitess, and Abigail, Nabal's wife, the Carmelite,** 1 Sam. 30, 5. V.3. **And his men that were with him did David bring up,** the six hundred men who had been faithful to him in his adversity, **every man with his household; and they dwelt in the cities of Hebron,** the suburbs in the vicinity. V.4. **And the men of Judah came,** the elders of his own tribe, **and there they anointed David king over the house of Judah,** the affairs of the northern tribes at that time being in a condition of chaos.

**And they told David, saying, that the men of Jabesh-gilead were they that buried Saul.** This seems to have been in answer to David's inquiry concerning the disposition of the bodies of Saul and Jonathan, his first official act after his crowning. V.5. **And David sent messengers unto the men of Jabesh-gilead,** the city east of Jordan, whose inhabitants had been rescued by Saul and had, in gratitude, gotten his body from the walls of Beth-shan, 1 Sam. 31, 11-13, **and said unto them, Blessed be ye of the Lord that ye have showed this kindness unto your lord, even unto Saul, and have buried him;** they had shown that grateful love which became them in their relation to Saul as their king. V.6. **And now the Lord show kindness and truth unto you,** favor, gracious, faithful love in fulfilling all His promises for their benefit; **and I also,** by virtue of the royal authority now vested in him, **will requite you this kindness,** by calling down the divine blessing upon them, **because ye have done this thing.** V.7. **Therefore, now, let your hands be strengthened,** with a strong and cheerful courage, **and be ye valiant,** literally, "sons of valor or bravery"; **for your master Saul is dead, and also the house of Judah have anointed me king over them.** This message of David was a wise diplomatic move, particularly since the remnant of Saul's army had fled to Gilead, and there was danger that the heads of the army would not acknowledge David. V.8. **But Abner, the son of Ner, captain of Saul's host, took Ishbosheth, the son of Saul,** this had evidently been done even before David sent his messengers, **and brought him over to Mahanaim,** a city in Gilead northeast of Jabesh, v.9. **and made him king over Gilead,** the country east of Jordan, **and over the Ashurites,** probably in the territory of the upper Jordan, **and over Jezreel,** the entire plain of the recent defeat, **and over Ephraim, and**

**over Benjamin, and over all Israel,** all the northern tribes. V.10. **Ishbosheth, Saul's son, was forty years old when he began to reign over Israel, and reigned two years. But the house of Judah,** with the descendants of Simeon living in their midst, **followed David.** V.11. **And the time,** the total number of days, **that David was king in Hebron over the house of Judah was seven years and six months.** Thus the suffering and persecution which had darkened the life of David was now turned into joy. Even so, days of refreshing joy follow days of darkness in the lives of the Christians; for when God finds that faith has been sufficiently tested through afflictions, He changes tribulation into glory.

DAVID'S WAR WITH ISHBOSHETH. — V.12. **And Abner, the son of Ner, and the servants of Ishbosheth, the son of Saul, went out from Mahanaim to Gibeon;** they crossed to the western side of Jordan, into the territory of Benjamin, in order to wage war against David and to conquer Judah. V.13. **And Joab, the son of Zeruiah,** a nephew of David and the general of his armies, **and the servants of David,** who had prepared for such an attack, **went out and met together by the Pool of Gibeon,** the two opposing armies meeting at the reservoir some six miles north of Jerusalem, **and they sat down,** encamped, **the one on the one side of the pool, and the other on the other side of the pool.** V.14. **And Abner said to Joab,** proposing to decide the matter by individual contests, **Let the young men now arise and play before us,** here said of a serious battle-play, a combat of arms which was more than a game. **And Joab,** agreeing to the proposal to avoid a bloody civil war, if possible, **said, Let them arise.** V.15. **Then there arose and went over by number twelve of Benjamin, which pertained to Ishbosheth, the son of Saul, and twelve**

**of the servants of David,** these chosen warriors meeting, apparently, midway between the lines. V.10. **And they caught every one his fellow,** his opponent, **by the head, and thrust his sword in his fellow's side,** in a quick motion showing their excellent military training, but also the bitterness usually present in a civil war; **so they fell down together,** in a mutual slaughter, the twenty-four being slain at the same time; **wherefore that place was called Helkath-hazzurim** (field of sword-edges), **which is in Gibeon.** V.17. **And,** the individual combats having been a failure in deciding the issue, **there was a very sore battle that day; and Abner was beaten, and the men of Israel, before the servants of David.** A special scene of the pursuit which followed the defeat of the men of Israel, featuring champions of the family of David, is now given. V.18. **And there were three sons of Zeruiah there,** all nephews of David, **Joab, and Abishai, and Asahel; and Asahel was as light of foot as a wild roe,** as swift as the gazelles of the field. V.19. **And Asahel pursued after Abner,** for his capture would be the decisive blow ending the battle; **and in going he turned not to the right hand nor to the left from following Abner,** determined to accomplish his purpose. V.20. **Then Abner looked behind him and said, Art thou Asahel?** For he had evidently heard of him. **And he answered, I am.** V.21. **And Abner said to him, Turn thee aside to thy right hand or to thy left, and lay thee hold on one of the young men,** one of the privates, **and take thee his armor,** for Be thought that Asahel was merely seeking the glory of having slain an enemy, knowing that his own skill was much more than a match for the eager young man. **But Asahel would not turn aside from following of him,** he wanted to realize his ambition. V.22. **And Abner said again to Asahel,** in a last attempt at warning him, **Turn thee aside from following me; wherefore should I smite thee to the ground? How, then, could I hold up my face to Joab, thy brother?** His former friendship for Joab was such as to make it very unpleasant for him in case he should meet David's general afterwards. V.23. **How-beit he,** Asahel, **refused to turn aside; wherefore Abner with the hinder end of the spear,** with the lower metallic point, **smote him under the fifth rib,** in the abdomen, **that the spear came out behind him; and he fell down there, and died in the same place.** **And it came to pass that as many as came to the place where Asahel fell down and died stood still;** for he had been held in high regard by all, and therefore his death caused a general mourning. V.24. **And Joab also and Abishai pursued after Abner,** with the same persistence. **And the sun went down when they were come to the hill of Ammah, that lieth before Giah by the way of the Wilderness of Gibeon.** So the pursuit ended east of Gibeon, after it had lasted all day. V.25. **And the children of Benjamin gathered themselves together after Abner,** rallying for a last decided stand, **and became one troop, and stood on the top of an hill,** a favorable position to await an attack. V.26. **Then Abner called to Joab and said, Shall the sword devour forever,** in an endless bloody combat? **Knowest thou not that it will be bitterness in the latter end?** in a civil war of this kind there was always danger that sullen despair would cause such a wave of embittered feeling to arise as to make reconciliation extremely difficult. **How long shall it be, then, ere thou bid the people return from following their brethren?** It was an urgent demand to suspend hostilities at once and to agree to a truce. V.27. **And Joab said, As God liveth, unless thou hadst spoken,** suggesting the method of individual combat,

**surely then in the morning the people had gone up, every one, from following his brother.** He held that Abner was responsible for the stubborn battle of the day, for they might have come to an agreement without bloodshed. V.28. **So Joab blew a trumpet, and all the people stood still,** the battle was discontinued, **and pursued after Israel no more, neither fought they any more,** they concluded a truce. V.29. **And Abner and his men walked all that night through the plain,** marching up the valley of the Jordan to the place where they had forded, **and passed over Jordan, and went through all Bithron,** evidently a district on the Jabbok; **and they came to Mahanaim,** where their headquarters were at the time. V.30. **And Joab returned from following Abner; and when he had gathered all the people together, there lacked of David's servants nineteen men and Asahel,** very likely including the twelve that fell in single combat. V.31. **But the servants of David had smitten of Benjamin and of Abner's men, so that three hundred and threescore men died.** Joab had in his army only veteran soldiers, tried by many severe battles and steeled by many privations, while Abner had merely the remains of an army which had but recently been defeated by the Philistines, and which may otherwise have been weakened and discouraged. V.32. **And they took up Asahel, and buried him in the sepulcher of his father, which was in Bethlehem,** only a little to the left of the direct road to Hebron. **And Joab and his men went all night, and they came to Hebron at break of day.** Note: Christians should be glad to take upon themselves the disgrace and suffering of Christ, the Son of David, to be zealous for Him and His honor, to battle for His cause with the weapons of the Spirit, in order that the kingdom and rule of the Anointed may be spread over the world.

# 35

# 2 Samuel 3

**Abner, having Joined David, Murdered by Joab.**

ABNER LEAVES ISHBOSHETH FOR DAVID. — V.1. **Now, there was long war between the house of Saul and the house of David,** literally, "the war was protracted," a state of war continued to exist, since neither acknowledged the other as king, although outward hostilities were apparently not renewed; **but David,** patiently waiting and relying upon the promise of Jehovah, **waxed stronger and stronger, and the house of Saul waxed weaker and weaker;** David gained in adherents in the same measure as Ishbosheth lost them. V.2. **And unto David were sons born in Hebron; and his first-born was Amnon, of Ahinoam, the Jezreelitess;** v.3. **and his second, Chileab** (or Daniel, 1 Chron. 3, 1), **of Abigail, the wife of Nabal, the Carmelite; and the third, Absalom, the son of Maacah, the daughter of Talmai, king of Geshur,** a small principality in Syria; v.4. **and the fourth, Adonijah, the son of Haggith; and the fifth, Shephatiah, the son of Abital;** v.5. **and the sixth Ithream, by Eglah, David's wife.** The three women mentioned last are otherwise unknown. **These were**

**born to David in Hebron,** the fruit of his strange polygamous marriages. V.6. **And it came to pass, while there was war between the house of Saul and the house of David,** while the state of hostility continued, **that Abner made himself strong for the house of Saul,** his strong influence enabled the house of Saul to maintain itself. V.7. **And Saul had a concubine whose name was Rizpah, the daughter of Aiah; and Ishbosheth said to Abner, Wherefore hast thou gone in unto my father's concubine?** The reproof was given because Abner, by his action, had presumed upon royal rights, for in the ancient Orient claim to the harem was claim to the throne, the suspicion thus being that he aspired to be king. V.8. **Then was Abner very wroth for the words of Ishbosheth,** for he seems to have been self-willed and presumptuous in his conduct toward the weak man whom he had made king, **and said, Am I a dog's head,** a low, contemptible person, **which against Judah,** who sides with Judah? (I) **do show kindness this day unto the house of Saul, thy father, to his brethren, and to his friends, and have not delivered thee in to the hand of David, that thou chargest me to-day with a fault concerning this woman?** Ishbosheth owed position, kingdom, everything to Abner, who seems to have been on his side merely out of loyalty for Saul; but there was no personal bond between them, and Abner regarded the charge flung into his face as an insult. V.9. **So do God to Abner, and more also,** a strong oath of a vigorous, autocratic man, **except, as the Lord hath sworn to David, even so I do to him,** v.10. **to translate the kingdom from the house of Saul,** to take it away and transfer it, **and to set up the throne of David over Israel and over Judah, from Dan even to Beersheba,** from the extreme north to the extreme south of Canaan. Abner had evidently recognized the fact, even before this, that Ishbosheth was wholly unfit for the kingly rule, and the latter's charge now brought matters to a head. V.11. **And he,** Ishbosheth, **could not answer Abner a word again, because he feared him,** he was too feeble, too cowardly, to back up his reproof with action. V.12. **And Abner sent messengers to David on his behalf,** as an embassy representing him, **saying, Whose is the land?** His pride caused him to intimate that he was the real master of Israel. **Saying also, Make thy league with me, and, behold, my hand shall be with thee to bring about all Israel unto thee,** to get all the northern tribes to acknowledge David, with the expectation that he would be given a high position in the army of the united country. V.13. **And he,** David, **said, Well; I will make a league with thee; but one thing I require of thee,** this was his one condition upon whose fulfillment he insisted, **that is, Thou shalt not see my face except thou first bring Michal, Saul's daughter, when thou comest to see my face.** It was not merely that Michal was his lawful wife, but David had also a political reason in his union with Israel's princess, namely, that of gaining the favor of the northern tribes. V.14. **And David sent messengers to Ishbosheth, Saul's son, saying, Deliver me my wife Michal, which I espoused to me for an hundred foreskins of the Philistines,** that being the purchase price, the morning gift which Saul had demanded, 1 Sam. 18, 25, V.15. **And Ishbosheth,** who would not have been able to refuse the demand of David even if he had been so inclined, **sent and took her from her husband, even from Phaltiel, the son of Laish,** the man who seems to have taken her in good faith, 1 Sam. 25, 44. V.16. **And her husband went with her along weeping behind her to Bahurim,** on the boundary of Judah, his behavior showing that he was truly fond of

Michal. **Then said Abner,** who, in accordance with David's condition, had taken charge of this mission, **unto him, Go, return. And he returned. V.17. And Abner,** even before he restored Michal to her rightful husband, **had communication with the elders of Israel, saying, Ye sought for David in times past,** literally, "yesterday as well as the day before," **to be king over you,** their dissatisfaction with Ishbosheth had probably been voiced more than once; v.18. **now, then, do it: for the Lord hath spoken of David, saying, By the hand of My servant David I will save My people Israel out of the hand of the Philistines and out of the hand of all their enemies.** This was the promise implied in the prophetic tradition and the duty laid upon the king chosen by Jehovah. V.19. **And Abner also spake in the ears of Benjamin,** here distinguished from the northern tribes, because its members had been very strongly attached to the house of Saul; **and Abner went also to speak in the ears of David in Hebron all that seemed good to Israel, and that seemed good to the whole house of Benjamin.** In return for their recognition of David's royal authority they wanted the same advantages as the men of Judah; they were fully ready to acknowledge him. V.20. **So Abner came to David to Hebron, and twenty men with him,** as representatives of all Israel, as witnesses of the covenant. **And David made Abner and the men that were with him a feast,** a formal festival meal. V.21. **And Abner said unto David, I will arise and go, and will gather all Israel unto my lord the king that they may make a league with thee,** acknowledging him as the chosen king of Jehovah, through whom, as His instrument, the Lord Himself would rule over His people, **and that thou mayest reign over all that thine heart desireth,** over the entire people of God. **And David sent Abner away; and he went in peace,** regarded by David as a true friend to his cause. Even the adversaries of God and Christ are often instrumental in carrying out the counsel of God and in furthering the cause of Christ. And many a person who first strongly opposed the Lord has been brought to a better understanding and has embraced the good cause.

ABNER MURDERED BY JOAB, MOURNED BY DAVID. — V.22. **And, behold, the servants of David and Joab,** the latter being the general of the army of Judah, **came from pursuing a troop,** they had been out on a raid against one of the neighboring nations, **and brought in a great spoil with them,** such expeditions being necessary at that time to support the army. **But Abner was not with David in Hebron; for he had sent him away, and he was gone in peace,** dismissed as on the best footing with David. V.23. **When Joab and all the host that was with him were come, they told Joab,** some people promptly informed him, **saying, Abner, the son of Ner, came to the king, and he hath sent him away, and he is gone in peace.** V.24. **Then Joab,** who was filled with hatred against Abner, **came to the king and said, What hast thou done? Behold, Abner came unto thee; why is it that thou hast sent him away,** instead of holding him captive? **And he is quite gone;** no one had made a move to secure him. V.25. **Thou knowest Abner, the son of Ner, that he came to deceive thee,** with an evil and hostile purpose, **and to know thy going out and thy coming in, and to know all that thou doest.** In his reproach of David, Joab accused Abner of being a spy, a traitor, who was seeking information favorable to his schemes. The object was, of course, to make David so unfavorably disposed toward Abner that he would overlook the revenge which Joab was planning. V.26. **And when Joab was come out from David,** after this interview, **he sent**

**messengers after Abner, which brought him again from the well,** or cistern, **of Sirah,** for he had progressed to that point when the messengers reached him; **but David knew it not,** he was unacquainted with Joab's plans, much less did he approve of them. V.27. **And when Abner was returned to Hebron,** undoubtedly under the impression that David had some further instructions for him, **Joab took him aside in the gate to speak with him quietly,** in secret, in private, his attendants therefore retiring, **and smote him there under the fifth rib,** in the abdomen, **that he died, for the blood of Asahel, his brother,** for whom Joab considered himself an avenger. Joab's deed was murder and cast false suspicions on David; his real ground for committing it was false ambition and envy, for he feared that lie would be superseded by the more renowned Abner. V.28. **And afterward, when David heard it, he said, I and my kingdom are guiltless before the Lord forever from the blood of Abner, the son of Ner.** V.29. **Let it,** the guilt, **rest on the head of Joab and on all his father's house,** the punishment of God should turn, roll, plunge upon the entire family of Joab; **and let there not fail from the house of Joab,** not one escaping this fate, **one that hath an issue,** Lev. 15, 2, **or that is a leper, or that leaneth on a staff,** being a cripple, **or that falleth on the sword,** finding his death in battle, **or that lacketh bread.** Terrible sicknesses, violent deaths: and poverty: those were the afflictions with which the posterity of Joab was ever to be punished. V.30. **So Joab and Abishai, his brother,** who was an accomplice, **slew Abner because he had slain their brother Asahel at Gibeon in the battle.** The deed showed traits in Joab's character which appeared once more at a later time, in the murder of Amasa, chap. 20, 10. V.31. **And David said to Joab and to all**

**the people that were with him, Rend your clothes, and gird you with sackcloth,** the signs of deepest grief, **and mourn before Abner,** in the presence of his corpse, by an official lamentation. **And King David himself followed the bier,** his share in the ceremonies showing the deep personal sorrow which he felt. V.32. **And they buried Abner in Hebron; and the king lifted up his voice and wept at the grave of Abner,** his tears being further evidence of the genuineness of his grief; **and all the people wept,** sharing his trouble and his sympathy. V.33. **And the king lamented over Abner,** in an elegy expressing his deepest sorrow over Abner's innocent and shameful death, **and said, Died Abner as a fool dieth,** like a good-for-nothing, worthless fellow? V.34. **Thy hands were not bound, nor thy feet put into fetters,** he was not guilty of any crime; **as a man falleth before wicked men,** before assassins, **so fellest thou,** murdered in malice. **And all the people,** moved by the lament of this elegy, **wept again over him.** V.35. **And when all the people came to cause David to eat meat,** to partake of food, **while it was yet day, David sware, saying, So do God to me and more also if I taste bread or aught else till the sun be down;** his grief culminated in his voluntary fasting. V.36. **And all the people took notice of it, and it pleased them; as whatsoever the king did pleased all the people,** he won the love and confidence of the people by his manner of acting and freed himself from all suspicion of complicity in the murder of Abner. V.37. **For all the people,** those present in Hebron, **and all Israel,** to whom the news was brought, **understood that day that it was not of the king to slay Abner, the son of Ner.** V.38. **And the king said unto his servants, Know ye not that there is a prince and a great man fallen this day in Israel?** Abner had been a prince by reason of his distinguished military ability, and a great man on account of his lofty character and virtues of value to the nation. V.39. **And I am this day weak,** still powerless to act as the occasion really required, **though anointed king; and these men, the sons of Zeruiah, be too hard for me,** he did not feel able as yet to bring them to justice. **The Lord shall reward the doer of evil according to his wickedness.** Into Jehovah's hands, for the present, David placed this matter for adjustment. If fleshly zeal, anger, jealousy, revenge, are the motives actuating a person, the Lord will punish him in due time.

# 36

# 2 Samuel 4

**M**urder of Ishbosheth.

ISHBOSHETH MURDERED. — V.1. **And when Saul's son, Ishbosheth, heard that Abner was dead in Hebron, his hands were feeble,** slack, he completely lost heart, **and all the Israelites were troubled,** not only terrified, but completely at a loss what to do next. Things became altogether unsettled, chaos reigned in Israel. V.2. **And Saul's son had two men that were captains of bands,** bold, adventurous men who had divisions of the former Israelitish army under their command. **The name of the one was Baanah, and the name of the other Rechab, the son of Rimmon, a Beerothite, of the children of Benjamin. (For Beeroth,** although on its extreme western boundary, **also was reckoned to Benjamin,** Josh. 18, 25. V.3. **And the Beerothites fled to Gittaim,** probably because the Philistines had captured Beeroth, **and were sojourners there until this day.)** V.4. **And Jonathan, Saul's son, had a son that was lame of his feet,** the last representative of Saul's house after Ishbosheth, a cripple and a minor. **He was five years old when the tidings**

**came of Saul and Jonathan out of Jezreel,** at the time of the great defeat by the Philistines, 1 Sam. 29, 1. 11, **and his nurse took him up and fled; and it came to pass, as she made haste to flee, that he fell and became lame. And his name was Mephibosheth** (or Meribbaal, 1 Chron. 8, 34). V.5. **And the sons of Rimmon, the Beerothite, Rechab and Baanah, went and came about the heat of the day to the house of Ishbosheth, who lay on a bed at noon,** on the midday-bed, during the drowsiest part of the day, the time of the daily siesta, when men were not so alert as at other times. V.6. **And they came thither into the midst of the house, as though they would have fetched wheat,** grain to distribute to their soldiers, which was probably stored off the court or open space in the center of the house. Their presence for such a purpose would attract no attention. **And they smote him under the fifth rib,** through the abdomen; **and Rechab and Baanah, his brother, escaped.** V.7. **For when they came in to the house,** which was open to them by reason of their position in the army, **he lay on his bed in his bedchamber,** in the inner, more remote section of the house, **and they smote him, and slew him, and beheaded him, and took his head, and gat them away through the plain all night,** they fled down the valley of the Jordan. V.8. **And they brought the head of Ishbosheth unto David to Hebron, and said to the king, Behold the head of Ishbosheth, the son of Saul, thine enemy, which sought thy life; and the Lord hath avenged my lord the king this day of Saul and of his seed.** To their crime of cold-blooded assassination they added that of blasphemy by ascribing the success of their deed to Jehovah. The object of the murderers evidently was to commend themselves to David and to obtain a reward of some kind. It is impossible to correct a wrong by committing a wrong, for the punishment of all crimes is in the hands of the authorities, who have received their power from God.

THE MURDER AVENGED. — V.9. **And David answered Rechab and Baanah, his brother, the sons of Rimmon, the Beerothite, and said unto them, As the Lord liveth, who hath redeemed my soul out of all adversity,** from all the suffering with which he had been afflicted, thus putting him beyond the necessity of freeing himself from his enemies by crime, v.10. **when one told me, saying, Behold, Saul is dead,** namely, the Amalekite who came to Ziklag, chap. 1, 2, **thinking to have brought good tidings,** literally, "and he was as a bringer of good tidings in his own eyes," **I took hold of him and slew him in Ziklag, who thought that I would have given him a reward for his tidings,** or, in order to give him the reward, to inflict on him the punishment which he deserved; v.11. **how much more, when wicked men have slain a righteous person in his own house upon his bed?** Ishbosheth, although connected with a wrong cause, was himself without falsehood and blameless; he was not out on a raiding expedition or engaged in anything wrong, but was at home, doing no one any harm. **Shall I not, therefore, now require his blood of your hand,** God Himself being the chief avenger of blood and the king His instrument in carrying out justice upon the murderers, **and take you away from the earth?** V.12. **And David commanded his young men, and they slew them, and cut off their hands,** which had committed the murder, **and their feet,** which had hurried after the reward, **and hanged them up over the pool in Hebron,** a public place visited by many people, as a testimony to David's just severity against criminals of this kind. **But they took the head of Ishbosheth,** which the murderers had brought along as a trophy of their deed, **and buried it in the sepulcher of Abner in Hebron.** Note: As David finally subdued all his enemies who challenged his right to be king over Israel, so Christ, the Son of David, having conquered all enemies of mankind, will finally obtain the eternal victory.

# 37

# 2 Samuel 5

**D**avid King of the Entire Nation.
DAVID ANOINTED KING OVER ALL ISRAEL. — V.1.
**Then,** after the death of both Abner and Ishbosheth, **came all the tribes of Israel to David unto Hebron, and spake, saying, Behold, we are thy bone and thy flesh,** they were all kinsmen of blood by descent from a common ancestor, David not being a foreign usurper, a stranger coming into the country from elsewhere. V.2. **Also in time past, when Saul was king over us, thou wast he that leddest out and broughtest in Israel,** 1 Sam. 18, 13. 16, he had been the most trusted leader in their military campaigns; **and the Lord said to thee, Thou shalt feed My people Israel,** like a shepherd taking the most tender care of the sheep entrusted to him, **and thou shalt be a captain over Israel,** their prince in defending them from their enemies. This was the last and strongest ground for their proposal, the Lord's immediate call, as based upon the word of God to Samuel, 1 Sam. 15, 28; for the prophets of Naioth in Ramah undoubtedly made this fact known. Note that the king's function as shepherd of the people is mentioned first, a

hint for the rulers of all times. V.3. **So all the elders of Israel came to the king to Hebron,** as the representatives of the tribes; **and King David made a league with them in Hebron before the Lord,** a covenant in the presence of God, David accepting their promise of obedience and assuring them of a just and merciful reign. **And they anointed David king over Israel,** the anointing by Samuel, 1 Sam. 16, l. 12, being now confirmed by that of the entire people. V.4. **David was thirty years old when he began to reign, and he reigned forty years.** V.5. **In Hebron he reigned over Judah seven years and six months; and in Jerusalem he reigned thirty and three years over all Israel and Judah.** Cp. 1 Chron. 29, 27. After the long years of suffering, privations, and persecutions, David now enjoyed the fulfillment of God's promise to him. In the midst of all tribulations and afflictions the believers still look up to God, knowing that they mill yet bless Him who is the help of their countenance and their God.

JERUSALEM MADE THE CAPITAL. — V.6. **And the king and his men,** all the soldiers of the regular army, **went to Jerusalem unto the Jebusites, the inhabitants of the land,** for this heathen tribe of the hill country still held the fortress of the city, Judg. 1, 21; **which spake unto David, saying, Except thou take away the blind and the lame, thou shalt not come in hither,** literally, "Not wilt thou come in, but there will drive thee away the blind and the lame"; **thinking,** the Jebusites meant to say, **David cannot come in hither.** They were so firmly convinced that their fortress was impregnable that they considered the blind and the lame a sufficient guard for the defense of its walls. V.7. **Nevertheless David took the stronghold of Zion,** the southern and highest hill of Jerusalem; **the same is the City of David.** The name Zion afterwards was applied to the Temple of Jehovah situated on this hill, and so finally was used as a designation of the Church of God, both in the Old and in the New Testament. A special incident of the siege of Jerusalem is now mentioned. V.8. **And David said on that day,** while preparing to storm the fortress, **Whosoever getteth up to the gutter and smiteth the Jebusites and the lame and the blind, that are hated of David's soul, he shall be chief and captain,** 1 Chron. 11, 6-9. The difficult passage is best rendered: Every one who conquers the Jebusites, let him cast into the waterfall both the lame and the blind, hated of David's soul. The expression "blind and lame" applied to all the Jebusites, and the order to throw the slain down the declivity was given in order to gain space for the hand-to-hand encounter in the fortress. **Wherefore they said,** it became a proverbial saying, **The blind and the lame,** undesirable people like the Jebusites, **shall not come in to the house.** V.9. **So David dwelt in the fort,** making the castle his residence, **and called it the City of David. And David built round about from Millo,** the citadel or fortification proper, **and inward;** the fort being on the most exposed point, he strengthened the defenses between it and his residence. Thus the entire upper city became one huge fortress. V.10. **And David went on and grew great,** he continued to gain in power, influence, and prestige, **and the Lord God of hosts,** Jehovah God of Sabaoth, **was with him.** He owed not only his kingdom, but all the success which attended him to the blessing of the covenant God. Jerusalem, nearer to the center of Canaan than Hebron, was now the capital of all the tribes. V.11. **And Hiram, king of Tyre, sent messengers to David,** a formal embassy, in order to establish friendly relations with the neighboring state, **and cedar-trees,** whose wood was much used for costly buildings, **and carpenters, and masons; and they built David an house,** the first fine palace of the kings of Judah. V.12. **And David perceived,** from the success which attended all his undertakings, **that the Lord had established him king over Israel, and that he had exalted his kingdom for His people Israel's sake,** because He had chosen Israel for His people and promised to make it great and powerful. V.13. **And David took him more concubines and wives of Jerusalem,** according to the custom of Oriental monarchs, **after he was come from Hebron.** In the law pertaining to kings, Deut. 17, 17, the taking of many wives had indeed been forbidden the kings of Israel, and David found out to his sorrow that his following the custom of the heathen kings brought him much trouble and heartache. **And there were yet sons and daughters born to David.** V.14. **And these be the names of those that were born unto him in Jerusalem; Shammuah, and Shobab, and Nathan, and Solomon,** v.15. **Ibhar also, and Elishua** (or Elishama, 1 Chron. 3, 6), **and Nepheg, and Jephia,** v.16. **and Elishama, and Eliada** (or Beeliada, 1 Chron. 14, 7), **and Eliphalet.** Thus God was with David and established his rule, for under His blessing alone true progress is possible.

TWO VICTORIES OF DAVID OVER THE PHILISTINES. — V.17. **But when the Philistines heard that they,** the people of Israel, **had anointed David king over Israel, all the Philistines,** all the armies of the confederate city-states, **came up to seek David,** marching up from the lowlands, where they had mobilized their forces, to the highlands of Judah, to attack and subdue this new king before he had become too strong. **And David heard of it, and went down,** from his palace, **to the hold,** the citadel of Mount Zion, where he could make preparations for either an offensive or a defensive campaign.

V.18. **The Philistines also came and spread themselves in,** occupied and used for their camp, **the Valley of Rephaim,** a fruitful plain southwest of Jerusalem, well suited for military maneuvers. V.19. **And David enquired of the Lord,** in the usual manner, by means of the Urim and Thummim, Ex. 28, 30, **saying, Shall I go up to the Philistines,** venture to attack them? **Wilt Thou deliver them in to mine hand? And the Lord said unto David, Go up; for I will doubtless deliver the Philistines in to thine hand.** V.20. **And David came to Baal-perazim. And David smote them there,** in a sudden, violent attack, **and said, The Lord hath broken forth upon mine enemies before me as the breach of waters,** as when a strong torrent breaks down all obstructions and sweeps everything before it. **Therefore he called the name of that place Baal-perazim** (plain of breaches). V.21. **And there they,** the Philistines, **left their images,** the figures of their idols, which they had taken along to assure them the victory. **And David and his men burned them.** Thus the disgrace of the capture of the Ark of the Covenant by the Philistines was avenged. V.22. **And the Philistines came up yet again,** venturing a second campaign in their anxiety to regain their power over Israel, **and spread themselves in the Valley of Rephaim,** as upon the first invasion. V.23. **And when David enquired of the Lord,** as before, **he said, Thou shalt not go up,** not in a direct attack in the front; **but fetch a compass behind them,** make a wide detour around to their rear, **and come upon them over against the mulberry-trees,** the baca-trees, small, shrublike trees which exude sap like tears when their twigs or leaves are bruised. V.24. **And let it be, when thou hearest the sound of a going,** as of an advancing army, **in the tops of the mulberry-trees,** they being moved as by a strong wind, while there was no mind blowing, **that then thou shalt bestir thyself,** be sharp, rush quickly to the attack; **for then shall the Lord go out before thee,** with His own invincible army, **to smite the host of the Philistines.** V.25. **And David did so, as the Lord had commanded him, and smote the Philistines from Geba,** northwest of Jerusalem, **until thou come to Gazer,** on the northern edge of the Philistine plain. It was the Lord who gave the enemies into the hands of David. Note: David is a type of Christ. Those who accept Him as their King are assured of His blessing. But all the kings and nations that rebel against His rule will not continue. The King of Grace blesses, strengthens, and protects His kingdom on earth.

# 38

# 2 Samuel 6

**T**he Ark Brought to Jerusalem.
THE FIRST ATTEMPT ENDS SADLY. — V.1. **Again, David gathered together all the chosen men of Israel,** the captains and leaders of the army, together with the best soldiers of the nation, **thirty thousand.** V.2. **And David arose and went with all the people that were with him, from Baale of Judah,** to Kirjath-baal or Kirjath-jearim, **to bring up from thence the ark of God,** which had been in the house of Abinadab some seventy years, since the time that the Philistines had returned this trophy, 1 Sam. 7, **whose name is called by the name of the Lord of hosts that dwelleth between the cherubim;** for at the ark, before the ark, the name of Jehovah Sabaoth, who appeared over the cover of the ark, between the cherubim on the mercy-seat, was invoked. V.3. **And they set the ark of God,** literally, "let it ride," **upon a new cart, and brought it out of the house of Abinadab that was in Gibeah,** on the hill; **and Uzzah and Ahio, the sons of Abinadab,** here probably in the sense of grandsons of Abinadab, and sons of Eleazar, who had been the first

guardian of the ark, **drave the new cart.** Strictly speaking, this mode of transporting the ark did not agree with the legal requirement, which demanded that the ark should always be carried by Levitical priests, Num. 7, 9. V.4. **And they brought it out of the house of Abinadab which was at Gibeah,** on the hill, **accompanying the ark of God,** the two men acting as guardians; **and Ahio went before the ark,** while Uzzah walked along at the side of the cart. V.5. **And David and all the house of Israel,** the entire assembled multitude, **played before the Lord, in His honor, on all manner of instruments made of fir-wood,** with all their might, and with songs, 1 Chron. 13, 8, **even on harps,** the Jewish zithers, **and on psalteries,** small harps held in the hand, **and on timbrels,** tabrets or hand-drums, **and on cornets,** sistrums, instruments which gave forth a musical sound when shaken in time with the rest of the music, **and on cymbals,** the well-known metal plates used to this day. V.6. **And when they came to Nachon's threshing-floor,** a permanent floor along the road leading to Jerusalem, probably covered with a roof, **Uzzah put forth his hand to the ark of God and took hold of it, for the oxen shook it;** in stepping to the side of the road or in slipping they jostled the ark, so that it seemed about to fall off. V.7. **And the anger of the Lord was kindled against Uzzah,** for the unauthorized touching of the ark, as of the throne of God's glory in the midst of Israel, was a profanation of the Lord's majesty; **and God smote him there for his error,** for his rash mistake in touching the ark; **and there he died by the ark of God,** he was struck down immediately. V.8. **And David was displeased,** becoming angry that his undertaking had resulted in such a misfortune, **because the Lord had made a breach upon Uzzah,** by inflicting this stroke; **and he called**

**the name of the place Perez-uzzah** (the breach of Uzzah) **to this day.** V.9. **And David was afraid of the Lord that day,** the anger over his misfortune gradually turned to apprehension and then to fear, as he considered that his disregard of the Lord's command about transporting the ark had evidently been the cause of the unfortunate happening, **and said, How shall the ark of the Lord come to me?** David felt that he was guilty before the Lord and unworthy of His presence. V.10. **So David would not remove the ark of the Lord unto him in to the city of David,** fearing that misfortune might strike his entire family if he proceeded with his plan; **but David carried it aside into the house of Obed-edom the Gittite,** who hailed from Gath-Rimmon, the Levitical city in Dan, a musician and also a porter at the Sanctuary in Jerusalem. V.11. **And the ark of the Lord continued in the house of Obed-edom, the Gittite, three months; and the Lord blessed Obed-edom and all his household.** To the believers of the New Testament the most holy thing is God's Word and Sacrament, for where the means of grace are administered, there the Triune God dwells. To the believing Christians the Word of God is a savor of life unto life, but to those who despise His grace it is a savor of death unto death.

THE SECOND ATTEMPT SUCCESSFUL. — V.12. **And it was told King David, saying, the Lord hath blessed the house of Obed-edom, and all that pertaineth unto him, because of the ark of God.** So the mere presence of the ark did not bring misfortune, as David had feared. All depended, rather, upon one's attitude toward the Lord, whether that was one of rash presumption or of humble faith. **So David went and brought up the ark of God from the house of Obed-edom in to the city of David,** where he had prepared a place and pitched a tent for it, 1 Chron. 15, 1, **with gladness,** with festival joy, in solemn procession. V.13. **And it was so that, when they that bare the ark of the Lord,** for David did not repeat his first mistake of transporting it on a cart, **had gone six paces, he sacrificed oxen and fatlings,** literally, "he caused to be sacrificed an ox and a fat calf," in order to consecrate the procession, which had started so auspiciously. V.14. **And David,** when the procession moved on, **danced before the Lord with all his might,** in an ecstasy of holy joy; **and David was girded with a linen ephod,** a copy of those worn by the priests, for David, as the head of a nation of priests, wore this garment in honor of Jehovah. V.15. **So David and all the house of Israel brought up the ark of the Lord with shouting,** amid the joyful acclamation of the people, **and with the sound of the trumpet,** used on all festive occasions. V.16. **And as the ark of the Lord came in to the City of David, Michal, Saul's daughter,** showing the characteristics of her father rather than those of her husband, **looked through a window,** for she had probably disdained to mingle with the common people, **and saw King David leaping and dancing before the Lord,** placing himself on a level with the multitude; **and she despised him in her heart,** considering his behavior unseemly and unbecoming his royal dignity. V.17. **And they brought in the ark of the Lord, and set it in his place,** in a space marked off as particularly holy, **in the midst of the tabernacle that David had pitched for it,** a large tent with costly curtains. **And David offered burnt offerings and peace-offerings before the Lord,** preparing for the sacrificial meal which was then celebrated. V.18. **And as soon as David had made an end of offering burnt offerings and peace-offerings, he blessed the people in the name of the Lord of hosts,** not with the blessing of Aaron, which pertained to the priests only, but in an address in which he called down upon them the blessings of Jehovah. V.19. **And,** after the ceremony of dedication, **he dealt among all the people, even among the whole multitude of Israel, as well to the women as men, to every one a cake of bread,** like those baked for sacrificial meals, Ex. 29, 23; Lev. 8, 24. 25, **and a good piece of flesh,** either a slab of bread or a measure of wine, the word in the original meaning "measure," **and a flagon of wine,** a cake of pressed raisins. **So all the people departed every one to his house,** at the completion of the festival meal. V.20. **Then David,** still filled with elation over the success of his undertaking, **returned to bless his household,** as he had blessed the entire assembly **And Michal, the daughter of Saul,** still under the influence of her feeling of disgust, **came out to meet David and said, How glorious was the king of Israel to-day,** emphasizing his title in bitter irony, **who uncovered himself to-day in the eyes of the handmaids of his servants,** degrading himself by exchanging his long royal garments for the light and comparatively short priestly dress, **as one of the vain fellows shamelessly uncovereth himself!** She accused him of forgetting his royal dignity and acting the buffoon, the common street-dancer. V.21. **And David said unto Michal,** in a gentle, but very effective reproof of her pride, **It was before the Lord, which chose me before thy father and before all his house,** the sons who might have been his successors, **to appoint me ruler over the people of the Lord, over Israel.** Saul had been rejected by God on account of his pride, and here the same ugly trait showed in his daughter. But David had been placed ahead of Saul and his own family, hence he adds: **Therefore will I play before the Lord,** willing to abase himself in the presence of Jehovah.

V.22. **And I will yet be more vile than thus,** ready to bear still greater contempt on the part of men, **and will be base in mine own sight; and of the maid-servants which thou hast spoken of, of them shall I be had in honor,** fully satisfied with the homage given him by the lowest in the nation. He that humbleth himself shall be exalted. V.23. **Therefore,** because she had exhibited such unwarranted pride, **Michal, the daughter of Saul, had no child unto the day of her death,** one of the severest punishments known in the Old Testament. Like David and the children of Israel, the believers rejoice in the Lord and in His Word and gladly sing praises to Him, nor will they be deterred by the contempt of the world.

# 39

## 2 Samuel 7

**T**he Promise of the Messiah.

THE NEWS ANNOUNCED TO DAVID. — V.1. **And it came to pass, when the king sat in his house,** an expression referring to his permanent abode after having attended to all the external affairs of the kingdom, **and the Lord had given him rest round about from all his enemies,** all those nations which still felt strong enough to dispute the growing power of Israel having been vanquished, v.2. **that the king said unto Nathan, the prophet,** whom he regarded highly as a confidential adviser, **See, now, I dwell in an house of cedar,** in a fine palace, **but the ark of God dwelleth within curtains.** Even though David had provided a tabernacle in his city which consisted of very fine and costly curtains, like those of the first Tabernacle, yet the contrast was too obvious and too incongruous; it did not seem right and fitting to David that he should have a finer palace than that used for housing the ark. V.3. **And Nathan,** understanding the suggestion of the king and approving his intention, **said to the king, Go, do all that is in thine heart,** all that David had resolved upon;

**for the Lord is with thee.** This approval of David's purpose, however, came out of Nathan's own mind, not by divine revelation. V.4. **And it came to pass that night that the word of the Lord came unto Nathan, saying,** v.5. **Go and tell My servant David,** an honoring designation for the king, **Thus saith the Lord, Shalt thou build Me an house for Me to dwell in?** The question implies, of course, a very decided denial of his request, a rejection of his proposal to build a temple. V.6. **Whereas I have not dwelt in any house,** any permanent building, **since the time that I brought up the children of Israel out of Egypt, even to this day, but have walked in a tent and in a tabernacle,** literally, "I was a wanderer in tent and dwelling-place"; for even after the children of Israel had reached Canaan, the tent had been moved from Gilgal to Shiloh, and then to the hill between Gibeah and Gibeon. The Tabernacle, the structure as built by Moses, Ex. 35, 11, had been Jehovah's dwelling-place. V.7. **In all the places wherein I have walked with all the children of Israel, spake I a word with any of the tribes of Israel, whom I commanded to feed My people Israel, saying, Why build ye not Me an house of cedar?** Neither during the desert journey, nor during the entire period of the Judges, when the leadership passed from one tribe of the more important ones to another, had the Lord ever commanded the children of Israel to build Him a permanent and costly sanctuary, worthy of His glory. V.8. **Now, therefore, so shalt thou say unto My servant David, Thus saith the Lord of hosts,** Jehovah Sabaoth, the King of the whole earth, **I took thee from the sheepcote,** from the meadows where the sheep were pastured, **from following the sheep, to be ruler over My people, over Israel.** That was an act of God's merciful favor. V.9. **And I was with**

**thee whithersoever thou wentest,** David had always been sure of the merciful presence of Jehovah, even during the years when Saul persecuted him, **and have cut off all thine enemies out of thy sight,** from before thy face, **and have made thee a great name like unto the name of the great men that are in the earth;** for David's victories had brought him into prominent attention in all the surrounding nations. Of so much concerning his outward success Nathan was to remind David first, of the fact that he owed his position and all his success to the Lord alone. V.10. **Moreover, I will appoint a place for My people Israel and will plant them,** rather, "I have established and I have planted," **that they may dwell in a place of their own and move no more,** not be troubled, distressed, and driven from one place to another; **neither shall the children of wickedness afflict them any more, as beforetime,** in the time of the Egyptian oppression, v.11. **and as since the time that I commanded judges to be over My people Israel, and have caused thee to rest from all thine enemies.** The former days of slavery and tribulation were to return no more. Those were the blessings which the Lord had provided for the people as such. And now comes the most wonderful promise of all, one affecting both king and people to the most remote descendants. **Also the Lord telleth thee that he will make thee an house,** literally, "And there announces to thee Jehovah that a house will make to thee Jehovah," a very solemn announcement preparing for the prophecy proper. V.12. **And when thy days be fulfilled and thou shalt sleep with thy fathers,** after David would have been laid to rest in the hope of a glorious resurrection to eternal life, **I will set up thy Seed after thee,** one of David's descendants, **which shall proceed out of thy bowels,** as a true descendant according to the flesh, **and I will establish His kingdom,** confirm the royal office in His case. V.13. **He shall build an house for My name,** to the name of Jehovah, **and I will stablish the throne of His kingdom forever.** The descendant of David to whom this prophecy looked forward was to be confirmed in regal honor and dignity in a most singular way, in a kingdom which would have everlasting duration. His building of a house to Jehovah, moreover, would be the same as that of Jehovah making a house to Himself, v.11. The two statements refer to the same event. The relation between Jehovah and this singular descendant of David is now described in detail. V.14. **I will be His Father, and He shall be My Son. If he commit iniquity,** literally, "whom, if He transgresses," **I will chasten Him with the rod of men and with the stripes of the children of men.** That this is not spoken of Solomon, as most modern commentators will have it, may be seen from the fact that Solomon was a mere man, and there would have been nothing unusual in his being punished for any transgressions after the manner of men. This singular descendant of David, if found guilty of the sins of men, the implication being that the latter would be imputed to Him, would have to bear the penalty of a sinner. V.15. **But my mercy shall not depart away from Him, as I took it from Saul, whom I put away before thee,** "from before thy face." The descendant of David to whom the Lord refers would not experience the rejection which struck Saul, because He would not become guilty of such disobedience to Jehovah. V.16. **And thine house and thy kingdom,** the royal power in lineal descendants of David, **shall be established forever before thee; thy throne shall be established forever.** The constant repetition of the phrase "forever, for eternity," again forces the conclusion that we must look beyond Solomon, to the eternal existence of the Son here concerned, to One who is Himself possessor of eternal life and of a kingdom which shall never have an end. This, of course, may rightly be said only of Christ, for it was in His case alone that there was so complete an identification with the sons of men as to make the expression possible: "He was made sin for us," 2 Cor. 5, 21. V.17. **According to all these words and according to all this vision, so did Nathan speak unto David.** The temple here spoken of is that of the Christian Church, the communion of saints, which is the habitation of God in the Spirit. Christ is the Lord, and the believers cling to this Head in the Kingdom which shall last through all eternity.

DAVID'S PRAYER OF THANKSGIVING. — V.18. **Then went King David in and sat before the Lord,** he spent some time in the tent where the ark of the Lord's presence was; for it took him a long while to become familiar with the miraculous contents of the message announced to him; **and he said, Who am I, O Lord God, and what is my house,** his entire family, **that thou hast brought me hitherto?** He humbly acknowledged that all the blessings and benefits bestowed upon him by the Lord were expressions of His free love and mercy. V.19. **And this,** the wonderful external favors, **was yet a small thing in Thy sight, O Lord God; but Thou hast spoken also of thy servant's house for a great while to come. And is this the manner of man, O Lord God?** literally, "And this is the law of the man, namely, Lord Jehovah." David not only understood that the Messianic prophecy was given to his family, that the eternal establishment of his house and kingdom, in the person of Messiah, was included in the prophecy which had come to him, but it was also clear to him that this singular descendant would, in His person, combine two natures, the human and the divine. Messiah, the true man, would at the same time be the Lord Jehovah. V.20. **And what can David say more unto Thee?** Human language is inadequate to convey the gratitude which filled his heart. **For Thou, Lord God, knowest Thy servant.** V.21. **For Thy word's sake,** the promise transmitted to him by Nathan, **and according to Thine own heart,** out of free grace and mercy, **hast thou done all these great things,** for David even now considered the promises fulfilled, **to make thy servant know them.** V.22. **Wherefore Thou art great, O Lord God,** in the revelation of His grace toward all mankind; **for there is none like Thee, neither is there any God beside Thee, according to all that we have heard with our ears,** namely, of the great deeds whereby in the past God had revealed Himself to His people as such a God. V.23. **And what one nation in the earth is like thy people, even like Israel,** an emphatic statement of the singular position Israel enjoyed in the grace of Jehovah, **whom God went to redeem for a people to Himself, and to make Him a name, and to do for you great things and terrible, for Thy land, before thy people, which Thou redeemedst to Thee from Egypt, from the nations and their gods?** it is a short review of all the great and mighty wonders with which God had visited His people since He had chosen them for His own, down to the time when He had driven out the heathen of Canaan and their idols before Israel's victorious armies. V.24. **For Thou hast confirmed to Thyself thy people Israel to be a people unto Thee forever; and Thou, Lord, art become their God.** The Lord's free grace had been the source of the covenant which existed, and Israel's obedience was the condition of the continuance of this relation. V.25. **And now, O Lord God, the word that Thou hast spoken concerning**

**Thy servant,** the special Messianic promise, **and concerning his house, establish it forever, as Thou hast said,** so that it would truly be fulfilled. V.26. **And let Thy name be magnified forever, saying, The Lord of hosts is the God over Israel,** the almighty God, who rules heaven and earth, is the Defender and Protector of Israel. **And let the house of Thy servant David be established before Thee.** V.27. **For Thou, O Lord of hosts, God of Israel, hast revealed to thy servant,** literally, "hast uncovered the ear," by the announcement of Nathan, **saying, I will build Thee an house; therefore hath thy servant found in his heart,** gained the courage, **to pray this prayer unto Thee;** for out of the fullness of the heart his mouth spoke. V.28. **And now, O Lord God, Thou art that God,** the one true God, **and Thy words be true, and Thou hast promised this goodness unto thy servant.** V.29. **Therefore, now, let it please Thee to bless,** rather, begin to bless, **the house of thy servant, that it may continue for ever before Thee;** having determined upon His course, the Lord is begged to set Himself to the fulfillment of His promise, to take it in hand speedily; **for Thou, O Lord, hast spoken it, and with Thy blessing let the house of thy servant be blessed forever.** David completes his prayer of thanksgiving by expressing his confident hope, his firm trust, that the word of the Lord will certainly come to pass. True faith clings to the promises of God and applies them to ourselves.

# 40

## 2 Samuel 8

David's Wars and Victories.

VICTORIES OVER VARIOUS NATIONS. — V.1. **And after this it came to pass that David smote the Philistines and subdued them,** brought them completely into his power. **And David took Metheg-ammah out of the hand of the Philistines,** literally, "the bridle of the mother," of the chief city, the figurative saying being understood of the complete yielding to the control of another. V.2. **And he smote Moab,** east and southeast of the Dead Sea, **and measured them with a line, casting them down to the ground; even with two lines measured he to put to death, and with one full line to keep alive.** It was a very severe punishment which was here meted out to the Moabites, since their soldiers were compelled to lie down on the ground, two thirds of them being measured for death and one-third for life. **And so the Moabites,** with only a third of their warriors remaining, **became David's servants and brought gifts,** that is, paid tribute-money. V.3. **David smote also Hadadezer, the son of Rehob, king of Zobah,** a district of Syria, **as he went**

**to recover his border at the river Euphrates;** for Saul had already successfully fought against this nation, 1 Sam. 14, 47. When Hadadezer attempted to recover his shattered power on the Euphrates, David completed the work begun by Saul and brought the entire territory into subjection to him. V.4. **And David took from him a thousand chariots and seven hundred horsemen** (some read seven thousand, 1 Chron. 18, 4) **and twenty thousand footmen. And David houghed all the chariot horses,** by cutting the sinews of their hind feet, **but reserved of them for an hundred chariots,** probably to display them in a triumphal procession or for the use of his guard. V.5. **And when the Syrians of Damascus came to succor Hadadezer, king of Zobah, David slew of the Syrians,** or, Arameans, **two and twenty thousand men.** V.6. **Then David put garrisons in Syria of Damascus,** in the country of the Arameans, whose capital was Damascus, a city still situated in its ancient location on the Pharpar River and on the great caravan route between Central Asia and the Mediterranean: **and the Syrians became servants to David,** tributary to Israel, **and brought gifts. And the Lord preserved David whithersoever he went;** his success was due entirely to the blessing of Jehovah. V.7. **And David took the shields of gold that were on the servants of Hadadezer,** for the officers of this king could afford such costly weapons, **and brought them to Jerusalem,** as a part of the rich booty made in this war. V.8. **And from Betah and from Berothai, cities of Hadadezer, King David took exceeding much brass,** for it seems that there were very productive copper-mines in this part of Syria. Note: If a believer undertakes his work in the fear of God and to His glory, the Lord will grant His blessing according to His promise.

DAVID'S PRESTIGE RECOGNIZED. — V.9. **When Toi, king of Hamath,** a district of Syria on the Orontes River, **heard that David had smitten all the host of Hadadezer, v.10. then Toi sent Joram, his son** (also known as Hadoram), **unto King David, to salute him,** with the usual greetings of peace, **and to bless him, because he had fought against Hadadezer and smitten him; for Hadadezer had wars with Toi,** he had been waging continual war with Toi with the purpose of subduing his land. David's victory had freed him from a dangerous enemy, and therefore Toi wisely sought an alliance with the powerful victor. **And Joram brought with him vessels of silver and vessels of gold and vessels of brass,** gifts almost like those of a tributary king, v.11. **which also,** like the metal brought as booty from the Syrian war, **King David did dedicate unto the Lord,** placing them into the treasury of the Tabernacle, **with the silver and gold that he had dedicated of all nations which he subdued,** including the Ammonites, the Amalekites, and the Edomites; v.12. **of Syria, and of Moab, and of the children of Ammon, and of the Philistines, and of Amalek, and of the spoil of Hadadezer, son of Rehob, king of Zobah. V.13. And David gat him a name,** he gained renown, his fame spread far and wide, when **he returned from smiting of the Syrians in the Valley of Salt, being eighteen thousand men,** namely, of the Edomites. It seems that the children of Edom took the opportunity offered by David's absence in the Syrian country to make an attack on Southern Canaan. They had advanced to the Southern end of the Dead Sea when the army of David, just back from the Syrian war, fell upon them with such disastrous results. V.14. **And he put garrisons in Edom; through out all Edom put he garrisons,** the character of the country demanding such a complete garrisoning, **and**

**all they of Edom became David's servants,** tributary vassals. **And the lord preserved David whithersoever he went;** it was due to God's protection, to his blessing, that David was so successful in his campaign. V.15. **And David reigned over all Israel,** the reunited nation. **And David,** taking advantage of the peaceful conditions following the conquest of the various nations, **executed judgment and justice unto all his people;** he built up his influence among his own people by a wise and just rule, ordering and administering the affairs of the nation with great care. V.16. **And Joab, the son of Zeruiah,** was over the host, had supreme command of the army; and Jehoshaphat, the son of Ahilud, **was recorder,** chronicler and preserver of the most important happenings in the kingdom; v.17. **and Zadok, the son of Ahitub,** of the line of Eleazar, Aaron's son, **and Ahimelech, the son of Abiathar,** of the line of Eli, **were the priests,** that is, the high priests, one probably officiating at the Tabernacle on the heights of Gibeon, 1 Chron. 16. 39, the other in the tent at Jerusalem; **and Seraiah was the scribe,** secretary of state; v.18. **and Benaiah, the son of Jehoiada, was over both the Cherethites and the Pelethites,** the king's body-guard, who not only carried out the royal orders, but also executed the royal death sentences, being executioners and runners; **and David's sons were chief rulers,** serving as confidential counselors. Like David, all believers labor and battle during their whole life for the honor of the Lord, serve Him with body and soul, and willingly sacrifice of the blessing which the Lord has given them.

# 41

## 2 Samuel 9

**D**avid's Kindness to Mephibosheth.
DAVID RECEIVES MEPHIBOSHETH GRACIOUSLY.
— V.1. **And David said,** at the time when his victories had given him comparative peace for the time being, **Is there yet any that is left of the house of Saul,** any descendant of his, any member of his family, **that I may show him kindness for Jonathan's sake?** The word here used applies to such kindness as the Lord shows, which is an outflow of the kindness and love of God living in the hearts of the believers. His question implies the answer: There certainly must be some relative living, in whose case I may fulfill my promise to Jonathan, 1 Sam. 20, 14. 15. V.2. **And there was of the house of Saul a servant whose name was Ziba,** probably known to some of David's men and hunted up by them for the purpose of obtaining the information required by the king. **And when they had called him unto David, the king said unto him, Art thou Ziba? And he said, thy servant is he.** V.3. **And the king said, Is there not yet any of the house of Saul that I may show the kindness of God unto him?** David felt under

obligations that, as he had received the mercy of the Lord, so he would pass on its kindness even to the descendants of the man who had pursued him for years. **And Ziba said unto the king, Jonathan hath yet a son, which is lame on his feet,** chap. 4, 4. V.4. **And the king said unto him, Where is he? And Ziba said unto the king, Behold, he is in the house of Machir, the son of Ammiel, in Lodebar.** Machir evidently was a well-to-do and influential man, living on the east side of Jordan, near Mahanaim and Rabboth-Ammon, who had offered his house as a place of refuge to the poor cripple. V.5. **Then King David sent and fetched him out of the house of Machir, the son of Ammiel, from Lodebar.** He lost no time in fulfilling his promise and in showing mercy, for postponing a good work is often equivalent to abandoning it altogether. V.6. **Now, when Mephibosheth** (or, Meribbaal, 1 Chron. 8, 34), **the son of Jonathan, the son of Saul, was come unto David, he fell on his face and did reverence,** acknowledging him as king with tokens of fear. **And David said, Mephibosheth! And he answered, Behold thy servant!** V.7. **And David said unto him, fear not,** he was to have no apprehension of losing his life, according to the custom of Oriental monarchs of putting all the members of the former dynasty to death; **for I will surely show thee kindness for Jonathan, thy father's sake, and will restore thee all the land of Saul, thy father,** which had either passed into the possession of the crown or into that of remote kinsmen of Saul; **and thou shalt eat bread at my table continually,** receive his sustenance from the king's bounty. This threefold promise was intended fully to reassure Mephibosheth, whose great misfortunes, the loss of his parents, his lameness, and his poverty, cast a shadow upon his whole life. V.8. **And he,** Mephibosheth, **bowed himself,** in

245

grateful appreciation of the king's kindness, **and said,** with words wherein he confessed himself unworthy of such great goodness, **what is thy servant that thou shouldest look upon such a dead dog as I am?** The comparison, as in 1 Sam. 24, 14, is intended to convey the feeling of utter worthlessness, of despicable lowliness. David's forbearance and love, the eager zeal with which he entered upon the performance of good works, are an example to all believers.

DAVID GIVES ORDERS FOB MEPHIBOSHETH'S CARE. — V.9. **Then the king called to Ziba, Saul's servant,** who may have resided upon the property of the family of Saul at Gibeah as steward, **and said unto him, I have given unto thy master's son all that pertained to Saul and to all his house,** thereby giving him all the rights of the sole heir. V.10. **Thou, therefore, and thy sons and thy servants shall till the land for him, and thou shalt bring in the fruits,** have entire charge of the farm-lands and be responsible for the crop, **that thy master's son may have food to eat,** that his house or family might be taken care of; **but Mephibosheth, thy master's son, shall eat bread alway at my table,** he personally was to have this honor of dining daily at the king's table. **Now, Ziba had fifteen sons and twenty servants,** he was therefore in a position to manage so large an estate as that hereby transferred to Mephibosheth. V.11. **Then said Ziba unto the king, According to all that my lord the king hath commanded his servant, so shall thy servant do. As for Mephibosheth, said the king, he shall eat at my table as one of the king's sons.** Ziba repeated the exact words of the king, to show his full agreement and ready obedience. He thought it expedient to show himself as tractable as possible, in order to get into David's good graces. V.12. **And Mephibosheth had a young son, whose name was**

**Micha,** 1 Chron. 8, 34. **And all that dwelt in the house of Ziba were servants unto Mephibosheth,** they took care of the estate at Gibeah, according to David's orders. V.13. **So Mephibosheth dwelt in Jerusalem; for he did eat continually at the king's table,** as David had arranged, a companion of the royal family in the house and at the table; **and was lame on both his feet.** David's manner of acting was noble, truly royal in showing such kindness to Mephibosheth, a type of the loving-kindness and tender mercies of his great descendant, Jesus Christ, in His care for all those who are poor, miserable, and heavy laden.

# 42

# 2 Samuel 10

The Syro-Ammonite War.

DAVID'S SERVANTS SHAMEFULLY TREATED. —
V.1. **And it came to pass after this that the king of the children of Ammon died, and Hanun, his son, reigned in his stead. V.2. Then said David, I will show kindness unto Hanun, the son of Nahash, as his father showed kindness unto me.** Nahash had been defeated by Saul at Jabesh, 1 Sam. 11, but had maintained a friendly attitude toward David, probably also by rendering him some form of assistance during the years of his persecution. **And David sent to comfort him by the hand of his servants for his father,** he dispatched an embassy to express his sympathy at the bereavement of Hanun. **And David's servants came in to the land of the children of Ammon,** as David supposed, to a nation friendly to Israel under his reign. V.3. **And the princes of the children of Ammon said unto Hanun, their lord, Thinkest thou that David doth honor thy father,** literally, "Is David in thine eyes an honorer of thy father," **that he hath sent comforters unto thee? Hath not David**

**rather sent his servants unto thee to search the city, and to spy it out, and to overthrow it?** The suggestion that the messengers of David were spies was made with the purpose of causing Hanun to adopt a hostile attitude toward David which would be a challenge to war, for the Ammonites now felt themselves strong enough again to try conclusions with Israel. V.4. **Wherefore Hanun,** listening to the counsel of his princes, especially as this implied a criticism of his carelessness, **took David's servants and shaved off the one half of their beards,** the one side, one of the grossest insults that can be offered an Oriental, who considers his beard the sign of manly dignity and freedom, **and cut off their garments in the middle, even to their buttocks,** thus exposing them before the eyes of all men, **and sent them away,** heaped with this double insult and disgrace. V.5. **When they told it unto David,** when the news of this shameful treatment came to him, **he sent to meet them, because the men were greatly ashamed,** disgrace had been heaped upon them; **and the king said, Tarry at Jericho,** the district where that city had formerly stood, **until your beards be grown, and then return.** He himself did not want to witness their shame. To seek occasion for wars, to provoke quarrels, is a great wrong, which has often been punished by the Lord with great severity.

THE FIRST DEFEAT OF THE ENEMIES. — V.6. **And when the children of Ammon saw that they stank before David,** that they had become hateful to him 1 Sam. 13, 4, **the children of Ammon sent and hired the Syrians of Beth-rehob, and the Syrians of Zoba,** chap. 8, 3. 5, **twenty thousand footmen, and of King Maacah,** on the northern border of Bashan, **a thousand men, and of Ishtob,** of the men of Tob, a district east or northeast of the Ammonite territory, **twelve thousand**

**men.** It was a mighty army of infantry, cavalry, and mar-chariots. V.7. **And when David heard of it, he sent Joab and all the host of the mighty men,** literally, "the whole host, the mighty men," the veterans of the many wars in which David had engaged. V.8. **And the children of Ammon came out,** namely, from the strong fortifications of their capital city, **and put the battle in array at the entering in of the gate,** they formed their battle-front immediately before the city; **and the Syrians of Zoba, and of Rehob, and Ishtob, and Maacah,** their auxiliaries or allies, **were by themselves in the field,** in the broad Plain of Medeba, the two armies preferring to maneuver separately. V.9. **When Joab saw that the front of the battle was against him before and behind,** that he could be attacked by the Syrians in the front, by the Ammonites in the rear, **he chose of all the choice men of Israel,** the best men of his veteran army, **and put them in array against the Syrians,** whom he evidently considered the more dangerous enemies; v.10. **and the rest of the people he delivered in to the hand of Abishai, his brother, that he might put them in array against the children of Ammon.** Thus Joab was covered in his rear when he attacked the Syrians and might have support if he needed it. V.11. **And he said, if the Syrians be too strong for me,** for he intended to attack and defeat the Syrians first, **then thou shalt help me; but if the children of Ammon be too strong for thee, then I will come and help thee.** All depended upon the quickness and the force of the double blow as Joab had planned it. V.12. **Be of good courage,** Abishai himself should be of a fearless temper of mind, **and let us play the men for our people,** true leaders in warlike action, **and for the cities of our God,** for the cities of Israel, for which they were contending, were really the gift of God to His people; **and the Lord do that**

**which seemeth Him good.** "These words express trust in God combined with unconditional submission," V.13. **And Joab drew nigh, and the people that were with him, unto the battle against the Syrians,** in a quick and vigorous attack against their well-disciplined forges; **and they fled before him,** their lines broke at the first onslaught. V.14. **And when the children of Ammon saw that the Syrians were fled, then fled they also before Abishai, and entered in to the city,** they retired into their fortifications. **So Joab returned from the children of Ammon, and came to Jerusalem.** His was a brilliant exploit, but not a decisive defeat of the Syrians. The siege of Rabbah he did not undertake, either because the season was too far advanced, or because he did not have the materials for such a siege. Both Joab and Abishai, trusting in the God of Israel, had done their duty, for a just war may well be carried on by believers.

THE FINAL DEFEAT of THE SYRIANS. — V.15. **And when the Syrians saw that they were smitten before Israel,** in the battle near Rabbah, **they gathered themselves together,** anxious to wipe out the disgrace of their defeat. V.16. **And Hadarezer,** the mightiest Syrian king, **sent, and brought out the Syrians that were beyond the river,** in Mesopotamia: **and they came to Helam,** in the neighborhood of Hamath: **and Shobach, the captain of the host of Hadarezer, went before them.** V.17. **And when it was told David, he gathered all Israel together,** all the men that were trained for warfare, **and passed over Jordan, and came to Helam.** The importance which David attached to this campaign is seen from the fact that he took command in person, for he had lost none of his military ability. **And the Syrians set themselves in array against David and fought with him.** V.18. **And the Syrians**

**fled before Israel,** unable to withstand the fury of their attack; **and David slew the men of seven hundred chariots of the Syrians, and forty thousand horsemen, and smote Shobach, the captain of their host, who died there,** he was so severely wounded that he did not survive the battle. V.19. **And when all the kings that were servants,** vassals, **to Hadarezer saw that they were smitten before Israel, they made peace with Israel and served them,** became tributary to them together with their former lord. **So the Syrians feared to help the children of Ammon any more.** "Nothing is here said of the wars with Damascus and Edom, to which Joab turned in the south, while David was gaining his victories in the north, because the narrative is here occupied with the fortunes of Rabbah only because of their connection with those of Uriah." (Lange.) Thus Jehovah crowns the work, the battle of those who trust in Him with His blessing and good fortune. The Ammonites experienced what many others have since found out, namely, that those who begin a war without cause will in the end have the greatest misfortune on account of their crime.

# 43

# 2 Samuel 11

**D**avid's Double Transgression.
DAVID'S ADULTERY. — V.1. **And it came to pass, after the year was expired,** literally, "at the return of the year," when spring set in, when the close of the rainy season made operations in the field possible, **at the time when kings go forth to battle,** starting out for the season's campaigns, **that David sent Joab and his servants with him and all Israel,** the military chieftains with the entire regular army; **and they destroyed the children of Ammon,** overthrowing their smaller cities, devastating their land, and putting the inhabitants to death, **and besieged Rabbah,** the capital, which was strongly fortified. **But David,** instead of joining his army in the field, **tarried still at Jerusalem,** this life of comparative ease offering the occasion for the transgression: for, as the proverb has it: An idle brain is the devil's workshop. V.2. **And it came to pass in an evening tide that David arose from off his bed,** after the noonday siesta, when the cool of the evening invited people outside, **and walked upon the roof of the king's house,** which was

flat and parapeted, like all the houses of the Orient; **and from the roof,** which offered an all the wider view, since it was on Mount Zion, **he saw a woman washing herself,** taking a bath in the uncovered court of her house; **and the woman was very beautiful to look upon.** There is a warning here to every woman against in tent ional or unintentional exposure, whether at bathing-beaches, in street-dress, or about the house. V.3. **And David,** inflamed with sensual desire, **sent and enquired after the woman,** made inquiry concerning her person and family relation. **And one said, Is not this Bathsheba** (or Bath-shuah. 1 Chron. 3, 5), **the daughter of Eliam,** also known as Ammiel, **the wife of Uriah, the Hittite?** Uriah was one of the heroes in David's army, being at that time in the field with Joab. V.4. **And David sent messengers and took her,** Bathsheba evidently coming and submitting to his demands without opposition. **And she came in unto him, and he lay with her; for she was purified from her uncleanness,** literally, "and she cleansed herself from her defilement," this being demanded by the Law, Lev. 15, 18; **and she returned unto her house.** The great sin of adultery she had committed without serious thought, but the act of purification she religiously observed, just as many people living in open transgressions of God's holy Law believe they may salve their consciences by small acts of charity. V.5. **And the woman conceived, and sent and told David, and said, I am with child.** This message was sent with the object of having David find some means of avoiding the consequences of their mutual sin, since, according to the Law, Lev. 20, 10, both of the guilty ones should die. V.6. **And David,** acting upon Bathsheba's hint, **sent to Joab, saying, Send me Uriah, the Hittite. And Joab sent Uriah to David.**

**V.7. And when Uriah was come unto him, David demanded of him how Joab did, and how the people did, and how the war prospered.** Uriah, as one of Joab's officers, could easily give this information. The entire move, of course, was merely a blind, as the sequel shows. **V.8. And David said to Uriah, Go down to thy house and wash thy feet.** It was, apparently, a gracious dismissal, with the suggestion that Uriah should take his rest and refreshment at home. The object was, of course, that Uriah, having been at his house, might pass for the father of the child begotten in adultery. **And Uriah departed out of the king's house, and there followed him a mess of meat from the king.** The present was probably a dish of honor, Esther 2, 18, which he was to enjoy at home, a second inducement to have him visit his house. **V.9. But Uriah,** whether his suspicions had been aroused or not, **slept at the door of the king's house with all the servants of his lord,** in the guard-room with the royal court officials, **and went not down to his house. V.10. And when they had told David, saying, Uriah went not down unto his house, David said unto Uriah,** with a displeasure caused by his growing uneasiness over the frustration of his plans, **Camest thou not from thy journey? Why, then, didst thou not go down unto thine house?** The conduct of Uriah was strange, and not at all in conformity with the manner of the average person. **V.11. And Uriah said unto David, the ark and Israel and Judah abide in tents,** in camp before Rabbah; **and my lord Joab and the servants of my lord are encamped in the open fields,** without the comforts of home, lying on the bare ground; **shall I, then, go into mine house to eat and to drink, and to lie with my wife? As thou livest and as thy soul liveth, I will not do this thing.** It was a solemn explanation and asseveration declaring his inability to meet the king's wishes at this time, under these conditions. V.12. **And David said to Uriah. Tarry here to-day also, and to-morrow I will let thee depart.** He wanted to try once more to gain his object of having Uriah return to his house. **So Uriah abode in Jerusalem that day and the morrow,** waiting to be dismissed to the army. V.13. **And when David had called him,** invited him to partake of a meal at his own table, **he did eat and drink before him; and he,** David, **made him drunk,** hoping that in this condition he would surely pass the night with his wife; **and at even he went out to lie on his bed with the servants of his lord, but went not down to his house.** Even in his befuddled condition his sense of duty or his suspicion of the king's plan kept him from spending the night at home. David's example shows how a person who has fallen into sin will try to hide his disgrace from the eyes of men. God and His will are disregarded entirely. But it is impossible to remove the consequences of sin in this manner, as David was to find out.

DAVID'S MURDER OF URIAH. — V.14. **And it came to pass in the morning that David wrote a letter to Joab and sent it by the hand of Uriah.** His first plan having failed, his sin-darkened heart now made ready to add murder to adultery. V.15. **And he wrote in the letter, saying, set ye Uriah in the forefront of the hottest battle,** opposite the place where the most bitter attack might be expected, **and retire ye from him,** falling away from behind him while he was busily engaged in warding off the blows of the attacking enemies, **that he may be smitten and die.** His own bravery being of a kind to he relied upon at all times, and his retreat cut off, the supposition was that Uriah would surely fall. V.16. **And it came to pass, when Joab observed the city,** literally, "watched, found out the place where the fiercest sallies might be expected," **that he assigned Uriah unto a place where he knew that valiant men were,** namely, on the part of the enemy. V.17. **And the men of the city,** accepting the challenge, **went out and fought with Joab; and there fell some of the people of the servants of David; and Uriah, the Hittite, died also.** Thus Joab carried out the command of the king in permitting a man to be killed whose seemingly accidental death was desired for some special reason. V.18. **Then Joab sent and told David all the things concerning the war,** with a report of this special engagement; v.19. **and charged the messenger, saying, When thou hast made an end of telling the matters of the war unto the king,** the general circumstantial report, v.20. **and if so be that the kings wrath arise and he say unto thee, Wherefore approached ye so nigh unto the city when ye did fight? Knew ye not that they would shoot from the wall?** Joab felt that such a real or simulated outburst of anger on the part of the king might be expected. V.21. **Who smote Abimelech, the son of Jerubbesheth? Did not a woman cast a piece of a millstone upon him from the wall that he died in Thebez?** Cp. Judg. 6, 32; 9, 53. **Why went ye nigh the wall? Then say thou, thy servant Uriah, the Hittite, is dead also.** Joab was sure that this information would have the desired effect in taking away the king's anger. V.22. **So the messenger went, and came and showed David all that Joab had sent him for,** his report being even briefer than that outlined by Joab. V.23. **And the messenger said unto David, Surely The men prevailed against us,** proved too mighty at the point of attack, **and came out unto us into the field,** in a sharp sally, **and we were upon them even unto the entering of the gate,** in repulsing the sally. V.24. **And the shooters,** the archers stationed on the ramparts, **shot from off the wall upon thy servants,** as the pressed so near the gate; **and some of the king's servants be dead, and thy servant Uriah, the Hittite, is dead also.** V.25. **Then David said unto the messenger,** apparently with the quiet of a commander whom such evil news could not disturb in his equanimity and in his certainty of eventual victory, **Thus shalt thou say unto Joab, Let not this thing displease thee, for the sword devoureth one as well as another,** literally, "so and so devours the sword," that is the fortune of war: **make thy battle more strong against the city and overthrow it,** the siege should be pressed until the city was taken; **and encourage thou him,** for the messenger evidently himself was one of the officers in the army. He indicated his confidence that the courage and ability of the soldiers of Joab would surely bring the campaign to a successful close. V.26. **And when the wife of Uriah heard that Uriah, her husband, was dead, she mourned for her husband,** probably the usual seven days, Gen. 50, 10; 1 Sam. 31, 13. V.27. **And when the mourning was past, David,** still with the same passionate desire for the woman as before, **sent and fetched her to his house, and she became his wife, and bare him a son,** the child begotten in adultery. The two guilty ones wanted it to appear that the interval between their marriage and the birth of Bathsheba's child was long enough to make its birth in wedlock seem possible, an evil plan still resorted to by fornicators or adulterers to hide their sin. **But the thing that David had done displeased the Lord.** He took note of the transgression and prepared to punish it in due time. Sins of adultery and murder are of a nature to take faith out of the hearts of the believers and to make them children of wrath and damnation.

# 44

# 2 Samuel 12

**D**avid's Repentance.

NATHAN'S REPROOF AND ITS SUCCESS. — V.1. **And the Lord,** almost a year after the first transgression, **sent Nathan unto David. And he came unto him and said unto him, There were two men in one city, the one rich and the other poor.** Nathan chose the parable in order to bring home his reproof with all the greater force. V.2. **The rich man had exceeding many flocks and herds,** he is purposely represented as possessing all that his heart might desire; v.3. **but the poor man had nothing,** literally, "nothing at all." **save one little ewe lamb,** the only property which his slender means allowed, **which he had bought and nourished up; and it grew up together with him and with his children; it did eat of his own meat,** since he shared even his last morsel with it, **and drank of his own cup, and lay in his bosom,** carefully tended and shielded against all harm and danger, **and was unto him as a daughter.** Note that all the circumstances are pictured in such a manner as to heighten both the pity and the indignation of the hearer. V.4. **And there** came a traveler unto the rich man, and he, the latter, **spared to take of his own flock and of his own herd to dress for the way faring man that was come unto him, but,** in an excess of base selfishness, **took the poor man's lamb and dressed it for the man that was come to him.** V.5. **And David's anger was greatly kindled against the man,** as Nathan had intended for the sake of the effective application of his parable; **and he said to Nathan, as the Lord liveth, the man that hath done this thing shall surely die,** literally, "is a son of death," since his robbery of the one ewe lamb was almost like that of a human being; v.6. **and he shall restore the lamb fourfold,** as the Law required, Ex. 21, 37, **because he did this thing, and because he had no pity.** The parable had been so chosen that David could have no idea of its application to his own crime against Uriah. V.7. **And Nathan said to David, Thou art the man.** The accusation came with all the greater force since David was not aware of the fact that he himself was concerned. The wisdom, tact, and firmness with which Nathan approached the king are truly admirable. **Thus saith the Lord God of Israel, I anointed thee king over Israel,** therefore his crime had been one against the royal office, **and I delivered thee out of the hand of Saul,** an act of divine kindness and grace; v.8. **and I gave thee thy master's house and thy master's wives in to thy bosom,** both the property and the harem of the king being legally given into the hands of his successor, although it does not follow that David actually married Saul's wife, **and gave thee the house of Israel and of Judah;** the entire nation had promised him allegiance, and he might have had his choice of the virgins of the country; **and if that had been too little, I would moreover have given unto thee such and such things;** His bountiful goodness was not yet exhausted. V.9. **Wherefore**

**hast thou despised the commandment of the Lord,** literally, "the word," that is, the law, of God, **to do evil in His sight,** in this double transgression? **Thou hast killed Uriah, the Hittite, with the sword,** in fact, though not in person, **and hast taken his wife to be thy wife,** she who still should have been Uriah's wife now lived in a guilty marriage with David, **and hast slain him with the sword of the children of Ammon,** according to a well-laid plan. V.10. **Now, therefore, the sword shall never depart from thine house,** its bloodiness being evident in the murder of Amnon, the death of Absalom, and the execution of Adonijah; **because thou hast despised Me,** since he who despises God's Word despises Him, **and hast taken the wife of Uriah, the Hittite, to be thy wife.** This was the first punishment. But more was to come. V.11. **Thus saith the Lord, Behold, I will raise up evil against thee out of thine own house,** as a punishment for the sin of adultery, **and I will take thy wives before thine eyes, and give them unto thy neighbor, and he shall lie with thy wives,** in open, incestuous intercourse, **in the sight of this sun.** V.12. **For thou didst it secretly; but I will do this thing before all Israel and before the sun,** in broad daylight, in flagrant shamelessness. Cp. chap. 16, 22. V.13. **And David said unto Nathan,** in full acknowledgment of his sin, without the slightest attempt at excusing himself or depreciating the sin, **I have sinned against the Lord,** His confession is given in only a few words, but the feelings of his heart are expressed in Psalm 51. **And Nathan said unto David, The Lord also hath put away thy sin,** literally, "has caused thy sin to pass over," not to remain before Him, to vanish, to be forgiven; **thou shalt not die,** the punishment which his sin properly merited. V.14. **Howbeit, because by this deed thou hast given great occasion to the**

**enemies of the Lord to blaspheme,** to despise the God of Israel for permitting such sins to be committed, for so they would construe the matter, **the child also that is born unto thee shall surely die,** the fruit of the adulterous union would be destroyed, to show the severity of God's justice upon the transgressors of His Lam. God has no pleasure in the death of the sinner, but wants him to repent and live. Even those who hare fallen into serious sins the Lord seeks with His Word and Spirit and admonishes them to repent. Note that the purpose of every reproof of sins is to move the heart and conscience of sinners, to cause them to forsake their transgressions, and to turn to the mercy and grace of God.

THE DEATH OF DAVID'S CHILD. — V.15. **And Nathan,** having delivered the sentence of the Lord, **departed unto his house. And the Lord struck the child that Uriah's wife bare unto David,** the phrasing once more calling attention to the sin, **and it was very sick.** The sickness in this case was a direct punishment of God upon the parents. V.16. **David, therefore, besought God for the child,** to spare its life; **and David fasted,** as a sign of deep sorrow and repentance, **and went in,** to a quiet room or retired spot of his house, **and lay all night upon the earth.** He bowed in meekness under the punishing hand of God, but also pleaded for merciful consideration, if he might expect such. V.17. **And the elders of his house,** his oldest and most confidential servants, **arose and went to him to raise him up from the earth; but he would not, neither did he eat bread with them.** His grief was too great to Field to their appeals and admonitions. V.18. **And it came to pass on the seventh day that the child died,** God had deemed it best to carry out the punishment decided upon. **And the servants of David feared to tell him that the child was** dead; for they said, Behold, while the child was yet alive, we spake unto him, and he would mot hearken unto our voice; how will he, then, vex himself, by being plunged into still deeper grief, in which he might do himself harm, if we tell him that the child is dead? V.19. But when David saw that his servants whispered, not daring to approach him with the sad news, David perceived that the child was dead, he drew his conclusions from their behavior; therefore David said unto his servants, Is the child dead? And they said, he is dead. V.20. Then David arose from the earth, and washed and anointed himself, and changed his apparel, and came into the house of the Lord, the tent where the Ark of the Covenant had been placed, and worshiped, his humble yielding to God's chastening hand enabling him joyfully to bear the burden laid upon him. Then he came to his own house; and when he required, they set bread before him, and he did eat. V.21. Then said his servants unto him, What thing is this that thou hast done? They could not explain David's conduct to themselves. Thou didst fast and weep for the child while it was alive, but when the child was dead, thou didst rise and eat bread. V.22. And he said, While the child was yet alive, I fasted and wept; for I said, he thought in his heart, Who can tell whether God will be gracious to me that the child may live? If God had spared his child. David would have regarded the fact as a proof of God's special mercy upon him. V.23. But now he is dead, wherefore should I fast? Can I bring him back again? He humbled himself under the mighty hand of God without giving way to fruitless grief. I shall go to him, but he shall not return to me, a clear confession of the belief in a life after death. V.24. And David comforted Bathsheba, his wife, with the same comfort which he himself had received, **and went in unto her and lay with her; and she bare a son, and he called his name Solomon,** undoubtedly with the prayer that God might grant him peace in every way. **And the Lord loved him,** gave the child special evidences of His loving-kindness. V.25. **And He,** the Lord, **sent by the hand of Nathan, the prophet,** as His official representative in this case; **and he called his name Jedidiah** (beloved of the lord), **because of the Lord.** All this points forward to the object of Christ's coming in the flesh. For He is come to cover over our nakedness and disgrace before God, to change the scarlet color of our guilt into the white of perfect innocence, through the atonement gained by His blood.

SUCCESS AGAINST THE AMMONITES. — V.26. **And Joab,** in the second year of the campaign, **fought against Rabbah of the children of Ammon, and took the royal city,** the city proper, without the citadel. V.27. **And Joab sent messengers to David and said, I have fought against Rabbah, and have taken the city of waters,** for it lap on both banks of the Upper Jabbok, in a narrow valley beneath its fort or acropolis. V.28. **Now, therefore, gather the rest of the people together,** mustering all those able to bear arms, **and encamp against the city,** the citadel on the heights, **and take it, lest I take the city and it be called after my name.** Joab here acted either as a devoted servant of David, who honestly wished him to have all the honor in the campaign, or as a shrewd politician, who would run no risks by gaining extraordinary successes. V.29. **And David gathered all the people together, and went to Rabbah, and fought against it, and took it,** he conquered the strong acropolis. V.30. **And he took their king's crown from off his head, the weight whereof was a talent of gold with the precious stones** (about one hundred

264

pounds avoirdupois); **and it was set on David's head,** at least during the coronation ceremonies, which proclaimed him lord of the Ammonite kingdom. **And he brought forth the spoil of the city in great abundance.** V.31. **And he brought forth the people that were there in,** in the acropolis, **and put them under saws,** putting them to death by sawing them apart, **and under harrows,** instruments or axes, **of iron, and under axes of iron,** knives or other cutting instruments, **and made them pass through the brick-kiln,** the place where they burned their children to their idol Moloch; **and thus did he unto all the cities of the children of Ammon.** The purpose was to inflict a striking punishment upon idolatry, for the war was a holy war. **So David and all the people returned unto Jerusalem.** This great victory was another proof of God's grace and favor, for He is kind and gracious, and abundant in mercy and truth, forgiving iniquities, and transgressions, and sins.

# 45

# 2 Samuel 13

**A**mnon's Incest and Its Punishment.

AMNON'S CRIME. — V.1. **And it came to pass after this that Absalom, the son of David,** chap. 3, 3, **had a fair sister,** a full sister to him, who was a very beautiful young woman, **whose name was Tamar; and Amnon, the son of David,** her half-brother by another of David's wives, **loved her.** V.2. **And Amnon was so vexed,** his passion preyed on him to such an extent, **that he fell sick for his sister Tamar, for she was a virgin; and Amnon thought it hard for him to do anything to her,** literally, "it was difficult to accomplish in the eyes of Amnon," he found it impossible to gratify his passion because of Tamar's maidenly reserve and her inaccessibility in the harem. V.3. **But Amnon had a friend whose name was Jonadab, the son of Shimeah, David's brother,** his own cousin; **and Jonadab was a very subtle man,** known for his craftiness. V.4. **And he said unto him, Why art thou, being the king's son,** in whose case there was no apparent reason for such a condition, **lean from day to day?** He looked more wretched from one morning to the next, since his nights were made sleepless by his torturing passion, **Wilt thou not tell me? And Amnon said unto him, I love Tamar, my brother Absalom's sister.** V.5. **And Jonadab said unto him, Lay thee down on thy bed and make thyself sick,** feigning illness; **and when thy father cometh to see thee,** to visit the son who had been reported sick, **say unto him, I pray thee, let my sister Tamar come and give me meat,** prepare food, **and dress them eat in my sight,** make ready some special dish for the sick, **that I may see it, and eat it at her hand.** He intimated that the sight of the food in such circumstances would give him an appetite. Evidently every wife of the king with her children occupied her own apartments in the royal palace, but the intercourse between the children was fairly free. V.6. **So Amnon,** following the advice of his shrewd cousin with all that it implied, **lay down and made himself sick; and when the king was come to see him, Amnon said unto the king, I pray thee, let Tamar, my sister,** whose skill in cooking was evidently well known, **come and make me a couple of cakes in my sight,** two heart-cakes, made of rolled dough, something on the order of pancakes, considered very strengthening for the heart, **that I may eat at her hand.** V.7. **Then David sent home to Tamar, saying, Go now to thy brother Amnon's house,** who apparently occupied apartments of his own, **and dress him meat,** prepare him some strengthening food. V.8. **So Tamar went to her brother Amnon's house; and he was laid down. And she took flour,** a mixture or paste of dough, **and kneaded it, and made cakes in his sight, and did bake the cakes,** used the batter to bake the special cakes for which he had asked. V.9. **And she took a pan,** or the cakes prepared by her, **and poured them out before him,** served them for him to eat; **but he refused to eat. And Amnon said, have out**

**all men from me,** he ordered all his attendants to leave the room. **And they went out, every man, from him.** V.10. **And Amnon said unto Tamar, Bring the meat in to the chamber,** the inner room where his couch was, **that I may eat of thine hand.** He acted like a capricious patient. **And Tamar took the cakes which she had made, and brought them in to the chamber to Amnon, her brother.** V.11. **And when she had brought them unto him to eat, he took hold of her,** throwing aside all his feigned weakness, **and said unto her, Come, lie with me, my sister.** V.12. **And she,** in the attempt to save her honor, **answered him, Nay, my brother, do not force me,** humbling her by this crime; **for no such thing ought to be done in Israel,** it was strictly in opposition to the Law, Lev. 18, 9; 20, 17; Deut. 27, 22; **do not thou this folly.** Cp. Gen. 34, 7, the passage which Tamar probably had in mind. V.13. **And I, whither shall I cause my shame to go?** Disgrace and contempt would be sure to strike her wherever she would go. **And as for thee, thou shalt be as one of the fools in Israel,** a person who foolishly and to his own condemnation committed a heinous transgression. **Now, therefore, I pray thee, speak unto the king; for he will not withhold me from thee.** She did not hold out an actual hope that the king would sanction the forbidden marriage, but spoke in the height of her fear, wishing to escape his passion for the present, trying to put him off by the prospect that he might be able to gratify his passion with a show of right, if lie would but wait. V.14. **Howbeit, he would not hearken unto her voice; but, being stronger than she, forced her, and lay with her,** gratified his passionate lust. Such is the power of sin if it is not kept in check by the fear of God or by love toward the Lord.

AMNON SPURNS TAMAR. — V.15. **Then Amnon,** having

gratified his bestial lust, **hated her exceedingly,** this being the usual consequence of a relation such as pictured in this chapter, **so that the hatred wherewith he hated her was greater than the love wherewith he had loved her;** he now loathed the object of his former intense passion. **And Amnon said unto her, Arise, be gone!** V.16. **And she said unto him, there is no cause; this evil in sending me away is greater than the other that thou didst unto me.** The Hebrew text shows an unfinished sentence, spoken in great agitation: On account of this greater evil than the other which thou didst to me in sending me away-. If he persisted in driving her from his house, men might believe that she had given him occasion to act toward her in such a manner, and the disgrace would be all the greater. **But he would not hearken unto her,** did not, in fact, even let her finish her protest. V.17. **Then he called his servant that ministered unto him,** his own private attendant, **and said, Put now this woman out from me, and bolt the door after her,** just as if she had tempted him to a shameful act and he wanted to insure against a repetition of her shamelessness. V.18. **And she had a garment of divers colors upon her,** a coat or upper garment with long sleeves; **for with such robes were the king's daughters that were virgins appareled.** Although she was a virgin and a princess, Amnon treated Tamar like a common prostitute. **Then his servant brought her out, and bolted the door after her.** V.19. **And Tamar,** as a sign of her great grief over the shame laid upon her, **put ashes on her head, and rent her garment of divers colors that was on her, and laid her hand on her head,** as a token of the fact that the hand of God lay heavily on her in this visitation, **and went on crying,** bewailing the greatness of her shame and disgrace. V.20. **And Absalom, her brother,**

**said unto her, Hath Amnon, thy brother, been with thee?** He guessed the state of affairs at once, expressing his opinion thus delicately. **But hold now thy peace, my sister; he is thy brother; regard not this thing,** lay it not to heart. He feigned a carelessness which he was far from feeling, because he wanted to conceal his purpose to revenge himself in the sight of all men. If Tamar would act in the same manner, he would have a better opportunity to carry out his design. **So Tamar remained desolate in her brother Absalom's house,** literally, "as desolated," as one whose happiness in life had been destroyed. V.21. **But when King David heard of all these things, he was very wroth.** His anger, unfortunately, did not cause him to act, to punish Amnon. Either the consciousness of his own recent sin held him back, or he practiced a false indulgence toward his first-born son. V.22. **And Absalom,** true to his plan of hiding his feelings for the time being and lulling Amnon to security, **spake unto his brother Amnon neither good nor bad,** he simply avoided him; **for Absalom hated Amnon because he had forced his sister Tamar.** Such examples of sin as here narrated instill a loathing and a horror of sin. They show that every sin and especially such sins of the flesh are an abomination in the sight of God, evils which cause only sorrow and heartache among men.

ABSALOM'S REVENGE. — V.23. **And it came to pass after two full years,** during all of which time Absalom carried his grudge toward Amnon in his heart, **that Absalom had sheep-shearers in Baal-hazor, which is beside Ephraim,** some miles northeast of Bethel, where he had a ranch; **and Absalom invited all the king's sons,** for sheep-shearing was a joyous festival. V.24. **And Absalom came to the king and said, Behold now, thy servant hath sheep-shearers; let the**

**king, I beseech thee, and his servants go with thy servant,**
The invitation had originally been made to the king and his
body-guard. V.25. **And the king said to Absalom, Nay, my
son, let us not all now go, lest we be chargeable unto thee,**
too large a number of invited guests might make the festival
too expensive for Absalom. **And he,** Absalom, **pressed him,**
tried to make him change his mind; **howbeit he would not go,
but blessed him,** wished him success for the festival. V.26.
**Then said Absalom,** who craftily saw that this arrangement
favored his plans of revenge, **if not, I pray thee, let my brother
Amnon go with us. And the king said unto him, Why should
he go with thee?** He may have had some premonition of evil
in hesitating about letting the heir apparent go along at this
time. V.27. **But Absalom pressed him that he let Amnon and
all the king's sons go with him.** Here was another instance
of David's weakness in yielding to Absalom's urgent request.
V.28. **Now, Absalom had commanded his servants, saying,
Mark ye now when Amnon's heart is merry with wine,** when,
under the influence of wine, he would throw aside caution, **and
when I say unto you, Smite Amnon, then kill him, fear not;
have not I commanded you?** He would take the responsibility
of the murder upon himself, his purpose being chiefly to
avenge his sister Tamar, but probably also to remove the crown
prince, an act which would make him the heir apparent to
the throne. **Be courageous, and be valiant.** The servants of
Absalom needed this encouragement very much since they
stood in awe of the king and his anger. V.29. **And the servants
of Absalom did unto Amnon,** in the course of the festival meal,
**as Absalom had commanded. Then all the king's sons arose,
and every man gat him up upon his mule and fled,** fearing
for his own life. V.30. **And it came to pass, while they,** the

princes, **were in the way,** on their flight to Jerusalem, **that tidings came to David, saying, Absalom hath slain all the king's sons, and there is not one of them left.** This shows the usual exaggeration of rumors. V.31. **Then the king arose and tare his garments,** in token of his great grief, **and lay on the earth; and all his servants,** following the example of their master, **stood by with their clothes rent.** V.32. **And Jonadab, the son of Shimeah, David's brother,** who had followed the development of matters with sharp eyes, **answered and said, Let not my lord suppose that they have slain all the young men, the king's sons; for Amnon only is dead; for by the appointment of Absalom this hath been determined from the day that he forced his sister Tamar,** his determination to avenge the crime had been written in his features, in the fixed position of his mouth. V.33. **Now, therefore, let not my lord the king take the thing to his heart, to think that all the king's sons are dead,** that was not the state of affairs; **for Amnon only is dead.** V.34. **But Absalom fled;** having accomplished his purpose, he thought it best to evade the king's wrath. **And the young man that kept the watch lifted up his eyes,** watching the return of the people from the festival with double interest, **and looked, and, behold, there came much people by the way of the hillside behind him,** the princes coming in from the west, the shortest and quickest way. V.35. **And Jonadab said unto the king, Behold, the king's sons come; as thy servant said, so it is.** This confirmed Jonadab's keen guess. V.36. **And it came to pass, as soon as he had made an end of speaking, that, behold, the king's sons came, and lifted up their voice and wept,** in deep mourning over the death of Amnon; **and the king also and all his servants wept very sore.** V.37. **But Absalom fled**

**and went to Talmai, the son of Ammihud, king of Geshur,** his grandfather, chap. 3, 3. **And David mourned for his son,** namely, for Amnon, **every day,** literally, "all his days," all his life. V.38. **So Absalom fled and went to Geshur, and was there three years.** V.39. **And the soul of King David longed to go forth unto Absalom,** literally, "And held back, refrained, David, the king, from going forth to Absalom"; **for he was comforted concerning Amnon, seeing he was dead,** the grief gradually became less sharp, and therefore David abandoned the idea of calling Absalom to account for his revenge. The word of the Lord that the sword would not depart from the house of David had begun to be fulfilled. A sin is quickly committed, and there may be a momentary gratification, but in the end the consequences are such as to make all its fruits appear apples of Sodom, as they really are.

# 46

# 2 Samuel 14

**T**he Reconciliation between David and Absalom.
THE WISE WOMAN OF TEKOAH. — V.1. **Now, Joab,
the son of Zeruiah, perceived that the king's heart
was toward Absalom,** or, more exactly, against Absalom;
David continued in his aversion to the slayer of the crown
prince. V.2. **And Joab,** either from genuine goodness of heart
or with the shrewdness which sought to get into the good
graces of Absalom and the people, **sent to Tekoah,** some fire
or six miles south of Bethlehem, **and fetched thence a wise
woman,** one known for the readiness of her speech, for her
boldness and shrewdness, **and said unto her, I pray thee,
feign thyself to be a mourner, and put on now mourning
apparel, and anoint not thyself with oil, but be as a woman
that had a long time mourned for the dead,** one whose
greatness of sorrow caused her to continue her mourning for
a very long time; v.3. **and come to the king and speak on
this manner unto him. So Joab put the words in her mouth,**
giving her exact and detailed instructions concerning her
behavior and speech. V.4. **And when the woman of Tekoah,**

in accordance with the instructions received, **spake to the king, she fell on her face to the ground and did obeisance,** her great humility serving to draw the king's attention to her, **and said, Help, O king!** V.5. **And the king said unto her, What aileth thee?** Her feigned distress caused him deep concern. **And she answered, I am indeed a widow woman, and mine husband is dead,** the double statement being intended to arouse sympathy. V.6. **And thy handmaid had two sons, and they two strove together in the field, and there was none to part them,** to act as arbitrator and deliverer between them, **but the one smote the other and slew him.** V.7. **And, behold, the whole family,** the entire relationship, **is risen against thine handmaid, and they said, Deliver him that smote his brother that we may kill him for the life of his brother whom he slew,** according to the law of blood-vengeance; **and we will destroy the heir also,** namely, the remaining son, whose death would make the other relatives the heirs; **and so they shall quench my coal which is left,** a figurative expression for the one son through whom her house could be built up, **and shall not leave to my husband neither name nor remainder upon the earth.** "The woman's purpose was not only to bring out the design of the kinsmen in their blood-avenging as harshly as possible, but also, with reference to David's hostile feeling to Absalom, to emphasize the point that the latter was the heir to David's throne, and to save him as such from his father's anger." V.8. **And the king said unto the woman,** in granting her request, **Go to thine house, and I will give charge concerning thee,** to protect her son from the pursuing relatives. V.9. **And the woman of Tekoah said unto the king, My lord, O king, the iniquity be on me and on my father's house,** namely, in case some wrong should be connected with the fact that the

275

unintentional murder was not avenged, **and the king and his throne be guiltless,** no blame should be attached to David's government. V.10. **And the king said, Whosoever saith aught unto thee, bring him to me, and he shall not touch thee any more.** The matter was to be adjusted so that no one would dare to annoy the woman any more. V.11. **Then said she,** pursuing the advantage she had gained till now, **I pray thee, let the king remember the Lord, thy God,** she pleaded with the king for his interference to the point of assuring her son's safety by an oath, **that thou wouldest not suffer the revengers of blood to destroy any more, lest they destroy my son.** The destruction already wrought should not be increased. **And he,** David, **said. As the Lord liveth, there shall not one hair of thy son fall to the earth.** As her appeals grew in fervor, so his assurances in emphasis. V.12. **Then the woman said, Let thine handmaid, I pray thee, speak one word unto my lord the king.** She acted as if she had another matter to present. **And he said, Say on.** V.13. **And the woman said, Wherefore, then,** after voicing such sentiments as she had just obtained from him, **hast thou thought such a thing against the people of God?** She has some difficulty in making the application to the king's own case, because she cannot speak openly, but may only, in passing, allude to Absalom. Her implication was that on account of the attitude of David toward Absalom at least some of the people were suffering. **For the king doth speak this thing,** in announcing the decision in her own case, **as one which is faulty, in that the king doth not fetch home again his banished.** To be just, he must apply the same mildness in the case of Absalom which he decided for in her case. V.14. **For we,** men in general, and Absalom in particular, **must needs die and are as water spilt on the ground, which cannot**

**be gathered up again,** which fate may come upon Absalom before David is aware of the fact; **neither doth God respect any person,** in calling him away by death at the time appointed by Him; **yet doth he devise means that His banished be not expelled from Him,** literally, "And not takes away God a soul but He thinks out plans not to banish a banished one"; He does not cut off the life of the sinner outright, but is merciful and changes His sentence of rejection in the case of a repentant sinner. V.15. **Now, therefore, that I am come to speak of this thing unto my lord the king, it is because the people have made me afraid,** namely, by their demand to deliver her son to the avenger of blood; **and thy handmaid said, I will now speak unto the king; it may be that the king will perform the request of his handmaid.** Thus she skillfully returned to her own case. V.16. **For the king will hear to deliver his handmaid out of the hand of the man that would destroy me and my son together out of the inheritance of God.** This was the point which was so awful in her sight, that of being cut off from the people of the Lord. V.17. **Then thine handmaid said, The word of my lord the king shall now be comfortable,** serve for her reassurance; **for as an angel of God,** the great Angel of the Covenant, **so is my lord the king to discern good and bad,** to hear the crying of his oppressed subjects and to come to the assistance of those who were in trouble; **therefore the Lord, thy God, will be with thee.** V.18. **Then the king answered and said unto the woman,** since he had drawn his own conclusions from the skill with which she presented her matter, **Hide not from me, I pray thee, the thing that I shall ask thee. And the woman said, Let my lord the king now speak.** V.19. **And the king said, Is not the hand of Joab with thee in all this?** The entire manner in which the case had been presented and handled reminded him of his general. **And the woman answered and said,** with a sincere acknowledgment of the king's sagacity, **As thy soul liveth, my lord the king, none can turn to the right hand or to the left from aught that my lord the king hath spoken,** David, according to her praise, always hit the nail on the head; **for thy servant Joab, he bade me, and he put all these words in the mouth of thine handmaid.** V.20. **To fetch about this form of speech,** literally, "to turn about entirely the face of this matter," to change the relation then obtaining between David and Absalom, to bring about a reconciliation, **hath thy servant Joab done this thing; and my lord is wise, according to the wisdom of an angel of God, to know all things that are in the earth.** The woman certainly made use of fine tact and wisdom. It is a noble thing to act as advocate for another and to intercede where this will bring about better relations. Where such sagacity succeeds in convincing others, it is well-pleasing to God.

THE RECONCILIATION EFFECTED. — V.21. **And the king said unto Joab, Behold, now, I have done this thing,** in fulfilling the request preferred through the woman of Tekoah; **go, therefore, bring the young man Absalom again.** V.22. **And Joab fell to the ground on his face, and bowed himself, and thanked the king; and Joab said, Today thy servant knoweth that I have found grace in thy sight, my lord, O King, in that the king hath fulfilled the request of his servant.** His intercession had finally succeeded. V.23. **So Joab arose and went to Geshur, and brought Absalom to Jerusalem.** V.24. **And the king,** still unable to forget the crime which Absalom had committed, **said, Let him turn to his own house, and let him not see my face.** David's forgiveness was not yet perfect, it lacked sincerity. **So Absalom returned to his own**

**house, and saw not the king's face;** he was, to all intents and purposes, still banished. V.25. **But in all Israel there was none to be so much praised as Absalom for his beauty,** there was no other man physically so perfect as he; **from the sole of his foot even to the crown of his head there was no blemish in him.** V.26. **And when he polled his head,** when he had his hair cut, **(for it was at every year's end that he polled it; because the hair was heavy on him, therefore he polled it,) he weighed the hair of his head at two hundred shekels after the king's weight** (about six pounds). V.27. **And unto Absalom there were born three sons and one daughter, whose name was Tamar** bearing the same name as her father's sister; **she was a woman of fair countenance,** very beautiful. V.28. **So Absalom dwelt two full years in Jerusalem, and saw not the king's face.** David persisted in punishing him by keeping him at a distance. V.29. **Therefore Absalom sent for Joab to have sent him to the king,** to have this unbearable relation terminated; **but he would not come to him,** probably in order not to incur the king's displeasure: **and when he sent again the second time, he would not come.** V.30. **Therefore he said unto his servants, See, Joab's field is near mine,** alongside of his own ground, a parcel of land which he cultivated near the city, **and he hath barley there; go and set it on fire. And Absalom's servants set the field on fire.** V.31. **Then Joab arose and came to Absalom unto his house,** as the latter had foreseen, **and said unto him, Wherefore have thy servants set my field on fire?** V.32. **And Absalom answered Joab, Behold, I sent unto thee, saying, Come hither that I may send thee to the king to say, Wherefore am I come from Geshur? It had been good for me to have been there still,** he would have fared far better if he had remained there, as circumstances were now. **Now, therefore, let me see the king's face; and if there be any iniquity in me, let him kill me.** Instead of showing sorrow and confessing his guilt, he denies it and challenges his father to punish him at this time. It was a defiant and bitter spirit which spoke here. David had made a mistake in the first place by letting Absalom return without a penitent confession. V.33. **So Joab came to the king and told him; and when he** David, **had called for Absalom, he came to the king, and bowed himself on his face to the ground before the king,** as a token of the usual homage paid to the sovereign, but not as a mark of penitence; **and the king kissed Absalom.** So the matter was patched up, sincerely enough on the part of David, but without this spirit on the part of Absalom. Even believers find that it is altogether against their sinful nature really to forgive and to forget any wrong that has been done. But the fear of God will gradually overcome the evil with good, conquer hatred and revenge, and be reconciled to the person who has done wrong.

# 47

# 2 Samuel 15

The Rebellion of Absalom.

THE INSURRECTION BEGUN. — V.1. **And it came to pass after this,** shortly after Absalom had received the pardon of his father, **that Absalom prepared him chariots,** a state-chariot, **and horses, and fifty men to run before him,** to be runners or footmen. He thus appeared before the people in royal state and influenced their minds to think of him as the coming ruler. V.2. **And Absalom rose up early,** in order to impress people with his zeal in their behalf, **and stood beside the way of the gate,** at the entrance to the royal palace; **and it was so that, when any man that had a controversy came to the king for judgment,** if he had a matter in which he sought the king's decision, **then Absalom,** with every show of winning condescension, **called unto him and said, Of what city art thou?** Such an inquiry on the part of a royal prince was, of course, very flattering to the average member of the nation. **And he said, Thy servant is of one of the tribes of Israel,** a member of the Israelitish nation, belonging to this or that specific tribe. V.3. **And Absalom,** who had inquired also about his business, **said unto him, See, thy matters are good and right,** his decision being made without a thorough investigation of the matter; **but there is no man deputed of the king to hear thee.** The "hearers" of Oriental kings were judicial officers whose duty it was to investigate the matters brought to the king's court, the king usually deciding on the basis of their findings. It is possible that neglect and partiality had crept in without the knowledge of David, so that Absalom could avail himself of a dissatisfaction already existing. V.4. **Absalom said moreover,** in following up the advantage of the good impression made by this bid for the people's favor, **Oh that I were made judge in the land,** literally, "Who will establish me as judge in the land?" **that every man which hath any suit or cause might come unto me, and I would do him justice!** Absalom's imagination causes him to see the people crowding around him as he sits on the throne of judgment before them, eager to correct all the faults which had crept into the judicial procedure of the kingdom V.5. **And it was so that, when any man came nigh to him to do him obeisance,** to fall down before him and render him homage, **he put forth his hand, and took him, and kissed him,** thus feigning an affability which was ready to acknowledge all men as brothers. V.6. **And on this manner did Absalom to all Israel that came to the king for judgment; so Absalom stole the hearts of the men of Israel,** secretly, by guile, gained them for himself, made everything ready for the insurrection which he had planned. V.7. **And it came to pass after forty years,** about four gears after Absalom's return to Jerusalem, **that Absalom said unto the king, I pray thee, let me go and pay my vow which I have vowed unto the Lord in Hebron.** He pretended that his vow required a sacrifice in the city of his birth, but in reality he considered Hebron a city peculiarly suited for his temporary capital after he had been proclaimed king. V.8. **For thy servant vowed a vow while I abode at Geshur in Syria,** during his banishment, **saying, if the Lord shall bring me again indeed to Jerusalem, then I will serve the Lord,** namely, by a special sacrifice. V.9. **And the king said unto him, Go in peace.** Since full order had not yet been restored in the religious observances of Israel and the strict law of Leviticus, chap. 17, 3. 4, was not in practical operation, such sacrifices, especially in priestly cities, were not unusual at that time. **So he arose and went to Hebron,** to carry out his intention of gaining the kingdom. V.10. **But Absalom,** having gained the hearts of the people by the methods described above, **sent spies,** emissaries, **through out all the tribes of Israel, saying, As soon as ye hear the sound of the trumpet, then ye shall say, Absalom reigneth in Hebron.** The sound of the trumpet was to be a signal to all those who favored him to proclaim him as king over the entire nation. V.11. **And with Absalom went two hundred men out of Jerusalem that were called,** members of the king's household; such as usually accompanied the royal princes, invited to the sacrificial feast; **and they went in their simplicity, and they knew not anything,** they were in total ignorance of Absalom's intentions. V.12. **And Absalom sent for Ahithophel, the Gilonite, David's counselor, from his city, even from Giloh,** a city near Hebron, **while he offered sacrifices,** for he felt that the time for the open insurrection had now come. Ahithophel had probably joined Absalom's party some time before, turning traitor to David either from motives of ambition or on account of the affair with Bathsheba, who apparently was his relative. **And the conspiracy was strong; for the people increased continually with Absalom.**

His venture seemed to be very successful. Absalom is a type of a rebel who disregards the Fourth Commandment. Such people are disobedient to their parents and oppose the lawfully constituted government. Their stock in trade consists of deceits and treason, and they end by being murderers.

THE FLIGHT OF DAVID. — V.13. **And there came a messenger to David, saying, The hearts of the men of Israel are after Absalom.** Before David had been aware of any dissatisfaction, while he was attending to the affairs of his kingdom in calm security, the damage had been done. V.14. **And David,** seized with a sudden terror at this unexpected development, **said unto all his servants that were with him at Jerusalem, Arise, and let us flee; for we shall not else escape from Absalom. Make speed to depart, lest he overtake us suddenly, and bring evil upon us,** thrust upon them suddenly the threatened misfortune, **and smite the city with the edge of the sword.** Not knowing how strong Absalom's army was at that time nor how vigorous the spirit of the insurrection had grown, David's move was intended to avert a storming of the city with its attendant bloodshed. V.15. **And the king's servants said unto the king,** exhibiting a splendid faithfulness in the midst of the general defection, **Behold, thy servants are ready to do whatsoever my lord the king shall appoint.** They assured him of their unwavering loyalty. V.16. **And the king went forth, and all his household after him,** as his attendants and followers. **And the king left ten women, which were concubines,** a part of his harem, **to keep the house,** to guard the palace. V.17. **And the king went forth, and all the people after him, and tarried in a place that was far off,** he stopped for some time at Beth-merhak, possibly a fort which guarded the passage of the Kidron, in order to gather all the faithful followers about him. V.18. **And all his servants passed on beside him; and all the Cherethites and all the Pelethites,** chap. 8, 18, **and all the Gittites,** the men who had been with David in the wilderness and had followed him from Gath on, **six hundred men which came after him from Gath, passed on before the king.** These companions of his wilderness wanderings were the old guard, the heroes of David, who were ready now as ever to defend their master with their lives. V.19. **Then said the king to Ittai the Gittite,** a Philistine who had joined his forces, **Wherefore goest thou also with us? Return to thy place, and abide with the king,** to him who would occupy that position; **for thou art a stranger and also an exile,** wherefore it would not be advisable for him to take sides at this time. V.20. **Whereas thou camest but yesterday,** having cast his fortunes with David but recently, **should I this day make thee go up and down with us? Seeing I go whither I may, return thou, and take back thy brethren; mercy and truth be with thee.** Since the lot of David would at best be most uncertain in the near future, he did not want Ittai to share this uncertainty, which partook of the nature of a banishment, but commended him to the grace and faithfulness of God. V.21. **And Ittai answered the king and said,** with a solemn oath. **As the Lord liveth, and as my lord the king liveth, surely in what place my lord the king shall be, whether in death or life, even there also will thy servant be.** He thus expressed his unconditional devotion and fidelity to him unto death. V.22. **And David,** accepting this splendid vow of loyalty, **said to Ittai, Go and pass over. And Ittai the Gittite passed over, and all his men,** for he had a company of his own, **and all the little ones that were with him,** the members of his family. V.23. **And all the country,** the inhabitants of the countryside east of Jerusalem, along the line of march, **wept with a loud voice,** lamenting over the misfortune of their king; **and all the people,** those in the company of the king, **passed over. The king also himself passed over the brook Kidron,** the valley between Jerusalem and Mount Olivet, whose course is filled with water only during the winter or rainy season; **and all the people passed over toward the way of the wilderness,** the northern part of the wilderness of Judah, between Jerusalem and Jericho. V.24. **And lo, Zadok also and all the Levites were with him, bearing the Ark of the Covenant of God; and they set down the ark of God,** in order to give the people that were still coming time to join the procession. **And Abiathar went up,** on the road which led over Mount Olivet toward the east, **until all the people had done passing out of the city.** Abiathar was the high priest, and Zadok was the chief officer in charge of the ark. V.25. **And the king said unto Zadok, Carry back the ark of God into the city,** to its place in the sanctuary. **If I shall find favor in the eyes of the Lord, He will bring me again, and show me both it and His habitation;** v.26. **but if He thus say, I have no delight in thee, behold, here am I, let Him do to me as seemeth good unto Him.** David thus resigned himself to the Lord for evil or for good, for favor or for disfavor; for he saw in these events the hand of the Lord, as the Prophet Nathan had foretold. V.27. **The king said also unto Zadok, the priest, Art got thou a seer? Return into the city in peace, and your two sons with you, Ahimaaz, thy son, and Jonathan, the son of Abiathar.** David bade Zadok, as the second high priest and as a prophet of the Lord, to return to his place in the sanctuary, where he could, moreover, watch events as they transpired. V.28. **See, I will tarry in the plain of the wilderness,** near the fords of Jordan, **until there come**

**word from you to certify me;** he should observe the trend of events, and report to David. V.29. **Zadok, therefore, and Abiathar carried the ark of God again to Jerusalem; and they tarried there,** remaining to see what the outcome would be. V.30. **And David went up by the ascent of Mount Olivet,** the road which led up past its summit, **and wept as he went up, and had his head covered,** as the symbol of a sorrowful mind wholly withdrawn from the outer world, **and he went barefoot,** as a sign of great grief and humiliation; **and all the people that was with him,** following his example, **covered every man his head, and they went up, weeping as they went up.** In giving way to a superior force and taking the suffering sent by the Lord upon him, David prepared the way for the salvation of the people. He appears here as a type of Christ, who also entered upon His great suffering by passing over the brook Kidron.

HUSHAI GOES TO JERUSALEM. — V.31. **And one told David, saying, Ahithophel,** in whom David had trusted as his secret counselor, **is among the conspirators with Absalom. And David said,** in a brief sigh commending the matter to the Lord, **O Lord, I pray Thee, turn the counsel of Ahithophel into foolishness.** The way for the fulfillment of this prayer was immediately prepared. V.32. **And it came to pass that, when David was come to the top of the mount, where he worshiped God,** or, where men were wont to worship God, for the summits of hills, the so-called high places, were still used for that purpose at the time of David, **behold, Hushai the Archite, came to meet him with his coat rent and earth upon his head,** as a token of his sympathetic grief; v.33. **unto whom David said, if thou passest on with me,** joining his forces in the campaign which was sure to come, **then thou shalt be a burden unto me,** probably on account of his advanced age and feeble condition: v.34. **but if thou return to the city and say unto Absalom, I will be thy servant, O king; as I have been thy father's servant hitherto,** in the capacity of private counselor, chap. 16, 16; 1 Chron. 27, 33, **so will I now also be thy servant, then mayest thou for me,** in the interest of David, **defeat the counsel of Ahithophel.** In this way Hushai could be of assistance in defeating the insurrection and restoring the rightful king to the throne. V.35. **And hast thou not there with thee Zadok and Abiathar, the priests?** These two men also held to the cause of David. **Therefore it shall be that what thing so ever thou shalt hear out of the king's house, thou shalt tell it to Zadok and Abiathar, the priests,** with whom David had arranged to have such reports forwarded to him. V.36. **Behold, they have there with them their two sons, Ahimaaz, Zadok's son, and Jonathan, Abiathar's son; and by them ye shall send unto me everything that ye can hear.** V.37. **So Hushai, David's friend,** for such he remained during the events which followed, **came into the city, and Absalom came into Jerusalem,** at about the same time. Note: It is the duty of all Christians not only to pray against the evil projects of the enemies, but also, so far as in them lies, to do all in their power to thwart the evil designs of the enemies against the kingdom of Christ.

# 48

# 2 Samuel 16

Events during David's Flight.

ZIBA AND SHIMEI. — V.1. **And when David was a little past the top of the hill,** beyond the summit of Mount Olivet, **behold, Ziba, the servant of Mephibosheth, met him,** having gone on in advance of the army in order to approach David after the first disorder was over, **with a couple of asses saddled and upon them two hundred loaves of bread and an hundred bunches,** or cakes, **of raisins, and an hundred of summer fruits,** probably fig-cakes, **and a bottle,** a skin, **of wine.** V.2. **And the king said unto Ziba, What meanest thou by these?** literally, "What these to thee?" What object did he have in bringing them at this time? **And Ziba said, The asses be for the king's household to ride on, and the bread and the summer fruit for the young men,** the servants of the king, **to eat, and the wine, that such as be faint in the wilderness may drink.** This act was, unfortunately, no unselfish thoughtfulness, but rather a shrewd move to gain the king's favor, since Ziba felt sure that David would come out victor over his son. V.3. **And the king said, And where**

**is thy master's son,** Mephibosheth, the son of Jonathan? **And Zibah,** taking this opportunity to cast an unfounded suspicion upon his master, **said unto the king, Behold, he abideth at Jerusalem; for he said, To-day shall the house of Israel restore me the kingdom of my father.** Ziba intimated that Mephibosheth expected the present disorder to result in his being restored to royal dignity and power, this lie being told in order to obtain possession of the estate which he was now taking care of by the king's order, chap. 9, 9-11. V.4. **Then said the king to Ziba, Behold, thine are all that pertained unto Mephibosheth;** all the latter's lands were to be transferred to Ziba for this supposed act of loyalty, whereas, in reality, Ziba was not only a liar, but also a thief and traitor, as the sequel shows, chap. 19, 26-29. **And Ziba said,** still playing the part of a loyal friend of the king, though he was a hypocrite, **I humbly beseech thee that I may find grace in thy sight, my lord, O king.** He expressed the hope that David might continue to show himself a gracious sovereign to him. David, in the excitement of the flight and his consequent distracted state, became guilty of a double wrong, by treating the faithful Mephibosheth as a traitor without hearing his testimony and by rewarding the slander of the false Ziba without investigating the charges made by him. V.5. **And when King David came to Bahurim,** some little distance beyond Mount Olivet, **behold, thence came out a man of the family of the house of Saul,** a distant relative of Saul, **whose name was Shimei, the son of Gera; he came forth, and cursed still as he came,** literally, "Going forth he went forth, and cursed," that is, he cursed as he went along. V.6. **And he cast stones at David and at all the servants of King David,** those of his body-guard; **and all the people and all the mighty men were on his**

**right hand and on his left.** In spite of this fact Shimei dared to offer this insult. V.7. **And thus said Shimei when he cursed, Come out, come out,** literally, "Out, out," namely, out of the kingdom and out of the land, **thou bloody man,** probably with reference to Ishbosheth and Abner, for he falsely connected David with these murders, **and thou man of Belial,** vain and good-for-nothing scoundrel! V.8. **The Lord hath returned upon thee,** as a just recompense, **all the blood of the house of Saul, in whose stead thou hast reigned,** the implication being that this was done contrary to right and justice; **and the Lord hath delivered the kingdom into the hand of Absalom, thy son,** as a just punishment for the misdeeds of the past; **and, behold, thou art taken in thy mischief,** literally, "Behold thee in thy evil," **because thou art a bloody man,** a man of blood art thou, rejoicing in murders. This vile talk was all the more reprehensible since Shimei used the name of the Lord and ascribed the present state of affairs to Jehovah. V.9. **Then said Abishai, the son of Zeruiah,** one of David's generals and heroes, **unto the king, Why should this dead dog,** this despicable, vile cur, chap. 9, 8, **curse my lord the king? Let me go over, I pray thee, and take off his head,** making Shimei atone for his reviling with his life. V.10. **And the king said, What have I to do with you, ye sons of Zeruiah?** Joab had probably agreed with his brother Abishai on the need of swift and drastic measures against Shimei, and David declared with great emphasis that he could not share their attitude. **So let him curse, because the Lord hath said unto him, Curse David.** In his humility David was willing to consider it a special dispensation on the part of God, permitting Shimei to cast such aspersions upon him. **Who shall, then, say, Wherefore hast thou done so?** V.11. **And David said to Abishai and to all his**

servants, Behold, my son, which came forth of my bowels, whose true father he was, **seeketh my life; how much more now may this Benjamite do it?** It was far less surprising that a member of a hostile family should act in this manner. **Let him alone, and let him curse; for the Lord hath bidden him.** V.12. **It may be that the Lord will look on mine affliction,** on the guilt of sins which David really had, since he felt that he had deeply offended the Lord, though not in the matter mentioned by Shimei, **and that the Lord will requite me good for his cursing this day.** Note that David's humility is again apparent in this "perhaps"; he will not be sure of the divine blessing even now, but leaves the matter in the hands of God. V.13. **And as David and his men went by the way, Shimei went along on the hill's side over against him,** separated from the army of David by the valley, **and cursed as he went, and threw stones at him, and cast dust.** It seems, then, that David's quiet behavior only enraged Shimei all the more, causing him to become ever more challenging in his vile conduct. V.14. **And the king and all the people that were with him came weary,** they arrived at Ajephim, a caravansary, or camping-place for travelers, **and refreshed themselves there.** Like David, all believers are obliged occasionally to endure the mockery, the scorn, the blasphemy of the world. But in such cases they do not revenge themselves, leaving the matter, instead, in the hands of Him who has said: "Vengeance is Mine, I will repay."

THE COUNSEL OF AHITHOPHEL. — V.15. **And Absalom and all the people, the men of Israel, came to Jerusalem,** the men who had cast their lot with the rebellious son of David, **and Ahithophel with him,** the counselor who had turned traitor to David. V.16. **And it came to pass, when Hushai the Archite, David's friend,** whom the king had persuaded to return to

Jerusalem the better to serve his interests, **was come unto Absalom, that Hushai said unto Absalom, God save the king, God save the king,** the double "May the king live" being intended to express his best wishes, since he does not state the name of the king to whom he refers. V.17. **And Absalom,** who was astonished and even suspicious at this greeting, **said to Hushai, Is this thy kindness to thy friend? Why wentest thou not with thy friend?** Hushai's relation to David had been a matter of common knowledge. V.18. **And Hushai said unto Absalom,** deliberately casting dust into his eyes, **Nay; but whom the Lord and this people,** those who had joined the cause of Absalom, **and all the men of Israel,** the entire nation, **choose, his will I be, and with him will I abide.** He infers that the choice of the nation in this case is the choice of Jehovah. V.19. **And again,** his second reason, **whom should I serve? Should I not serve in the presence of his son?** This idea he presented to Absalom as self-evident. **As I have served in thy father's presence,** before the face of thy father, **so will I be in thy presence.** This flattered and satisfied Absalom, vain as he was, immensely, for he felt that the best minds of the nation were now on his side. V.20. **Then said Absalom to Ahithophel, Give counsel among you what we shall do.** He was anxious to take some steps by which his authority would definitely be announced and secured. V.21. **And Ahithophel said unto Absalom, Go in unto thy father's concubines,** in public carnal intercourse, **which he hath left to keep the house; and all Israel shall hear that thou art abhorred of thy father,** since the insult would be practically unforgivable and since the act, according to Oriental usage, would indicate actual dethronement of his father, since he would thereby take over his harem; **then shall the hands of all that are with**

**thee be strong,** they mould be greatly encouraged to decide in his favor. V.22. **So they spread Absalom a tent,** the tent commonly used as a protection against sun, wind, and rain, **upon the top of the house,** on the same roof where David's look at Bathsheba led him into the path of sin; **and Absalom went in unto his father's concubines in the sight of all Israel,** in an unspeakably filthy act, but one which fulfilled the words of Nathan against David, chap. 12, 8. V.23. **And the counsel of Ahithophel which he counseled in those days was as if a man had enquired at the oracle of God,** it was regarded and followed as if inspired by God Himself, a far too high estimate of any man's ability; **so was all the counsel of Ahithophel both with David and with Absalom.** Rebels who overthrow the order of God in rising against the government instituted by Him are very often the slaves of the most loathsome sins and vices, their hearts hardened against every influence for good.

# 49

# 2 Samuel 17

The Campaign against David.
HUSHAI'S COUNSEL ACCEPTED. — V.1. **Moreover, Ahithophel,** whose filthy counsel Absalom had just followed, **said unto Absalom, let me now choose out twelve thousand men,** a thousand for each of the twelve tribes, **and I will arise and pursue after David this night,** the very night after his flight; v.2. **and I will come upon him while he is weary and weak-handed,** the hand being the symbol of strength, **and will make him afraid,** cause terror to fall upon him; **and all the people that are with him shall flee; and I will smite the king only,** namely, while he is alone, forsaken by his men; v.3. **and I will bring back all the people unto thee,** also the men who had joined David: **the man whom thou seekest is as if all returned,** David alone being equivalent to all the people in influence and power, his death will cause all his adherents to espouse the cause of Absalom. **So all the people shall be in peace,** the one obstacle to this condition being removed with the fall of David. V.4. **And the saying pleased Absalom well and all the elders of Israel,** for it was in truth

the very best plan in favor of Absalom's cause. V.5. **Then said Absalom, by the dispensation of God, Call now Hushai the Archite also, and let us hear likewise what he saith,** what counsel is in his mouth. V.6. **And when Hushai was come to Absalom, Absalom spake unto him, saying, Ahithophel hath spoken after this manner,** outlining his plan briefly; **shall we do after his saying,** follow the word of his counsel? **If not, speak thou.** Hushai was in a delicate position, which required all the tact and wisdom he possessed; for it was necessary for him to feign the closest friendship for Absalom, while furthering the cause of David. V.7. **And Hushai said unto Absalom, The counsel that Ahithophel hath given is not good at this time.** The implication is that the first advice was fine and well worthy of taking, but in this case he overlooked certain facts. V.8. **For, said Hushai, thou knowest thy father and his men that they be mighty men,** valiant heroes, far from being exhausted by a short march, **and they be chafed in their minds,** embittered in spirit, **as a bear robbed of her whelps in the field,** doubly dangerous at such a time; **and thy father is a man of war,** acquainted with all the arts of warfare, **and will not lodge with the people,** he would not permit himself to be taken by surprise in an unfortified camp. V.9. **Behold, he is hid now in some pit or in some other place,** either in a natural stronghold or in a fortified position; **and it will come to pass, when some of them be overthrown at the first,** if Absalom's advance guard should be thrown back by a sudden attack on the part of David, **that whosoever heareth it will say, There is a slaughter among the people that follow Absalom.** The mere report of a surprise attack on the part of David would be exaggerated into a defeat of Absalom's entire force. V.10. **And he also that is valiant, whose heart is as the**

**heart of a lion,** the most courageous on the side of Absalom, **shall utterly melt; for all Israel knoweth that thy father is a mighty man, and they which be with him are valiant men.** Hushai purposely emphasized this point, in order to magnify the prowess of David and his men and to strike terror to the heart of Absalom. V.11. **Therefore I counsel that all Israel,** the entire army of the nation, all men able to bear arms, **be generally gathered unto thee, from Dan even to Beersheba, as the sand that is by the sea for multitude,** again said with willful exaggeration; **and that thou go to battle in thine own person,** Absalom was to lead his great army in person, a suggestion which could not fail of making a deep impression on his vanity. V.12. **So shall we,** for Hushai skillfully includes himself with the host of Absalom, **come upon him in some place where he shall be found,** no matter where this might be, **and we will light upon him as the dew falleth on the ground,** coming quietly, but covering, drenching, and submerging him and his army completely; **and of him and of all the men that are with him there shall not be left so much as one.** V.13, **Moreover, if he be gotten into a city, then shall all Israel bring ropes to that city, and we will draw it into the river,** on whose banks all the fortified cities were built, **until there be not one small stone found there.** In his exaggerated manner, Hushai pictures the entire city dragged into the neighboring brook or river, the walls with the houses and all the inhabitants. V.14. **And Absalom and all the men of Israel,** overcome by the boastful boldness and the skilful plausibility of the plan outlined, said, **the plan of Hushai the Archite is better than the counsel of Ahithophel. For the Lord had appointed to defeat the good counsel of Ahithophel,** for the latter would undoubtedly have been successful, **to the intent that the Lord**

**might bring evil upon Absalom.** He should be blind to his own advantage, fatuously believing that the entire nation would immediately rally around him, while David would gain time to perfect his plans and to overthrow the insurrection. Mark: It is well-pleasing to God if we oppose all rebels and scoundrels who attempt to overthrow divine and human order. And God, on His part, often blinds the eyes of such rebellious persons, especially such as oppose Christ and His government, causing them to fall from one foolish move into another and to bring destruction upon themselves.

DAVID IN THE COUNTRY EAST OF JORDAN. — V.15. **Then said Hushai unto Zadok and to Abiathar, the priests,** giving them a report of his efforts in David's behalf, **Thus and thus did Ahithophel counsel Absalom and the elders of Israel; and thus and thus have I counseled.** V.16. **Now, therefore, send quickly and tell David, saying,** offering him advice which he could not afford to ignore, **Lodge not this night in the plains of the wilderness,** near the fords on the west side of the river, **but speedily pass over; lest the king be swallowed up, and all the people that are with him.** There was always danger that an expedition might be sent against him before he had completed his plans and gotten ready to defend himself. He would be safer at any rate on the east side, where he might also find additional followers. V.17. **Now, Jonathan and Ahimaaz,** the sons of the high priests and their messengers to David, **stayed by En-rogel,** they were standing at this spring, near the southeast corner of Jerusalem; **for they might not be seen to come into the city; and a wench,** one of the high priest's servant girls, **went and told them,** delivered to them the advice of Hushai; **and they went and told King David,** they started out to deliver the message. V.18. **Nevertheless,**

**a lad saw them, and told Absalom,** probably being a spy set to watch the priests; **but they,** finding themselves discovered, **went both of them away quickly, and came to a man's house in Bahurim,** between Jerusalem and Jericho, chap. 16, 5, **which had a well,** evidently empty, **in his court, whither they went down,** to hide themselves from their pursuers. V.19. **And the woman,** the wife of this man, with quick presence of mind, **took and spread a covering over the well's mouth,** over the opening of the cistern, **and spread ground corn thereon,** as if she were drying barley-groats; **and the thing was not known,** for the opening was not visible and could therefore not arouse suspicions. V.20. **And when Absalom's servants,** in their pursuit of the two messengers, **came to the woman to the house, they said, Where is Ahimaaz and Jonathan? And the woman,** purposely dissembling to shield the messengers, **said unto them, They be gone over the brook of water,** some creek in the neighborhood to which she pointed. **And when they had sought and could not find them, they returned to Jerusalem.** V.21. **And it came to pass, after they were departed, that they came up out of the well, and went and told King David, and said unto David,** according to the counsel of Hushai, **Arise, and pass quickly over the water,** the Jordan; **for thus hath Ahithophel counseled against you,** and there was still danger that his counsel might be reconsidered. V.22. **And David arose, and all the people that were with him, and they passed over Jordan; by the morning light,** by the time the new day dawned, **there lacked not one of them that was not gone over Jordan,** they had passed over to the very last man. Thus God had protected David, the situation of affairs now being in his favor. V.23. **And when Ahithophel saw that his counsel was not followed,** his advice was not carried out, **he saddled**

**his ass, and arose, and gat him home to his house, to his city,** chap. 15, 12, **and put his household in order,** regulated all his affairs, **and hanged himself, and died,** a suicide from baffled ambition and despair, since he foresaw the overthrow of the insurrection, **and was buried in the sepulcher of his father.** The prayer of David, chap. 15, 31, was thus fulfilled. V.24. **Then David came to Mahanaim,** a fortified city of Gilead, near the ford of Jabbok. **And Absalom passed over Jordan, he and all the men of Israel with him,** all the warriors whom he had assembled according to the advice of Hushai. V.25. **And Absalom made Amasa captain of the host instead of Joab,** he occupied the same position in the rebel army which Joab held in that of David; **which Amasa was a man's son whose name was Ithra, an Israelite,** of Ishmaelite stock, 1 Chron. 2, 16. 17, **that went into Abigail, the daughter of Nahash** (or Jesse), **sister to Zeruiah, Joab's mother.** Amasa and Joab were cousins (step-cousins). V.26. **So Israel and Absalom pitched in the land of Gilead.** V.27. **And it came to pass, when David was come to Mahanaim, that Shobi, the son of Nahash, of Rabbah of the children of Ammon, and Machir, the son of Ammiel, of Lo-debar,** who had formerly sheltered Mephibosheth, chap. 9, 4, **and Barzillai, the Gileadite of Rogelim,** v.28. **brought beds,** quantities of bedding, **and basins,** vessels for preparing food, **and earthen vessels, and wheat, and barley, and flour, and parched corn,** roasted grain, **and beans, and lentils, and parched pulse,** roasted pulse-beans, v.29. **and honey, and butter, and sheep, and cheese of kine,** a milk-food on the order of cottage cheese, **for David, and for the people that were with him, to eat; for they said, The people is hungry and weary and thirsty in the wilderness.** So it was by no means all Israel that was on the side of Absalom, for here wealthy and influential men came to David's assistance. That was a noble deed, and similar works of love will be rewarded by the Lord according to His promise.

# 50

# 2 Samuel 18

The End of Absalom's Rebellion.
THE END OF ABSALOM. — V.1. **And David numbered the people that were with him, and set captains of thousands and captains of hundreds over them,** the mustering being done with the care of the experienced general. V.2. **And David,** having made three divisions of his army, **sent forth a third part of the people under the hand of Joab and a third part under the hand of Abishai, the son of Zeruiah, Joab's brother, and a third part under the hand of Ittai the Gittite,** the three divisions thus being sent forth under the command of these three tested warriors. **And the king said unto the people, I will surely go forth with you myself also,** in supreme command of all the forces. V.3. **But the people,** who loved him and were thoroughly loyal to him, **answered, Thou shalt not go forth; for if we flee away, they will not care for us,** that fact would have comparatively little weight with them; neither if half of us die, will they care for us, that also would not really satisfy their hearts; **but, now, thou art worth ten thousand of us,** his power and

influence was equivalent to that of ten thousand common soldiers; **therefore, now, it is better that thou succor us out of the city,** remaining with a reserve corps in case assistance should be needed at any point of the battle-line. V.4. **And the king said unto them, What seemeth you best I will do,** he agreed to this prudent suggestion. **And the king stood by the gate side,** in the entrance of the city gate, **and all the people came out by hundreds and by thousands,** he reviewed them as they marched by. V.5. **And the king commanded Joab and Abishai and Ittai, saying, Deal gently for my sake with the young man, even with Absalom;** they should abstain from all harshness against his person. **And all the people heard when the king gave all the captains charge concerning Absalom,** the command was given in the hearing of the entire army. V.6. **So the people went out into the field against Israel,** the army of David advancing to the attack; **and the battle was in the wood of Ephraim,** in the northeastern part of the country of Gilead; v.7. **where the people of Israel were slain before the servants of David,** completely defeated by the veteran army of the king, **and there was there a great slaughter that day of twenty thousand men.** V.8. **For the battle was there scattered over the face of all the country,** it was spread out over the entire woody mountain terrain, which was cut up by deep gorges; **and the wood devoured more people that day than the sword devoured,** for soldiers were lost in the mountain fastnesses and perished from exhaustion and hunger. V.9. **And Absalom met the servants of David,** he found himself face to face with the heroes of David and in imminent danger of being captured. **And Absalom rode upon a mule,** the animal used for riding by the royal children: **and the mule went under the thick boughs of a great oak,** one of the splendid terebinths of the forest, **and his head caught hold of the oak,** evidently because his long hair, of which he was so proud, wrapped around a limb; **and he was taken up between the heaven and the earth,** suspended from the tree by the hair of his head. **And the mule that was under him went away,** continuing his flight without his master. V.10. **And a certain man,** a private of the army of David, **saw it and told Joab,** making a report to his commander, **and said. Behold, I saw Absalom hanged in an oak.** V.11. **And Joab said unto the man that told him, And, behold, thou sawest him, and why didst thou not smite him there to the ground?** Joab severely reprimanded the private as though he had neglected an important duty. **And I would have given thee ten shekels of silver and a girdle,** as a reward for killing Absalom. V.12. **And the man said unto Joab, Though I should receive a thousand shekels of silver in mine hand,** literally, "weighed into my hand," that is, seven hundred dollars instead of the seven offered, **yet would I not put forth mine hand against the king's son; for in our hearing** v.5. **the king charged thee and Abishai and Ittai, saying, Beware that none touch the young man Absalom,** to harm his person or to take his life. V.13. **Otherwise I should have wrought falsehood against mine own life,** literally, "Had I dealt deceitfully against his life," by acting against the express prohibition of the king; **for there is no matter hid from the king, and thou thyself wouldest have set thyself against me,** appearing before the king as accuser and causing the private to be punished. V.14. **Then said Joab, I may not tarry thus with thee,** losing time in this discussion, instead of doing what he considered necessary. **And he took three darts in his hand,** wooden staffs sharpened to he weapons, **and thrust**

**them through the heart of Absalom, while he was yet alive in the midst of the oak,** suspended in the thicket of its branches. V.15. **And ten young men that bare Joab's armor compassed about and smote Absalom, and slew him,** completing the work of their master. V.16. **And Joab blew the trumpet,** since Absalom's death made further fighting unnecessary, **and the people returned from pursuing after Israel; for Joab held back the people,** since he wanted to spare the party of Absalom and not provoke a civil war. V.17. **And they took Absalom, and cast him into a great pit in the wood,** not granting him a proper burial, **and laid a very great heap of stones upon him,** a sign of embittered feeling for the rebel, a proper monument of shame for his crime; **and all Israel fled, every one to his tent,** to his own home. The rebellion was definitely broken. V.18. **Now, Absalom in his lifetime had taken and reared up for himself a pillar,** a monument of stone, **which is in the king's dale,** Gen. 28, 22; 31, 52, the valley of the Kidron, some distance east of Jerusalem; **for he said, I have no son to keep my name in remembrance,** those mentioned chap. 14, 27 evidently having died in early childhood; **and he called the pillar after his own name; and it is called unto this day Absalom's Place,** literally, "Absalom's Hand," recalling his memory like an uplifted hand. A significant contrast: the monument which his own vanity erected during his lifetime, and that actually placed over his body after his death! His example shows how jealously God guards the honor of parents and masters according to the Fourth Commandment, how severely He punishes disobedience and contempt of the authorities established by Him.

DAVID'S LAMENT FOR ABSALOM. — V.19. **Then said Ahimaaz, the son of Zadok,** who was with the troops, **let me**

now run and bear the king tidings how that the Lord hath
avenged him of his enemies, it was the direct divine interposition which had brought David justice. V.20. And Joab
said unto him, Thou shalt not bear tidings, be a messenger,
this day, but thou shalt bear tidings an other day; but this
day thou shalt bear no tidings because the king's son is
dead. Joab felt that the king might be angry because Absalom
had been put to death, and he did not want Ahimaaz to be
exposed to this anger. V.21. Then said Joab to Cushi, probably
an Egyptian slave in his service, Go tell the king what thou
hast seen. And Cushi bowed himself unto Joab and ran.
V.22. Then said Ahimaaz, the son of Zadok, yet again to
Joab, but, howsoever, no matter what may happen, let me,
I pray thee, also run after Cushi. He was anxious to convey
what he thought was excellent news to David. And Joab, still
unwilling to let the young man incur the anger of David, said,
Wherefore wilt thou run, my son, seeing that thou hast no
tidings ready? His message would not be profitable, since
the king was bound to consider it bad, from his standpoint,
and would therefore look upon him as a messenger of evil.
V.23. But, howsoever, just the same, said he, let me run.
He was willing to take the risk. And he said unto him, Run.
Then Ahimaaz ran by the way of the plain and overran Cushi,
reaching Mahanaim before the real messenger arrived. V.24.
And David sat between the two gates, the space between the
outer and the inner gates; and the watchman went up to the
roof over the gate unto the wall, over the outer gate, which
was connected with the city wall, and lifted up his eyes and
looked, and, behold, a man running alone. V.25. And the
watchman cried and told the king, whom his voice could
reach, as he sat beneath the entrance arch or vault. And the

**king said, if he be alone, there is tidings in his mouth,** he came as a messenger, for in the other event there would be several fugitives. **And he,** the runner, **came apace, and drew near.** V.26. **And the watchman saw another man running; and the watchman called unto the porter,** the keeper of the gate, **and said, Behold, another man running alone. And the king said, He also bringeth tidings,** he also must surely be a messenger. V.27. **And the watchman said, Me thinketh that the running of the foremost is like the running of Ahimaaz, the son of Zadok,** for by this time he could distinguish the peculiarities of the runner's gait. **And the king said, He is a good man, and cometh with good tidings,** since Joab would certainly not have chosen him for evil news. V.28. **And Ahimaaz,** as soon as he came into hailing distance, **called and said unto the king, All is well,** literally, "Peace!" or, "Hail!" **And he fell down to the earth upon his face before the king,** in an attitude of reverence, **and said, Blessed be the Lord, thy God, which hath delivered up the men that lifted up their hand against my lord the king.** The revolt was so effectually quenched that the rebels could no longer stir. V.29. **And the king said, Is the young man Absalom safe? And Ahimaaz,** in an attempt to temporize, to evade the question, **answered, When Joab sent the king's servant,** namely, Cushi, **and me, thy servant, I saw a great tumult, but I knew not what it was.** He made the impression that Absalom's fate was not get decided when Joab sent him off. V.30. **And the king said unto him, Turn aside and stand here,** making way for the second messenger. **And he turned aside and stood still.** V.31. **And, behold, Cushi came; and Cushi said, Tidings, my lord the king,** he came as an official messenger; **for the Lord hath avenged thee this day of all them that rose up against thee,**

that was the way in which the victory must be regarded, as a direct interposition of God. V.32. **And the king said unto Cushi, Is the young man Absalom safe? And Cushi answered, the enemies of my lord the king, and all that rise against thee to do thee hurt, be as that young man is.** It was an indirect announcement of Absalom's destruction, and in a manner which properly expressed condemnation of Absalom's hostile attempt against his father and king. V.33. **And the king,** weakly losing sight of the avenging hand of God in this death, **was much moved, and went up to the chamber over the gate,** probably that used by the watchmen of the city, **and wept, and as he went, thus he said, O my son Absalom, my son, my son Absalom! Would God I had died for thee, O Absalom, my son, my son!** He was more deeply afflicted by the death of this rebellious son than by any event in his life. It is a blessing of God if dangerous and rebellious people, who lead others into temptation and destruction, are destroyed by God's wrath. In such cases the believers have all reason to thank and praise God for the justice of His punishments.

# 51

# 2 Samuel 19

**R**estoration of David's Royal Authority.
DAVID REINSTATED IN HIS ROYAL POWER. — V.1. **And it was told Joab, Behold, the king weepeth and mourneth for Absalom.** He was immersed in his immoderate and sinful grief for Absalom, and did not even take time to greet his victorious army upon its return. V.2. **And the victory,** the deliverance or salvation from the hands of the murderous rebels under the leadership of Absalom, **was turned into mourning unto all the people; for the people heard say that day how the king was grieved for his son.** But while they respected his fatherly grief and, in a measure, shared his sorrow, they were gradually filled with dissatisfaction over the fact that the king did not seem to have one word of cheer or appreciation for them. V.3. **And the people,** the soldiers of the army, infected with the gloom which hung over the entire city and its vicinity, **gat them by stealth that day into the city,** instead of entering in military order and with shouts of victory, they stole away in small groups and crept into the city as unobtrusively as possible, **as people being**

**ashamed steal away when they flee in battle,** like disgraced fugitives who find it impossible to face their friends and relatives. V.4. **But the king covered his face,** in unrestrained grief and shame, **and the king cried with a loud voice. O my son Absalom, O Absalom, my son, my son!** He had almost worked himself into a hysteria over the loss of his worthless son, the rebel against the entire kingdom. V.5. **And Joab came into the house to the king and said,** in a stern reproof, which was intended to restore the king to his senses, **Thou hast shamed this day the faces of all thy servants,** behaved in a shameful manner toward them, **which this day have saved thy life, and the lives of thy sons and of thy daughters, and the lives of thy wives, and the lives of thy concubines,** for, according to Oriental custom, Absalom, if he had been victorious, might have slain the entire royal household; v.6. **in that thou lovest thine enemies,** those that hate thee, as his excessive lamenting for Absalom showed, **and hatest thy friends,** for that would be the logical conclusion. **For thou hast declared this day,** by his behavior, **that thou regardest neither princes nor servants,** for David acted as if they simply did not exist, paying no attention to them; **for this day I perceive that, if Absalom had lived and all we had died this day, then it had pleased thee well.** It was a rude reproof; with deductions which went too far; but it was intended to jolt David severely, to rouse him from his strange behavior. V.7. **Now, therefore, arise, go forth, and speak comfortably unto,** literally, "to the heart of," **thy servants,** showing them some measure of appreciation, satisfying and refreshing their minds; **for I swear by the Lord, if thou go not forth, there will not tarry one with thee this night,** not that he himself would lead the army away, but that the dissatisfaction had reached a stage where this result was inevitable; **and that will be worse unto thee than all the evil that befell thee from thy youth until now.** V.8. **Then the king,** accepting the reproof in the spirit in which it was given, **arose and sat in the gate. And they told unto all the people, saying, Behold, the king doth sit in the gate.** This news worked a joyful reaction in the hearts of the people. **And all the people came before the king,** apparently passing before him in review, in order to receive the expressions of his appreciation and gratitude; **for Israel had fled every man to his tent,** chap. 18, 17. V.9. **And all the people,** those who had been adherents of Absalom, **were at strife throughout all the tribes of Israel,** they began to discuss the matter, to argue, to reproach one another, **saying, the king saved us out of the hands of our enemies, and he delivered us out of the hand of the Philistines,** all these deeds of David now being recalled; **and now he is fled out of the land for Absalom,** a fugitive before his rebellious son. V.10. **And Absalom, whom we anointed over us, is dead in battle. Now, therefore, why speak ye not a word of bringing the king back?** So the representatives of the people consulted with one another about restoring the throne to David and declaring to him their renewed loyalty. V.11. **And King David sent to Zadok and to Abiathar, the priests, saying, Speak unto the elders of Judah, saying, Why are ye the last to bring the king back to his house? seeing the speech of all Israel is come to the king, even to his house.** So David had information concerning the movement in the other parts of the kingdom, and expressed surprise that the men in the capital and in the tribe of Judah were not taking similar steps. V.12. **Ye are my brethren, ye are my bones and my flesh,** they were of his tribe and of his kindred; **wherefore, then, are ye the last**

**to bring back the king?** "Conscious that they had offended David, and fearing Absalom's garrison in Zion, they did not dare to recall him." V.13. **And say ye to Amasa,** who had been the commander of Absalom's forces, chap. 17, 25, **Art thou not of my bone and of my flesh?** He was David's nephew. **God do so to me, and more also, if thou be not captain of the host, before me continually in the room of Joab.** He was to supersede Joab, who OR account of his rudeness and his plain disregard for the royal command had forfeited his post. V.14. **And he,** David, **bowed the heart of all the men of Judah, even as the heart of one man,** completely winning them for his side, **so that they sent this word unto the king, return thou and all thy servants.** David had been shrewd enough to see that it would have been poor policy to force himself upon his tribe, just as it would have been foolish to wait for a spontaneous, general invitation on their part. By assuring them of his favor, however, and by reminding them of the relationship between him and them, he removed all difficulties. V.15. **So the king returned and came to Jordan. And Judah,** the representatives of the entire tribe, **came to Gilgal,** in the valley of Jordan, **to go to meet the king, to conduct the king over Jordan.** All was ready for a solemn and joyous reception. V.16. **And Shimei, the son of Gera, a Benjamite, which was of Bahurim,** the man who had behaved himself in such a vile manner during David's flight, chap. 16, 7-14. **hasted and came down with the men of Judah to meet King David.** He wanted to undo his evil, if possible, before he would be called to account. V.17. **And there were a thousand men of Benjamin with him and Ziba, the servant of the house of Saul,** he who had slandered his master when he met David by the way, chap. 16, 3, **and his fifteen sons and his twenty servants with him; and they went over Jordan**

**before the king,** fording the river in order to meet him on the east side. V.18. **And there went over a ferry-boat to carry over the king's household, and to do what he thought good,** to be placed at the disposal of the king. **And Shimei, the son of Gera, fell down before the king, as he was come over Jordan,** as soon as he had crossed by the ford; v.19. **and said unto the king, let not my lord impute iniquity unto me,** charge up the guilt to him, **neither do thou remember that which thy servant did perversely the day that my lord the king went out of Jerusalem, that the king should take it to his heart,** bear him a grudge on account of it. V.20. **For thy servant doth know that I have sinned; therefore, behold, I am come the first this day of all the house of Joseph,** representing all the tribes of Israel outside of Judah, **to go down to meet my lord the king.** V.21. **But Abishai, the son of Zeruiah,** who, apparently with good reason, doubted the sincerity of Shimei, especially since the latter was moved to confess his sin only when David had returned to power, **answered and said, Shall not Shimei be put to death for this, because he cursed the Lord's anointed?** Cp. Ex. 22, 27; Lev. 24, 14. 15. V.22. **And David,** rejecting the proposal as once before, chap. 16, 10. 11, **said, What have I to do with you, ye sons of Zeruiah, that ye should this day be adversaries unto me?** The measure suggested by them was altogether out of harmony with his own inclination on this happy occasion. **Shall there any man be put to death this day in Israel? For do not I know that I am this day king over Israel?** He felt that his restoration to the kingdom really was a proof of his being accepted into the divine favor once more, and he wanted to show his appreciation by being merciful. V.23. **Therefore the king,** without further discussion of the matter, **said unto**

**Shimei, Thou shalt not die. And the king sware unto him.** The pardon was granted evidently chiefly for political reasons. Evidences of special assistance and favor of God so influence the hearts of the believers that they are glad to forgive their enemies.

DAVID'S TREATMENT OF MEPHIBOSHETH AND BARZIL-LAI. — V.24. **And Mephibosheth, the son of Saul** (in the wider sense, since lie was his grandson) **came down to meet the king, and had neither dressed his feet, nor trimmed his beard, nor washed his clothes,** all evidences of deepest mourning, signs of his sincere, faithful attachment to the house of David, **from the day the king departed until the day he came again in peace.** V.25. **And it came to pass, when he was come to Jerusalem to meet the king,** when the inhabitants of Jerusalem went down in a body to welcome David, Mephibosheth being in the procession also, **that the king said unto him, Wherefore wentest thou not with me, Mephibosheth?** This question was prompted by Ziba's slander, chap. 16, 3. V.26. **And he answered, My lord. O king, my servant** (Ziba) deceived me, he had injured him by lies, betrayed his confidence; **for thy servant** (Mephibosheth) **said, I will saddle me an ass,** Ziba being ordered to do this, **that I may ride thereon, and go to the king; because thy servant is lame,** he could not have joined the procession afoot. V.27. **And he** (Ziba) **hath slandered thy servant unto my lord the king,** as Mephibosheth had meanwhile found out; **but my lord the king is as an angel of God,** to know and to do what justice required in this case; **do, therefore, what is good in thine eyes.** V.28. **For all my father's house were but dead men before my lord the king,** who might, according to Oriental custom, have put them all to death upon his accession to the throne; **yet didst thou set thy servant among them that did eat at thine own table,** chap. 9, 7. 10. 13. **What right, therefore, have I yet to cry any more unto the king?** Being without rights, he willingly subjected himself to any order which the king might give. V.29. **And the king said unto him,** evidently unwilling to acknowledge that he had done wrong in accepting the slander of Ziba, **Why speakest thou any more of thy matters? I have said, Thou and Ziba divide the land.** This was not quite in conformity with the truth, since David had restored the entire inheritance of Saul to Mephibosheth and merely made Ziba the farmer or steward of the estate, chap. 9, 6-11. V.30. **And Mephibosheth,** without a word of protest against this manifest injustice, **said unto the king, Yea, let him take all, forasmuch as my lord the king is come again in peace unto his own house.** This fact was worth more to his loyal soul than the possession of the estate at Gibeah. Mark: Sin, also in the case of David, weakens the will, the evil consequences being seen in false decisions. V.31. **And Barzillai the Gileadite,** one of those men who had sent provisions for David and his army to Mahanaim, chap. 17, 27, **came down from Rogelim, and went over Jordan with the king to conduct him over Jordan,** intending only to accompany David to the other side of the river, and then to return. V.32. **Now, Barzillai was a very aged man, even fourscore years old; and he had provided the king of sustenance while he lay at Mahanaim,** before the army of the rebels had been dispersed; **for he was a very great man,** rich and influential V.33. **And the king said unto Barzillai, Come thou over with me, and I will feed thee with me in Jerusalem,** in return for the kindness shown him in Mahanaim. V.34. **And Barzillai said unto the king, How long have I to live that I should**

**go up with the king unto Jerusalem?** His expectation of life was so short that he did not want to plunge into the dissipations of court life. V.35. **I am this day fourscore years old; and can I discern between good and evil?** His intellect was becoming so dull that he would have made a poor counselor. **Can thy servant taste what I eat or what I drink? Can I hear any more the voice of singing men and singing women?** His senses becoming feeble, he could no longer enjoy the pleasures of court life. **Wherefore, then, should thy servant be yet a burden unto my lord the king?** V.36. **Thy servant will go a little way over Jordan with the king,** only to escort him across the river; **and why should the king recompense it me with such a reward?** He had not shown his kindness with the expectation of any return. V.37. **Let thy servant, I pray thee, turn back again that I may die in mine own city and be buried by the grave of my father and of my mother.** Since the king might have commanded him to go along to Jerusalem, Barzillai, in all simplicity and cheerfulness, requests permission to return home, since life at court held no allurement for him. **But behold thy servant Chimham,** his son, who had accompanied his aged father to the meeting with the king; **let him go over with my lord the king, and do to him what shall seem good unto thee.** He was still young enough to enter into the service of the king. V.38. **And the king answered, Chimham shall go over with me, and I will do to him that which shall seem good unto thee,** deferring to the aged father's wishes; **and whatsoever thou shalt require of me, that will I do for thee,** for he still considered himself under obligations to Barzillai. V.39. **And all the people went over Jordan,** the passage was finally effected. **And when the king was come over, the king kissed Barzillai, and blessed**

**him,** taking leave of him in an affectionate and respectful manner; **and he returned unto his own place.** V.40. **Then the king went on to Gilgal,** the ancient encampment near the site of Jericho, **and Chimham went on with him; and all the people of Judah conducted the king, and also half the people of Israel,** as many as had been able to assemble at this time. V.41. **And, behold, all the men of Israel,** representatives of all the other tribes, **came to the king, and said unto the king, Why have our brethren the men of Judah stolen thee away,** in arranging this reception, **and have brought the king and his household and all David's men with him over Jordan?** V.42. **And all the men of Judah answered the men of Israel, Because the king is near of kin to us,** being a member of their tribe; **wherefore, then, be ye angry for this matter? Have we eaten at all of the king's cost?** They had enjoyed no special privileges from him, had not been fed by the royal bounty. **Or hath he given us any gift?** It was a case where jealousy once more led to unpleasant rivalry and finally to hostility V.43. **And the men of Israel,** reacting to the sharp words of Judah in kind, **answered the men of Judah and said, We have ten parts in the king,** since theirs were ten tribes to the two of Judah and Benjamin, **and we have also more right in David than ye,** by virtue of their greater number; **why, then, did ye despise us,** by slighting them, by not inviting them, **that our advice should not be first had in bringing back our king?** Their word had been first, the suggestion to bring back the king had come from members of Israel. **And the words of the men of Judah,** in this unpleasant quarrel over precedence, in this jealous ill feeling, **were fiercer than the words of the men of Israel.** The entire scene led to a new, evil purpose on the part of Israel; it paved the way for Sheba's rebellion. The entire matter, in the Lands of God, was a means to keep David humble. For such is His way of dealing with His believers.

# 52

# 2 Samuel 20

**T**he Insurrection of Sheba.
THE MURDER OF AMASA. — V.1. **And there happened to be there a man of Belial,** a vain and worthless scoundrel, **whose name was Sheba, the son of Bichri, a Benjamite,** evidently one of the rabid party of Saul; **and he blew a trumpet,** as a call to all those who thought as he did on account of the strained relations between Judah and Israel, **and said, we have no part in David, neither have we inheritance in the son of Jesse,** the northern tribes had nothing in common with him, nothing to do with him; **every man to his tents, O Israel!** It was a call to rebellion. V.2. **So every man of Israel,** of the ten northern tribes, **went up from after David,** renouncing his allegiance to the king, **and followed Sheba, the son of Bichri; but the men of Judah clave unto their king, from Jordan even to Jerusalem.** They remained loyal, they did not permit their faithfulness to be shaken. V.3. **And David came to his house at Jerusalem,** after the outbreak of this rebellion; **and the king took the ten women, his concubines, whom he had left to keep the**

**house,** chap. 15, 16; 16, 21. 22, **and put them in ward,** in a house by themselves, **and fed,** maintained, **them, but went not in unto them,** for they were impure to him, having been approached by Absalom. **So they were shut up unto the day of their death, living in widowhood, in perpetual widowhood.** V.4. **Then said the king to Amasa, Assemble me the men of Judah within three days,** he was given orders to mobilize them for the purpose of punishing the rebel Sheba, **and be thou here present,** for David intended formally to appoint him commander-in-chief, chap. 19, 13, V.5. **So Amasa went to assemble the men of Judah; but he tarried longer than the set time which he had appointed him,** he delayed beyond the three days given him, the reason for this state of affairs not being mentioned. V.6. **And David said to Abishai,** one of his commanders, **Now shall Sheba, the son of Bichri, do us more harm than did Absalom,** on account of the delay in calling him to account; **take thou thy lord's servants,** the part of the standing army stationed at Jerusalem, **and pursue after him, lest he get him fenced cities and escape us,** literally, "and deliver himself from our eyes," or, "darken not our eight," by hiding himself and eventually harming the cause of David, V.7. **And there went out after him Joab's men,** for as such the standing army was known, **and the Cherethites and the Pelethites,** chap. 8, 18, **and all the mighty men; and they went out of Jerusalem to pursue after Sheba, the son of Bichri.** V.8. **When they were at the great stone which is in Gibeon,** northwest of Jerusalem, **Amasa went before them,** coming towards them with the levy of troops which he had raised. **And Joab's garment that he had put on was girded unto him,** his military garment being held close to his body by the girdle, **and upon it a girdle with a sword fastened upon**

320

**his loins in the sheath thereof; and as he went forth,** rather, the sheath slipped out, **it fell out,** that is, the sword fell to the ground. This apparent accident happened just before Amasa came up to Joab, and the fact that the latter picked up and held the sword in his left hand would arouse no suspicions. V.9. **And Joab,** apparently with sincere friendliness, **said to Amasa, Art thou in health, my brother? And Joab took Amasa by the beard with the right hand to kiss him,** drawing down his face with a caressing gesture. V.10. **But Amasa took no heed to the sword that was in Joab's hand,** namely, in his left, with which he had just picked it up; **so he,** Joab, **smote him therewith in the fifth rib,** in the abdomen, **and shed out his bowels to the ground, and struck him not again,** for there was no need for repeating the blow; **and he died.** It was a cold-blooded murder, an act of malice, the product of jealousy and the desire for revenge. **So Joab and Abishai,** after the murder of Amasa, **pursued after Sheba, the son of Bichri.** V.11. **And one of Joab's men stood by him,** Amasa, **and said, He that favoreth Joab,** has pleasure and confidence in him, **and he that is for David, let him go after Joab,** the cause of David thus being identified with that of Joab. V.12. **And Amasa wallowed in blood in the midst of the highway,** a conspicuous object. **And when the man who had been left behind by Joab saw that all the people stood still, he removed Amasa out of the highway into the field, and cast a cloth upon him,** so that his corpse would no longer draw attention, **when he saw that every one that came by him stood still.** Thus the danger of an unfavorable impression for Joab and his cause was removed, for the crowd now passed forward without inquiring into the matter. V.13. **When he was removed out of the highway, all the people went on after Joab to pursue after Sheba, the son**

**of Bichri.** The act of Joab in removing his rival in this manner is inexcusable. The higher the public office which a person holds, the more he must be able to overlook ingratitude and slights.

THE DEATH OF SHEBA. — V.14. **And he,** Joab, **went through all the tribes of Israel,** moving ever northward through the country of the ten tribes, **unto Abel and to Beth-maachah,** in the territory of Naphtali, **and all the Barites; and they were gathered together and went also after him,** his army was continually increased by the addition of chosen young men who flocked to his standards. V.15. **And they came and besieged him,** Sheba, **in Abel of Beth-maachah, and they cast up a bank,** threw up a high embankment, **against the city, and it stood in the trench,** it reached the height of, and was joined to, the outer wall or works of the fortress; **and all the people that were with Joab battered the wall,** the inner wall, **to throw it down.** V.16. **Then cried a wise woman out of the city, Hear, hear! Say, I pray you, unto Joab, Come near hither that I may speak with thee.** V.17. **And when he,** acting upon her suggestion, **was come near unto her, the woman said, Art thou Joab? And he answered, I am he. Then she said unto him, Hear the words of thine handmaid. And he answered, I do hear.** V.18. **Then she spake, saying, They were wont to speak in old time, saying,** it was a proverbial saying, **They shall surely ask counsel at Abel; and so they ended the matter.** The discretion and wisdom of the city's inhabitants were so widely known that their advice was acted upon without question. So in this case the inhabitants of Abel should first have been consulted before laying siege to the city. V.19. **I am one of them that are peaceable and faithful in Israel,** for she speaks in the name of the entire city. **Thou seekest to destroy a city and a mother in Israel,** one of the chief cities of the nation; **why wilt thou swallow up the inheritance of the Lord?** V.20. **And Joab,** struck by the sensibility of the argument, **answered and said, Far be it, far be it from me that I should swallow up or destroy,** in a ruthless and senseless manner. V.21. **The matter is not so,** he had no intention of being willfully cruel; **but a man of Mount Ephraim, Sheba, the son of Bichri, by name, hath lifted up his hand against the king, even against David; deliver him only, and I will depart from the city. And the woman said unto Joab, Behold, his head shall be thrown to-thee over the wall,** or "through the wall," through one of the openings or loopholes. V.22. **Then the woman went unto all the people,** the citizens of Abel, **in her wisdom,** laying the proposition of Joab before them, which she persuaded them to accept. **And they cut off the head of Sheba, the son of Bichri, and cast it out to Joab. And he,** his purpose having been attained, **blew a trumpet, and they retired from the city, every man to his tent.** The return march was begun at once. **And Joab returned to Jerusalem unto the king.** V.23. **Now, Joab was over all the host of Israel,** the commander-in-chief of the armies; **and Benaiah, the son of Jehoiada, was over the Cherethites and over the Pelethites,** the king's body-guard, including his runners and the official executioners; v.24. **and Adoram was over the tribute,** overseer of the public works; **and Jehoshaphat, the son of Ahilud, was recorder**; chancellor; v.25. **and Sheva was scribe,** secretary of state; **and Zadok and Abiathar were the priests;** v.26. **and Ira, also, the Jairite was a chief ruler about David,** confidential couselor. In spite of many mistakes of men the work of the Lord, also in His Church, must go forward according to His intentions.

# 53

# 2 Samuel 21

**F**amine and Expiation.
THE DIFFICULTY WITH THE GIBEONITES AD-
JUSTED. — V.1. **Then there was a famine in the days
of David three years, year after year,** three successive years,
a fact which made the visitation seem a special punishment;
**and David enquired of the Lord,** he sought the face of the Lord,
by consulting with the high priest, after earnest prayer. **And
the Lord answered, It is for Saul and for his bloody house,**
the house upon which blood-guiltiness rested, **because he
slew the Gibeonites,** he had put to death a number of those
people to whom Joshua and the princes of Israel had sworn
immunity, Josh. 9, 15. V.2. **And the king called the Gibeonites
and said unto them; (now the Gibeonites,** as the author here
inserts for the sake of the people of his time, **were not of
the children of Israel, but of the remnant of the Amorites,**
this name here designating the heathen nations of Canaan
in general; **and the children of Israel had sworn unto them;
and Saul,** disregarding the oath and the covenant, **sought
to slay,** to exterminate, **them in his zeal to the children**

of Israel and Judah;) v.3. **wherefore David said unto the Gibeonites, What shall I do for you? And wherewith shall I make the atonement,** expiate the wrong done and appease the Lord's anger, **that ye may bless the inheritance of the Lord?** He wanted them to change their maledictions upon Israel into blessings. V.4. **And the Gibeonites said unto him, we will have no silver nor gold of Saul,** they wanted no compensation of money in exchange for the blood shed by Saul, **nor of his house; neither for us shalt thou kill any man in Israel,** they had no right to put any one to death; they wanted blood revenge, but could not proceed without the consent and command of David. **And he said, What ye shall say, that will I do for you.** It is really a question asking them to express themselves more exactly, to state their request in specific terms. V.5. **And they answered the king, The man that consumed us,** who had slain the best of their tribe and practically annihilated them, **and that devised against us that we should be destroyed from remaining in any of the coasts of Israel,** v.6. **let seven men of his sons,** descendants, near relatives, **be delivered unto us, and we will hang them up,** punish them by crucifixion, **unto the Lord,** before His face, to appease His anger, **in Gibeah of Saul, whom the Lord did choose.** Saul had been the "chosen of Jehovah," king of Israel, when he had done this wrong, and therefore the whole people was being punished. **And the king said, I will give them.** He was ready to make the atonement. V.7. **But the king spared Mephibosheth, the son of Jonathan, the son of Saul, because of the Lord's oath that was between them, between David and Jonathan, the son of Saul.** The oath of the covenant between David and Jonathan had included the promise of sparing the sons of Jonathan, 1 Sam. 20, 15. 16. V.8.

**But the king took the two sons of Rizpah, the daughter of Aiah, whom she bare unto Saul, Armoni and Mephibosheth,** the sons of Saul's concubine, **and the five sons of Michal, the daughter of Saul, whom she brought up for,** literally, "had born to," **Adriel, the son of Barzillai the Meholathite.** Evidently Michal, who had originally been the wife of David, 1 Sam. 18, 27, and was later given to Phaltiel, 1 Sam. 25, 44, to be returned to David upon his accession to the throne, 2 Sam. 3, 15, had also, for some years, been the wife of this Adriel, for after her contemptuous behavior towards David, 2 Sam. 6, 23, she had no children, she bore no children to David. V.9. **And he,** David, **delivered them,** the seven men selected by him, **into the hands of the Gibeonites, and they hanged them,** impaled them with extended limbs, **in the hill before the Lord; and they fell all seven together, and were put to death in the days of harvest, in the first days, in the beginning of barley-harvest,** at the very beginning of the summer in that climate, about the middle of April, V.10. **And Rizpah, the daughter of Aiah,** the mother of two of the hanged men, **took sackcloth,** the usual garment of mourners, **and spread it for her upon the rock,** to serve as her bed, **from the beginning of harvest until water dropped upon them out of heaven,** until the falling of rain some time during the summer indicated that the anger of God was appeased, **and suffered neither the birds of the air to rest on them by day nor the beasts of the field by night.** This being a case where the bodies mere to serve as a sign of expiation, they were not taken do-m from the stakes in the evening, Deut. 21, 22. Since ravenous birds and beasts were not permitted to come near the bodies, they probably dried out quickly. V.11. **And it was told David what Rizpah, the daughter of Aiah, the concubine**

**of Saul, had done. V.12. And David,** touched by this evidence of a mother's faithfulness and loving care, **went and took the bones of Saul and the bones of Jonathan, his son, from the men of Jabesh-gilead,** in the country east of Jordan, **which had stolen them from the street,** from the open place near the city gate, where they had been fastened to the wall, 1 Sam. 31, 10-12, **of Bethshan, where the Philistines had hanged them, when the Philistines had slain Saul in Gilboa; v.13. and he brought up from thence the bones of Saul and the bones of Jonathan, his son; and they gathered the bones of them that were hanged. V.14. And the bones of Saul and Jonathan, his son, buried they,** most likely with those of the seven executed men, **in the country of Benjamin in Zelah, in the sepulcher of Kish, his father,** not far from Gibeah; **and they performed all that the king commanded. And after that God was intreated for the land,** He did not permit the famine to continue. Even the lowliest of men are in God's care, and He may punish an entire country for an injustice done to them. It is the duty of the believers, therefore, to help the poor and lowly obtain justice.

EXPLOITS DURING THE PHILISTINE WARS. — V.15. **Moreover, the Philistines had yet war again with Israel; and David went down, and his servants with him,** his standing army, his heroes, **and fought against the Philistines; and David waxed faint,** he was overcome with weariness. V.16. **And Ishbi-benob, which was of the sons of the giant,** one of the giant race of the Rephaim, to which also Goliath belonged, **the weight of whose spear weighed three hundred shekels of brass in weight,** that is, the brazen head of his lance weighed about eight pounds, **he being girded with a new sword, thought to have slain David. V.17. But Abishai, the** son of Zeruiah, one of David's commanders, **succored him, and smote the Philistine, and killed him,** thus saving the life of David. **Then the men of David swam unto him, saying, Thou shalt go no more out with us to battle,** not take part actively in battle, **that thou quench not the light of Israel,** for so David was regarded by his men, as a symbol of Israel's life in fortune and honor. V.18. **And it came to pass after this that there was again a battle with the Philistines at Gob,** probably a small place near Gezer; **then Sibbechai the Hushathite, a** general in the standing army, **slew Saph, which was of the sons of the giant,** also a member of the ancient giant race. V.19. **And there was again a battle in Gob with the Philistines, where Elhanan, the son of Jaare-oregim,** or simply Jair, 1 Chron. 20, 5, **a Bethlehemite, slew the brother of Goliath the Gittite, the staff of whose spear was like a weaver's beam.** V.20. **And there was yet a battle in Gath, where was a man of great stature that had on every hand six fingers and on every foot six toes, four and twenty in number; and he also was born to the giant,** he was likewise a member of the giant race. V.21. **And when he defied Israel,** as Goliath had done in the Valley of Elah, 1 Sam. 17, **Jonathan, the son of Shimeah, the brother of David, slew him.** V.22. **These four were born to the giant in Gath and fell by the hand of David and by the hand of his servants,** for they were killed by the heroes of David while he was their commander in the field. David here appears as an example to all believers, for they all should work while it is day; for the night cometh when no man can work.

# 54

## 2 Samuel 22

**D**avid's Psalm of Thanksgiving.

GRATITUDE FOR DELIVERANCE IN THE PAST. — V.1. **And David spake unto the Lord the words of this song,** which is simply another version of Ps. 18, from which it is distinguished only by slight deviations, **in the day that the Lord had delivered him out of the hand of all his enemies and out of the hand of Saul.** V.2. **And he said, The Lord is my Rock and my Fortress,** in whom he may confidently trust, **and my Deliverer;** v.3. **the God of my rock,** Deut. 32, 4, with reference to His unchangeable faithfulness; **in Him will I trust. He is my Shield,** covering him against the attacks of his enemies, **and: the Horn of my salvation,** yielding help and strength in overcoming the enemies, **my high Tower,** the inaccessible and safe stronghold, **and my Refuge, my Savior; Thou savest me from violence.** This is said of God by way of a general introduction. V.4. **I will call on the Lord, who is worthy to be praised,** or, upon Him whom I praised, who is the Praised One, I will call; **so shall I be saved from mine enemies.** The application is now made to

David's own case. V.5. **When the waves of death compassed me,** they came upon him from all sides like breakers on the shore of the ocean, **the floods of ungodly men,** the streams of destruction, **made me afraid.** V.6. **The sorrows of hell compassed me about,** like sudden pangs of pain, or like ropes which threatened to throttle him; **the snares of death prevented me,** fell on him in a treacherous attack, especially during the persecutions of Saul. V.7. **In my distress I called upon the Lord, and cried to my God; and he did hear my voice out of His temple,** out of the palace of His heavenly dwelling, **and my cry did enter into His ears.** The Lord's deliverance is next pictured. V.8. **Then the earth shook and trembled,** quaking to its very center; **the foundations of heaven moved and shook because He was wroth,** as when a terrible storm, with an accompanying earthquake, sweeps over the earth, sent by the wrath of His indignation. V.9. **There went up a smoke out of His nostrils,** the snorting being a sign of His anger, **and fire out of His mouth devoured,** like a fire ready to consume everything that comes into its path; **coals were kindled by it,** glowing coals burned out of Him. The picture is that of the rising of a storm-cloud and the flaming of the sheet-lightning which announces the storm. V.10. **He bowed the heavens also,** for the lowering storm-clouds seem to draw the heaven down to the earth, **and came down; and darkness was under His feet,** a symbol of the terror struck by God's wrath, as He hides His face in darkness. V.11. **And He rode upon a cherub,** as a bearer of the divine majesty and glory, **and did fly; and He was seen upon the wings of the wind,** as the bearers of the appearance of His glory. V.12. **And he made darkness pavilions round about Him,** like the tabernacles in which He made His habitation, **dark waters and thick clouds**

**of the skies,** they served as the booths in which He was hidden. V.13. **Through the brightness before Him were coals of fire kindled,** glowing forth from the intense gloom like live coals. V.14. **The Lord thundered from heaven, and the most High uttered His voice,** God's wrathful judgment, as that of the all-powerful, unapproachable Judge, burst forth upon the enemies. V.15. **And he sent out arrows and scattered them,** shafts of lightning, like a warrior armed with bow and arrow; **lightning, and discomfited them,** all this tending toward the complete destruction of the enemy. V.16. **And the channels of these a appeared,** the very beds of the ocean becoming visible, **the foundations of the world were discovered,** laid bare by the terrible storm and the earthquake, **at the rebuking of the Lord, at the blast of the breath of His nostrils,** at the noise of His angry crashes of thunder. V.17. **He sent from above, He took me,** stretching out His hand from heaven to the very abyss, in order to save the drowning man; **he drew me out of many waters.** V.18. **He delivered me from my strong enemy, and from them that hated me,** Saul being thought of as the principal one; **for they were too strong for me,** they were able to overpower him without the help of God. V.19. **They prevented me in the day of my calamity,** falling upon him in a sudden attack; **but the Lord was my Stay.** V.20. **He brought me forth also into a large place,** setting him free from all narrowness and straits, procuring for him a condition of freedom; **He delivered me because He delighted in me,** loving him because of his integrity which flowed from his faith in the God of his salvation. In a similar manner every believer praises his God, who was so often his Help and his Stay, delivering him in the midst of danger, distress, and death.

PRAISE AND PROPHECY. — V.21. **The Lord rewarded me according to my righteousness; according to the cleanness of my hands hath he recompensed me.** The righteousness of the heart is seen in the purity of the acts of his hands, in their abstaining from sin and unrighteousness. V.22. **For I have kept the ways of the Lord,** observing the rules of conduct laid down in His Law, **and have not wickedly departed from my God,** not fallen away from God through wickedness. V.23. **For all His judgments were before me,** the instructions to which He obligated all men; **and as for His statutes,** the precepts of His covenant, **I did not depart from them,** he was a sincere believer In, and follower of, Jehovah. V.24. **I was also upright before Him,** that was his immediate, inner relation to God, **and have kept myself from mine iniquity,** guarding himself against committing sin, and so contracting guilt. This testimony of David concerning himself agrees with that of the Lord, 1 Kings 14, 8; 15, 5. V.25. **Therefore the Lord hath recompensed me according to my righteousness, according to my cleanness in His eyesight,** rewarding every believer in accordance with the evidence presented in his life and works. V.26. **With the merciful Thou wilt show Thyself merciful, and with the upright man Thou wilt show Thyself upright.** V.27. **With the pure Thou wilt show Thyself pure, and with the froward,** the perverse, **Thou wilt show Thyself unsavory,** every man thus reaping as he sowed, being rewarded or punished according to his deeds. V.28. **And the afflicted people Thou wilt save,** those bowed down by a weight of misery; **but Thine eyes are upon the haughty,** those who look down upon and oppress the poor and afflicted, **that Thou mayest bring them down.** Cp. Luke 1, 52. V.29. **For Thou art my Lamp, O Lord,** as the Source of all his joy and good fortune; **and the Lord will lighten my darkness,** by taking away all affliction, wretchedness, and ruin. V.30. **For by Thee I have run through a troop,** running against the hostile forces and trampling them under foot; **by my God have I leaped over a wall,** conquering fortified places with ease. V.31. **As for God, His way is perfect,** He is altogether blameless in His government; **the Word of the Lord is tried,** without guile, pure, and true; **He is a buckler to all them that trust in Him,** offering protection against all dangers. V.32. **For who is God save the Lord?** He is the only true God. **And who is a rock save our God?** He only may be relied upon absolutely as trustworthy. V.33. **God is my strength and Power,** a Fortress of strength; **and he maketh my way perfect,** leading and guiding the perfect man on his way. V.34. **He maketh my feet like hinds' feet,** swift in strength and in the pursuit of the enemies; **and setteth me upon my high places,** which the singer victoriously holds against his enemies. V.35. **He teacheth my hands to war,** and thus to hold their own against the enemies, **so that a bow of steel is broken by mine arms,** so that his arms are able to bend the bronze bow without difficulty. V.36. **Thou hast also given me the shield of thy salvation,** whereby God protects and saves His people; **and Thy gentleness hath made me great,** by the favorable hearing of his prayer. V.37. **Thou hast enlarged my steps under me,** giving to the wanderer a wide space for free movement, **so that my feet did not slip,** his ankles standing unwavering and firm; he was able to move with a light and strong step. V.38. **I have pursued mine enemies and destroyed them, and turned not again until I had consumed them;** they could not rise for further contest; they fell under his feet in helpless submission. V.39. **And I have consumed them and wounded** them that they could not arise; yea, they are fallen under my feet. V.40. **For Thou hast girded me with strength to battle,** all his strength and prowess came from Jehovah; **them that rose up against me hast Thou subdued under me,** they had to bow down their necks like helpless slaves. V.41. **Thou hast also given me the necks of mine enemies,** causing them to turn their back in flight, **that I might destroy them that hate me.** V.42. **They looked, but there was none to save; even to the Lord, but he answered them not.** Though in their extreme need they cried to the God of Israel for help, they received no deliverance at His hands. V.43. **Then did I beat them as small as the dust of the earth,** rubbing, pulverizing, and scattering them; **I did stamp them as the mire of the street, and did spread them abroad,** contemptuously scorning and throwing them away as worthless. The result of this victorious conflict with the enemies is also pictured. V.44. **Thou also hast delivered me from the strivings of my people,** from the insurrections in the midst of his own nation; **Thou Hast kept me to be head of the heathen,** of all the surrounding nations; **a people which I knew not shall serve me,** Here the Messianic thought is included, that eventually even those outside 3f the chosen people of the Lord would learn to know the true God in Christ Jesus. V.45. **Strangers shall submit themselves unto me,** strange, foreign people would pay fawning, hypocritical homage, since they felt powerless before the Lord's king; **as soon as they hear, they shall be obedient unto me.** V.46. **Strangers shall fade away,** wither and shrivel up like a leaf in a hot wind, **and they shall be afraid out of their close places,** coming forth hobbling and trembling out of their fortresses. V.47. **The Lord liveth; and blessed be my Rock, and exalted be the God of the rock of my salvation.** These sentences return to the thought of the introduction, which dominated the entire psalm. V.48. **It is God that avengeth me, and that bringeth down the people under me,** subjecting the nations to his rule, v.49. **and that bringeth me forth from mine enemies,** delivering him from their power. **Thou also hast lifted me up on high above them that rose up against me; Thou hast delivered me from the violent man,** saving him from the persecution of Saul, as of the man of violent deeds, and from all those that followed the latter in his hatred. V.50. **Therefore I will give thanks unto Thee, O Lord, among the heathen, and I will sing praises unto Thy name,** as being expressive of all His deeds of deliverance, by which He has revealed Himself as the true God. V.51. **He is the Tower of Salvation for His king,** with the strong assurance of salvation, **and showeth mercy to His anointed, unto David, and to his seed forevermore;** the Messianic thought recurring here once more. Christ, the true Anointed of God, carried the Lord's cause to a still more victorious conclusion. He is the Head and King over all nations, over the spiritual Israel, the seed of Abraham gathered from all nations of the world.

# 55

# 2 Samuel 23

The Last Words of David. Catalog of His Heroes.

DAVID'S LAST PROPHETIC SONG. — V.1. **Now, these be the last words of David. David, the son of Jesse, said,** he uttered a divine, oracular saying based on immediate inspiration, **and the man who was raised up on high,** from his lowly position as the son of a shepherd, **the anointed of the God of Jacob,** who had the royal dignity conferred on him by God, **and the sweet psalmist of Israel,** he who was pleasant in the praise-songs of Israel, **said,** all in the power of the Holy Spirit, v.2. **The spirit of the Lord spake by me,** using him as His instrument to convey the divine truths to men, in his writings and psalms, **and His Word was in my tongue,** for the Spirit acts through the Word. V.3. **The God of Israel said,** He who chose Israel for His possession, **the Rock of Israel spake to me,** He who is unchangeable, faithful, and trustworthy, **he that ruleth over men must be just, ruling in the fear of God,** literally, "a ruler over men just, a ruler in the fear of God" (there will be), that is, such a Ruler would arise whose rule would be exercised in the fear of God. V.4.

**And he shall be as the light of the morning, when the sun riseth, even a morning without clouds; as the tender grass springing out of the earth by clear shining after rain.** The picture is that of a cloudless, beautiful morning after a night of ram, when all the plants, refreshed with moisture, respond to the coaxing warmth of the sunlight. That is the character of the Messianic period, such are the conditions following the coming of the promised King. V.5. **Although my house be not so with God** (the sentence is a question, like chap. 7, 18, expressing David's surprise over the goodness of God which was shown to his family), **yet He hath made with me an ever lasting covenant, ordered in all things, and sure,** chap. 7, 12 ff., the declaration of God ordering and arranging all things beyond the possibility of overthrow; **for this is all my salvation and all my desire,** the salvation promised by God being a constant source of pleasure to David, **although he make it not to grow,** literally, "Should He not make it sprout?" Messiah would surely be a righteous Branch, who would reign and prosper, Jer. 23, 5; 33, 15. The contrast between this excellent condition and the judgment upon the ungodly is now brought out. V.6. **But the sons of Belial,** the godless, vain, and worthless scoundrels, **shall be all of them as thorns thrust away because they cannot be taken with hands,** they are so hurtful and dangerous that one does not take his bare hands to handle them, but uses tools; v.7. **but the man that shall touch them must be fenced with iron and the staff of a spear,** in order to avoid all contact with them; **and they shall be utterly burned with fire in the same place,** so that there will be an end to them. The reference is to the final judgment upon the godless and unbelievers, Matt. 13, 30. Note: The first part of this prophecy is fulfilled. The wonderful grace of God in Christ Jesus has appeared to all men, the dawn of the Messianic day has come. All believers enjoy the light and the warmth of the grace of Jesus Christ, both in life and in death, and therefore bring forth, as long as they live, fruits of righteousness, to the honor and praise of God.

LIST OF DAVID'S HEROES. — V.8. **These be the names of the mighty men,** the heroes, **whom David had: The Tachmonite that sat in the seat, chief among the captains,** he belonged to the family of Hachmon, 1 Chron. 27, 32, and his name was Jashobeam, the most distinguished of the king's guard, the most eminent of the three greatest heroes. **The same was Adino the Eznite; he lifted up his spear against eight hundred, whom he slew at one time.** That was the greatest feat of this hero. V.9. **And after him,** next in the list, **was Eleazar, the son of Dodo the Ahohite, one of the three mighty men with David, when they defied the Philistines that were there gathered together to battle, and the men of Israel were gone away,** when they had marched against the Philistines, to meet them in battle. V.10. **He arose and smote the Philistines until his hand was weary, and his hand clave unto the sword,** cramped around the sword-hilt from excessive weariness; **and the Lord wrought a great victory that day; and the people,** who had apparently fallen back, **returned after him only to spoil.** V.11. **And after him was Shammah, the son of Agee the Hararite. And the Philistines were gathered together into a troop,** at Lehi or Ramath-lehi, **where was a piece of ground full of lentils; and the people fled from the Philistines.** V.12. **But he stood in the midst of the ground,** determined to hold it against the enemy, **and defended it, and slew the Philistines; and the Lord wrought a great victory,** for this was His gift. V.13. **And three of the**

**thirty chief,** of the knights of David, **went down, and came to David in the harvest time, unto the cave of Adullam,** 1 Sam. 22, l; **and the troop of the Philistines,** a plundering party, **pitched in the Valley of Rephaim,** 1 Sam. 5, 18. V.14. **And David was then in an hold,** in a mountain stronghold, **and the garrison of the Philistines was then in Bethlehem,** their camp was near Bethlehem. V.15. **And David longed,** he had a strong desire, **and said, Oh, that one would give me drink of the water of the well of Bethlehem which is by the gate!** The water of this well, which David had so often tasted as a lad, was exceptionally good, and he longed for it with the desire of home-sickness. V.16. **And the three mighty men brake through the host of the Philistines,** thrusting aside the enemies who tried to hinder their passage, **and drew water out of the well of Bethlehem that was by the gate,** some little distance outside, **and took it, and brought it to David. Nevertheless, he would not drink thereof, but poured it out unto the Lord,** as a drink-offering to Jehovah, to whom alone it ought to belong. V.17. **And he said, Be it far from me, O Lord, that I should do this,** namely, drink the water thus obtained. **Is not this the blood of the men that went in jeopardy of their lives?** They had brought it at the price of their lives, at the risk of their souls, and therefore it had the value of their blood, it was too precious to drink. **Therefore he would not drink it. These things did these three mighty men.** V.18. **And Abishai, the brother of Joab, the son of Zeruiah, was chief among three,** also distinguished for exceptional feats of valor. **And he lifted up his spear against three hundred,** brandishing it in battle, **and slew them, and had the name among three.** V.19. **Was he not most honorable of three,** among all the knights of David? **Therefore he was their captain,** becoming their leader; **howbeit, he attained not unto the first three,** the heroes whose exploits were described above. V.20. **And Benaiah, the son of Jehoiada,** the priest, who was captain of David's body-guard, chap. 8, 18; 20, 23, **the son of a valiant,** or honorable, honest, man, **of Kabzeel, who had done many acts,** having many feats to his credit; **he slew two lion like men of Moab,** two famous Moabite heroes; **he went down also and slew a lion in the midst of a pit in time of snow,** when the lion, searching for food, had fallen into a cistern or into a trap set for him. V.21. **And He slew an Egyptian,** a certain well-known enemy, **a goodly man; and the Egyptian had a spear in his hand; but he went down to him with a staff, and plucked the spear out of the Egyptian's hand,** showing both bravery and skill in snatching the weapon out of the enemy's hand, **and slew him with his own spear.** V.22. **These things did Benaiah, the son of Jehoiada, and had the name among three mighty men,** among the heroes of David. V.23. **He was more honorable than the thirty,** honored above the other knights, **but he attained not to the first three. And David set him over his guard,** chap. 8, 18; 20, 23. V.24. **Asahel, the brother of Joab, was one of the thirty,** a member of the corps of David's knights, chap. 2, 18; **Elhanan, the son of Dodo of Bethlehem;** v.25. **Shammah the Harodite; Elika the Harodite;** v.26. **Helez the Paltite; Ira, the son of Ikkesh, the Tekoite;** v.27. **Abiezer the Anethothite; Mebunnai the Hushathite;** v.28. **Zalmon the Ahohite; Maharai the Netophathite;** v.29. **Heleb, the son of Baanah, a Netophathite; Ittai, the son of Ribai, out of Gibeah of the children of Benjamin;** v.30. **Benaiah the Pirathonite; Hiddai of the brooks of Gaash;** v.31. **Abialbon the Arbathite; Azmaveth the Barhumite;** v.32. **Eliahba the Shaalbonite, of** the sons of Jashen, Jonathan: v.33. **Shammah the Hararite; Ahiam, the son of Sharar, the Hararite;** v.34. **Eliphelet, the son of Ahasbai, the son of the Maachathite; Eliam, the son of Ahithophel the Gilonite;** v.35. **Hezrai the Carmelite; Paarai the Arbite;** v.36. **Igal, the son of Nathan of Zobah; Bani the Gadite;** v.37. **Zelek the Ammonite; Nahari the Beerothite, armor-bearer to Joab, the son of Zeruiah;** v.38. **Ira, an Ithrite; Gareb, an Ithrite;** v.39. **Uriah the Hittite: thirty and seven in all,** namely, Joab as the commander-in-chief, three heroes of the first degree, three heroes of the second degree, and the thirty knights of David. As the names of these faithful followers of David were here entered into the catalog of heroes, so the names of the true servants of Christ are entered into the book of life, to be read on the last day, when all such men will receive the reward of mercy.

# 56

# 2 Samuel 24

The Numbering of the People and the Plague.
THE PEOPLE NUMBERED. — V.1. **And again the anger of the Lord was kindled against Israel,** as in the former famine, chap. 21, 1-14, **and He moved David against them,** namely, the members of the nation, by giving Satan leeway to tempt David, **to say, Go, number Israel and Judah,** by taking a census chiefly for military purposes. V.2. **For the king said to Joab, the captain of the host, which was with him,** having held his post as commander-in-chief of the army, **Go now through all the tribes of Israel, from Dan even to Beersheba,** from the extreme north to the extreme south end of the land, **and number ye the people that I may know the number of the people,** really get the exact statistics of the country's military strength. V.3. **And Joab said unto the king, Now the Lord, thy God, add unto the people, how many soever they be, an hundredfold, and that the eyes of my lord the king may see it! But why doth my lord the king delight in this thing?** Joab noticed that the pride of the king was his motive for instituting this census, that

he wanted to boast of the imposing and growing military strength of his people, and he feared that no good would come of it, especially since the people themselves might resent the procedure. Joab's native shrewdness here stood him in good stead. V.4. **Notwithstanding the king's word prevailed against Joab,** his sinful exaltation insisted upon having his command carried out, **and against the captains of the host,** for the practical sense of the latter had caused them to side with Joab. **And Joab and the captains of the host,** without further opposition, **went out from the presence of the king,** before his very eyes, **to number the people of Israel.** V.5. **And they passed over Jordan,** in order to begin the census in the southeastern part of the country, in the territory of Reuben, **and pitched in Aroer, on the right side of the city that lieth in the midst of the river,** that is, the valley, **of Gad, and toward Jazer,** preferring to camp in the open on account of the large numbers of people who had to be summoned to be enrolled in the census lists. V.6. **Then they came to Gilead,** the hill country along the Jabbok, **and to the land of Tahtim-hodshi,** probably a lower section of the east-Jordan country, which had but recently been settled; **and they came to Dan-jaan,** in Northern Perea, southwest of Damascus, **and about to Zidon,** as they turned to the west across the foothills of the Lebanon, v.7. **and came to the stronghold of Tyre,** still a Phenician city, **and to all the cities of the Hivites and of the Canaanites,** for here the heathen nations had never been fully exterminated, and the mixed population of Galilee was notorious even in Old Testament times; **and they went out to the south of Judah, even to Beersheba,** omitting Benjamin, however, and not including the Levites, 1 Chron. 21, 6. V.8. **So when they had gone through all the land, they came to**

**Jerusalem at the end of nine months and twenty days,** the census not being really finished, because wrath came upon Israel and caused the suspension of the project. V.9. **And Joab gave up,** reported, **the sum of the number of the people unto the king; and there were in Israel,** in the northern tribes, **eight hundred thousand valiant men that drew the sword; and the men of Judah were five hundred thousand men.** These were round numbers, and the statement in Chronicles, 1 Chron. 21, 5, includes either the standing army or the heathen proselytes. So David had yielded to the temptation of pride, an abomination to God, even as murder and adultery. Every believer must guard against this sin with all earnestness, lest it become a snare to him.

THE PESTILENCE. — V.10. **And David's heart smote him,** his conscience began to bother him, **after that he had numbered the people,** while the census was still being taken. **And David,** becoming conscious of the sinfulness of his act, **said unto the Lord, I have sinned greatly in that I have done,** the offense of his pride was directed against the Lord; **and now, I beseech Thee, O Lord, take away the iniquity of Thy servant,** the guilt which he had loaded upon himself by his transgression; **for I have done very foolishly.** It was a short penitential prayer, which he apparently sent up to God during a sleepless night. V.11. **For when David was up in the morning,** rather, when David got up in the morning, **the word of the Lord came unto the prophet Gad, David's seer,** his confidential counselor, who had evidently taken the place of Nathan, **saying,** v.12. **Go and say unto David, Thus saith the Lord,** in giving David his choice of three punishments, **I offer thee three things,** one of which would surely be laid upon him; **choose thee one of them that I may do it unto thee.** V.13. **So**

**Gad came to David, and told him, and said unto him,** naming the three forms of punishment selected by the Lord, **Shall seven years of famine come unto thee in thy land? Or wilt thou flee three months before thine enemies? or that there be three days' pestilence in thy land? Now advise and see what answer I shall return to Him that sent me;** the choice must be made at once. V.14. **And David said unto Gad, I am in a great strait,** in great fear and anguish. **Let us fall now into the hand of the Lord; for His mercies are great; and let me not fall into the hand of man.** The first two plague would have made David and his people dependent upon men, and he knew from experience that little favor might be expected there; the pestilence, however, was an immediate stroke of God's hand, and here he hoped for mercy, whence he might sooner hope to draw comfort and help. V.15. **So the Lord sent a pestilence upon Israel from the morning even to the time appointed,** which even now was fixed by the gracious will of God; **and there died of the people, from Dan even to Beersheba, seventy thousand men,** the entire people having deserved this punishment by various misdeeds, especially by the rebellions instituted under Absalom and Sheba. V.16. **And when the angel,** God's messenger of destruction, **stretched out his hand upon Jerusalem to destroy it, the Lord repented him of the evil,** this being the moment of the appointed time, **and said to the angel that destroyed the people, It is enough; stay now thine hand.** As yet the scourge had not struck Jerusalem. **And the angel of the Lord was by the threshing-place of Araunah the Jebusite,** northeast of Zion, on the summit of Moriah. V.17. **And David spake unto the Lord when he saw the angel that smote the people,** for the Lord opened his eyes and made the invisible visible to him, **and said, Lo,**

**I have sinned, and I have done wickedly,** upon him alone the blame really rested; **but these sheep,** the members of his people, **what have they done? Let Thine hand, I pray Thee, be against me and against my father's house.** He begged the Lord to visit the judgment upon him and his family, but to spare the people, whom he considered innocent. V.18. **And Gad came that day to David and said unto him, Go up, rear an altar unto the Lord in the threshing-floor of Araunah the Jebusite.** Thus the Lord's instructions were carried out, 1 Chron. 21, 18. V.19. **And David, according to the saying of Glad, went up as the Lord commanded.** V.20. **And Araunah,** who was busy threshing wheat, **looked,** bending forward to look more clearly in the distance, **and saw the king and his servants coming on toward him. And Araunah went out,** from the enclosure of the threshing-floor, **and bowed himself before the king on his face upon the ground,** rendering due honor to the king. V.21. **And Araunah said, Wherefore is my lord the king come to his servant? And David said, To buy the threshing-floor of thee, to build an altar unto the Lord, that the plague may be stayed from the people.** V.22. **And Araunah said unto David, Let my lord the king take,** as a present, **and offer up what seemeth good unto him,** for Araunah was just as anxious as David to have the plague stopped. **Behold, here be oxen,** those used by him on the floor, **for burnt sacrifice, and threshing instruments,** the threshing-sledges, which consisted of several iron-pointed rollers which were held together by a chain, **and other instruments of the oxen,** such as their yoke, **for wood.** V.23. **All these things did Araunah, as a king, give unto the king.** These words are a continuation of his speech: All this gives Araunah, O king, to the king. **And Araunah,** after a pause, **said unto the king, The**

**Lord, thy God, accept thee,** look with favor upon the sacrifice and prayer now to be made. V.24. **And the king,** unwilling to accept the offer thus made, **said unto Araunah, Nay, but I will surely buy it of thee at a price; neither will I offer burnt offerings unto the Lord, my God, of that which doth cost me nothing,** he felt that he could not properly, at this time, devote anything to Jehovah which he himself had gotten as a present. **So David bought the threshing-floor and the oxen for fifty shekels of silver** (about thirty dollars). This was apparently the price of the oxen only, since the land was worth more, 1 Chron. 21, 25. V.25. **And David built there an altar unto the Lord, and offered burnt offerings and peace-offerings,** the latter for the purpose of reestablishing the proper relation between him and the covenant God. **So the Lord was intreated for the land, and the plague was stayed from Israel.** At the same time the command to build an altar to the Lord included a hint that this place had been chosen by the Lord for the Temple to His name. We Christians of the New Testament have a far better atoning sacrifice, the blood of Jesus Christ, the Son of God, which cleanses us from all sins and keeps the plague of death and hell from us.

Made in the USA
Monee, IL
07 July 2026

56546313R00208